MATTHEW

Storyteller

Interpreter

Evangelist

MATTHEW

Storyteller

Interpreter

Evangelist

WARREN CARTER

© 1996 by Hendrickson Publishers, Inc.
P. O. Box 3473
Peabody, Massachusetts 01961–3473
All rights reserved
Printed in the United States of America

ISBN 1–56563–153–6

First Printing — April 1996

Library of Congress Cataloging-in-Publication Data

Carter, Warren, 1955–
    Matthew: storyteller, interpreter, evangelist /
Warren Carter.
    Includes bibliographical references and indexes.
    ISBN 1–56563–153–6 (alk. paper)
    1. Bible.   N.T.   Matthew—Criticism, interpretation, etc.
I. Title.
BS2575.2.C4   1996
226.2'06—dc20   96–1937
                                                              CIP

Material in chapters 10–11 previously appeared in W. Carter, "Kernels and Narrative Blocks: The Structure of Matthew's Gospel," *CBQ* 54 (1992) 463–81. Used with permission.

For Emma and Rebekah
two of the "little ones" (Matt 18:1–14)

Table of Contents

PART THREE: AFTER READING

Abbreviations

Int	*Interpretation*
JAAR	*Journal for the American Academy of Religion*
JBL	*Journal of Biblical Literature*
JSNT	*Journal for the Study of the New Testament*
JSNTSup	Journal for the Study of the New Testament Supplement Series
LCL	Loeb Classical Library
lit.	literally, that is, as the Greek reads
NCB	New Century Bible
NovTSup	Supplement to *Novum Testamentum*
NTS	*New Testament Studies*
OBO	Orbis biblicus et orientalis
RevExp	*Review and Expositor*
SBL	Society of Biblical Literature
SBLSBS	Society of Biblical Literature Sources for Biblical Study
SBLSP	*Society of Biblical Literature Seminar Papers*
SNTSMS	Society for New Testament Studies Monograph Series
UBS	United Bible Societies
WBC	Word Biblical Commentary

Preface

The Gospel of Matthew has been the object of the church's reflection for nearly two thousand years. Through the centuries, this gospel has guided everyday life (the Sermon on the Mount, Matt 5–7), shaped liturgy (the Lord's Prayer, 6:9–13; the Eucharist, 26:26–29), and formed ecclesial practices (Peter the "rock," 16:18–19; discipline, Matt 18; monastic traditions, 19:10–12). It has informed how people understand God and Jesus (the Virgin Birth, 1:18–25; the Trinity, 28:19–20). It has shaped how people of different faith traditions regard each other (the negative treatment of Jewish religious leaders [6:1–8; 23:1–29]). It has inspired the church to missionary work (25:31–46; 28:18–20). It has offered a vision of a life infused by the presence of Emmanuel, God with us (1:23). An encounter with this document can form an identity and shape a lifestyle.

The rich, diverse and, at times, tragic history of the interpretation of Matthew is a reminder of what is at stake in seeking to understand his gospel. It cautions us against excessive haste, presumption, or certainty in the task. The books about Matthew on my bookshelves constantly remind me of the complexity of the material, the lengthy debate about its interpretation, and the power of its story. Throughout this book I will discuss what I consider to be the major issues that have dominated debate about this gospel. I am primarily interested in the effect this gospel has on the identity and lifestyle of its audience.

I have written this book for college and seminary students who are either starting work in New Testament studies or who have completed an introductory course and have elected to study the gospels or Matthew's gospel. My audience also includes interested lay people who want to learn more about the First Gospel. I have written it as well for ministers who are either looking for resource material on Matthew for preaching and teaching or want to keep up with current work in gospel studies. The use of audience-oriented criticism will add another approach to the redaction method with which they are probably familiar. Finally, I hope that this book makes some contribution to the scholarly guild's ongoing study of this gospel.

Because of space limitations I have seldom quoted material from Matthew's gospel. Readers will find it helpful to refer to the biblical material indicated by citations. In some chapters readers will also find useful a gospel parallel or a synopsis which sets out gospel passages in parallel columns. When I have quoted verses I have used the New Revised Standard Version, unless otherwise indicated.

I wish to thank the president of Saint Paul School of Theology, Kansas City, Dr. Lovett Weems Jr., and its Trustees for the gracious provision of a sabbatical leave which enabled the writing of this book. I also wish to thank librarians David Coward, Logan Wright, and Bob Sallman of the Dana Dawson Library, Saint Paul School of Theology, for their energetic and efficient work. I am especially grateful to Sandra MacFarlane, Steve Kraftchick, and Stan Saunders for their careful and insightful reading of this manuscript. Their perceptive responses have clarified and enriched this study.

Chapter 1

Understanding Matthew's Gospel

Understanding can be expressed in two ways: (1) by restating, paraphrasing, or describing, and (2) by acting in a particular way or doing something. My aim in this book is to restate the story and concerns of Matthew's gospel, to describe its contents, and to express what I think its author is saying. While understanding as restatement predictably dominates this book, the question of appropriate action is never far off. I address this aspect at appropriate places throughout the book and discuss it briefly in the last chapter.

Determining how to restate the message of the author of Matthew's gospel is by no means self-evident. A number of options exist. No doubt the reading strategy or strategies we adopt for this task will to a great extent determine what we see. Choosing a strategy and explaining why I have chosen it are the tasks of this chapter.

Perhaps a personal story will help: Reading the Bible and hearing it read were important aspects of my upbringing. I was taught to read it not just because it was another interesting book but because in a special way it would guide me in living my life. My parents read it with me as a young child. This reading formed part of my bedtime ritual. When I was a little older they provided me with devotional booklets which designated a short Bible reading and then offered some thoughts about the passage.

With my parents' help I was learning a particular reading strategy. I was learning to read the Bible devotionally, personally, with an eye focused on my daily life and circumstances. This strategy assumed that the Bible was a contemporary book and provided guidance for daily living. It assumed that reading the Bible was profitable and that I had a responsibility to act on what I read.

So a specific practice of reading developed in my life. This involved asking certain questions about each Bible passage: What did I learn about God or Jesus in relation to my life? What did I learn about people and myself? Was there an example to follow, an action to avoid, a warning to heed, a comforting or encouraging word to hear? This made the Bible accessible and contemporary for me.

Then it occurred to me that reading the Bible in this way meant there were parts of it that did not connect with my world. I noticed geographical and historical references that made no sense to me. There were allusions to strange customs or figures of speech that were quite foreign to my experience. There were instructions that baffled me. I remember being puzzled about the instruction to carry the soldier's pack an extra mile. I wasn't sure what to do with the command to pray in one's room with the door shut because that seemed to limit where and when I could pray.

This meant two things. First, the Bible reflected a world different from my own. It bore the marks of a different time, place, and culture. Second, I was realizing that while my reading strategy served me well in some regards, there were aspects of the biblical material that were inaccessible to that particular approach.

I could have decided that, at this point, these other aspects didn't matter. After all, in any reading we cannot absorb everything an author sets before us. We ignore or filter out material. Sometimes, depending on circumstances, such as preparing for a test, writing a paper, or searching for information, we reread in an effort to discover more useful material.

Two things, however, prevented me from continuing with business as usual. First, my reading strategy had taught me to so value biblical material that it was difficult to ignore parts of it. Second, the reading strategy which had helped me to make sense out of biblical passages was also explicitly excluding parts of them. I realized that reading the Bible was more complex and required more questions than my strategy allowed.

Then I began studying the New Testament in a seminary. There I encountered a different set of questions and assumptions; a new reading strategy. This strategy is called historical criticism. It includes particular subsets called form, source, and redaction criticisms.[1] This strategy treats biblical writings not as bite-size pieces, but as individual documents. Historical criticism asks seven questions about each document in the New Testament:

- Who was the author?

- What sort of writing did he write? (It was always assumed to be a "he.")

- Who read it?

- How did he write it? Did he use sources?

- Where did the writer and the readers live?

- When did he and they live?

- What purpose did the author have?

In other words the historical conditions of the New Testament texts and their authors are of foremost importance. The focus is on an author's intentions and theological agenda. This strategy also assumes that the biblical texts are church texts written for communities of faith. The gospels and letters address the actual circumstances of communities of believers.

In this strategy information is the name of the game. This information is used to answer the seven questions. Competing theories also create overwhelming complexity and detail. It was exciting, complicated, and stimulating stuff.

It was also frustrating. On the one hand historical criticism opened up all sorts of new issues for me. It articulated many new questions and insights. On the other hand, it ignored much. While it took the texts apart and broke them down into sources, it often did not put them together again as whole units. It concentrated on authors, on how biblical texts were produced, where and how they originated, and for what purposes.

But it said little about the audience, about how the texts were received, and about their impact. Moreover, it seemed to say nothing about the present or about me, as had my other reading strategy. Historical criticism dug a huge ditch between the past and the present without offering a bridge across the ditch.

These two different reading strategies presented a puzzle. Could they be put together? Was it important to have different reading strategies for different purposes and situations? Was there a third strategy that embraced the respective strengths of the first two but overcame their weaknesses?

JOINING THE AUTHORIAL AUDIENCE

In this study I employ the notion of an authorial audience as a reading strategy.[2] This strategy invites us to read Matthew's gospel "as the author intended." This does not mean the author's inner intentions. These are lost to us forever. We could speculate on them, but since Matthew is not among us to adjudicate on our varied guesses, our efforts are futile.[3] Moreover, we know from conversation and other forms of communication that what we intend does not and cannot control the response of others. An innocent remark, for instance, can be interpreted as mean or critical. A serious comment can be treated as a joke.

Rather, to read "as the author intended" is to try and identify with and read along with the readers that the author has "in mind" in writing the gospel. Any author forms an image of those for whom he or she writes. This "authorial audience" is an ideal audience though it approximates an actual audience. The author images an audience that is able to respond appropriately to and understand everything in the text. The writing itself reveals an author's assumptions about or image of this audience. The choice of words, the simple or complex style adopted, the inclusion or omission of difficult concepts, the level of familiarity with the subject matter, the choice of figures of speech, allusions to places or events or figures, explanations of material, items that are ridiculed or held to be sacred, the advocacy of certain beliefs and values, indicate assumptions an author is making about the audience. By narrating actions, for instance, which display certain personal characteristics, the author will expect the audience to adopt certain attitudes toward these values. To read "as the author intended" is to identify with and read along with this audience imaged by the author.

This audience exists, of course, only in the author's mind. Its relationship to real or actual audiences can vary. If I agree with everything in a particular book, then considerable overlap exists between the actual and authorial audiences. I have adopted the roles and responses expected of the book's audience. This overlap is evident for example when I readily admire a character that the author expects me to admire. Likewise, if I read three pages and close the book declaring, "this is terrible," there is little overlap. I have decided that I will not play the author's game. In this case the gap between the role the author wants me to play as the authorial audience and my values, beliefs, or experiences is too large. So I refuse to read further.

A third option exists. Sometimes, even though there is a gap between the role, identity, and lifestyle required of the authorial audience and the actual audience, I decide to go along with the expected role. As the reader I can maintain my own identity yet still go along with the author. I enjoy a musical stage show, for instance, knowing that "in real life" a group of people does not suddenly burst forth into song. I consent to go along with the reality presented by the author because it offers other benefits.

In these circumstances the authorial audience goes along with its understanding of the roles, beliefs, commitments, knowledge, etc. advocated by the text. It adopts for awhile the identity and perspective which the text puts forward. To be an authorial audience is to join a "particular social/interpretive community . . . [and] to accept an author's invitation to read in a particular socially constituted way that is shared by the author and his or her expected readers."[4]

JOINING MATTHEW'S AUTHORIAL AUDIENCE

Three major obstacles present themselves as we consider joining Matthew's authorial audience. These three obstacles can be generally identified with the three temporal stages in the reading process.[5] These three stages provide the focus of this book's three parts, Part One, *Before Reading*; Part Two, *Reading Matthew*; Part Three, *After Reading*.

PART ONE: BEFORE READING

Matthew's gospel comes from a time and culture which differ greatly from our own. It bears the constraints of its historical location. It is written in Koiné Greek and it assumes its audience is familiar with this language. It refers to daily life, customs, social patterns, cultural values, and religious experience of the first-century world. Its metaphors sound strange to modern ears. Certain conventions of story-telling are utilized. The author assumes the reader is familiar with all this knowledge and experience. If we are to join the authorial audience we must educate ourselves to gain as much of this knowledge and experience as possible. Some can be accumulated as we read; some we need to identify before reading.

Accordingly, Part One, *Before Reading*, addresses some of the knowledge needed to read Matthew's gospel. The main methods employed to identify and gather this knowledge are historical criticism and redaction criticism. Historical criticism investigates the historical circumstances, social patterns, and cultural values of Matthew's world. Redaction criticism (which is featured in chs. 3–7) investigates the author's theological point of view as indicated by changes made to his sources and in relation to the community or audience being addressed. Both methods help to fill in the knowledge and experiences assumed of the authorial audience.

In the first six chapters, the reader takes five steps toward joining the authorial audience by examining five key aspects of Matthew's knowledge and experience. I am not claiming to convey *all* the knowledge assumed by the audience, only important elements of it.

(1) A Cross-Cultural Step

Chapter 2 discusses the author implied by the Gospel of Matthew. It considers his possible relation to his subject matter, his ethnicity, the time and place of writing, and a sense of what is important to the author. This starting point helps to register the distance between the present and the world of Matthew's gospel. It provides a point of introduction to the world encountered in this text. This information has important implications for determining the genre of the gospel and the roles of the authorial audience.

(2) Genre

The genre or form of any text imposes restrictions on an author and shapes the expectations of an audience. This is the topic of Chapter 3. For example, the genre of comedy restricts the author to providing humor. That choice creates expectations for an audience. The authorial audience expects to and is expected to laugh. An audience that refuses to laugh (for whatever reasons) does not carry out the roles expected of the authorial audience. Determining the genre of the gospel, and hence the expectations of the audience, has caused much debate among scholars of the Gospel of Matthew.

(3) The Audience's Religious Traditions

Matthew's gospel is a religious text belonging to the genre of ancient biography. It stands within a tradition of reflection about and proclamation of the significance of Jesus. The audience is assumed to have the identity and lifestyle of disciples of Jesus. It is familiar with traditions about Jesus. Chapter 4 examines some of the ways in which the author transmits and shapes these traditions, conserving and reconfiguring the identity and lifestyle of the audience. This alerts the reader to important emphases in the text.

(4) The Audience's Social and Religious Experiences

The gospel's origin and text offer clues about social and religious experiences assumed of the authorial audience. Chapters 5 and 6 investigate four aspects of the social and religious knowledge and experience assumed of the gospel's authorial audience.

(5) Narrative Conventions

An author employs various narrative conventions to guide the audience in its reading. The author assumes the audience is competent to recognize and utilize these conventions as it reads. Chapter 7 examines some of the conventions employed in Matthew's gospel.

By investigating these five areas in the next six chapters we will gain some familiarity with the world which the author and authorial audience share. In this way we can gain some of the knowledge and experience assumed of the authorial audience. Part One provides five steps toward joining the authorial audience.

PART TWO: READING MATTHEW

Joining the authorial audience requires the interpretation of extensive amounts of data. Texts can be interpreted in more than one way. Sometimes this is because of diverse information in the text. Sometimes different readers understand a text in different ways. Sometimes readers lack the knowledge assumed by the text or mistake a work's genre.

So, to join the authorial audience one cannot be passive. The audience is always actively involved in making meaning. This active role is assumed throughout chapters 8–16. These chapters discuss four very important aspects of the audience's work: constructing the gospel's point of view (8–9), plot (10–11), settings (12), and characters (13–16).

Reading is like making a jigsaw puzzle. The authorial audience seeks to unify the various pieces of the gospel into a coherent whole. This task involves the knowledge gained before reading as well as that acquired through reading. It recognizes the limits and guidelines provided by the gospel's author, genre, and narrative conventions. It involves taking into account the audience's assumed experiences and knowledge. It requires reading and re-reading, re-evaluating and re-describing the relationships among various aspects of the text. Such a process cannot eliminate differences of opinion about the work. But it will establish that some interpretations are inadequate in terms of joining the authorial audience.

PART THREE: AFTER READING

A third obstacle to joining the authorial audience is the gap between the role of the authorial audience and the values or experiences of actual readers. I have discussed this gap above in our general consideration of the authorial audience. A brief look at this in terms of Matthew's gospel is the concern of Part Three.

Some readers of this gospel find the roles, identity, and lifestyle required of the authorial audience familiar and easy to assume. Others find them very difficult. Four brief examples identify some problematical areas. (1) Throughout the gospel, the authorial audience is asked to recognize God's presence among human beings. If readers do not think God exists or do not experience God in daily life, this is difficult if not impossible. (2) The authorial audience understands that Jesus' death is a sacrifice. For some readers with strong antipathies to any taking of life, this is a difficult notion to accept. (3) The authorial audience, in siding with Jesus and the disciples, goes along with Jesus' strong condemnations of the Jewish religious leaders. For readers with knowledge of the church's tragic history of collusion with anti-Semitism, such condemnation is most problematic. (4) The authorial audience encounters many more male than female characters. For some the male-dominated world of the gospel may be difficult to connect with, and even offensive.[6]

I advocate reading the gospel as the authorial audience. But I am not claiming that this is the definitive reading of the gospel. It is not a privileged reading exempt from reflection and critique. Rather, to read as the authorial audience forms a basis for further reflection on the gospel. To find out what Matthew is saying is a step toward considering the implications and adequacy of this understanding of reality. The dual roles of *authorial* and *actual* audience provide the means for debate between the two. Joining the authorial audience is the bridge between Matthew's gospel and the world of the present. Some readers may find that no traffic can pass over this bridge. Others will find that there is much two-way traffic as they contemplate how this gospel shapes their identity and lifestyle as disciples of

Jesus in a world very different from that of Matthew. The final part entitled *After Reading* will briefly consider Matthew's gospel in relation to several aspects of contemporary religious experience. It invites the reader to explore these issues further.

To summarize, Part One, *Before Reading* (chs. 2–7), examines five aspects of the knowledge and experience assumed of the authorial audience:

- A sense of the gospel's author, time and place of origin.

- The gospel's genre and the expectations which it creates.

- The audience's religious traditions, its knowledge about and experience of Jesus.

- The audience's social and religious experiences as disciples of Jesus.

- The audience's reading skills.

Part Two, *Reading* (chs. 8–16), investigates how the authorial audience recognizes and constructs the gospel's point of view, plot, settings, and characters. Part Three, *After Reading* (ch. 17), considers the identity and lifestyle of the authorial audience in relation to actual audiences and some aspects of contemporary religious experience.

NOTES

1. I should note that the word "criticism" does not indicate an attack on the Bible. Rather it is used to designate a set of questions, a particular way of reading the Bible.

2. This approach is outlined in P. J. Rabinowitz, *Before Reading: Narrative Conventions and the Politics of Interpretation* (Ithaca: Cornell University, 1987) 15–46.

3. It is, after all, interpreters who formulate analyses and then claim that their interpretation realizes the authorial intention. Claiming one's interpretation as the author's intention has been identified as the "intentional fallacy." A plethora of claims about the author's purposes prompted a redaction critic to comment, "Perhaps it is an embarrassment that a method which purports to be especially suited for unearthing an author's purpose has produced so many purposes for Matthew." So D. Garland, "Review of J. D. Kingsbury, *Matthew*

(Proclamation; Philadelphia: Fortress, 1975)," in *RevExp* 74 (1977) 567–78. We will recognize below that even if authorial intention in this sense can be established, it may not be as central to the interpretive process as some have thought. So N. Petersen, *Literary Criticism for New Testament Critics* (Guides to Biblical Scholarship; Philadelphia: Fortress, 1978) 28.

4. Rabinowitz, *Before Reading,* 22.

5. I readily concede that what is ascribed here to these three linear stages probably happens in a much more integrated and simultaneous way; however, this structure enables various dimensions of this complex process to be identified and considered separately.

6. See, for example, the discussion of Elaine Mary Wainwright, *Towards a Feminist Critical Reading of the Gospel According to Matthew* (BZNW 60; Berlin and New York: de Gruyter, 1991).

PART ONE:
BEFORE READING

Chapter 2

A Cross-Cultural Step

To join Matthew's authorial audience we must take a cross-cultural step into another world. This chapter begins our orientation to this world by considering the author's identity, his ethnicity and cultural traditions, and his historical and geographical location. We will gain a sense of the gospel's author, its time, and its place of origin.

Inquiring into these areas provides a good starting point for two reasons. Understanding who the author of Matthew may or may not have been offers initial clues about the type of writing or genre of the gospel. This knowledge will help us understand the authorial audience's roles and expectations in interacting with the gospel. These implications are explored in chapter 3.

But investigating the identity, ethnicity, historical, and geographical location of the author has a more immediate payoff. It clearly demonstrates that this text did not originate in our time, our neighborhood, or our culture. It alerts us to the reality that some two thousand years and thousands of miles (depending on where we are) separate us from its world. It helps us understand that this foreign text assumes things of the authorial audience which are not familiar or commonplace for us. This realization provides the starting point for becoming familiar with the culture, values, and social practices which have left their mark on this text. To join Matthew's authorial audience we must engage in cross-cultural reading.

Our investigation of the author of the gospel according to Matthew will begin this process. Who is Matthew? Was this "Matthew" one of Jesus' twelve disciples? Or does the gospel's title designate a tradition influenced by or stemming from this person? Is the name added later to honor or to claim the authority of an important figure? To answer this question we must be open to notions of authorship that differ from our own culturally and historically shaped ideas.

These questions are difficult. No manuscript bears the name, ethnicity, date, and address of the author of the gospel. Nor is there an interview in which the author talks about the circumstances that influenced its writing and how the audience is to understand it. Two thousand years prevent any easy access to this information.

In the absence of any autobiographical evidence, two sources exist for obtaining information about the gospel's author. One source of information consists of *external* references to the gospel from other writers. But as we will see these references provide few reliable clues about the gospel's author. A second source is any information the text itself may contain. This is called an *internal* reference.

EXTERNAL REFERENCES

Numerous early second-century Christian writers quote material from Matthew's gospel. They do not, however, explicitly attribute their quotes to this gospel.

Irenaeus

The first major extant writing to refer unambiguously to the gospel "According to Matthew" is by Bishop Irenaeus of Lyons late in the second century.[1] Irenaeus provides the first evidence that this gospel was known as Matthew's gospel, some 100 years after the gospel's likely time of writing (see further below). He seems to know the contents of the gospel well, explicitly attributing citations to it and alluding to other passages in it.[2] However, the lateness of Irenaeus' evidence for the link between Matthew's name and the gospel raises questions about his claim that Matthew, one of Jesus' twelve disciples, wrote it.

Irenaeus' purposes for making claims about the gospel's origin also raise questions. The references appear in his work *Against Heresies,* written around 180–190, a time of much controversy and diversity of thinking. Irenaeus was defending and strengthening the "mainstream" church against those whose thinking and lifestyles he considered to be outside its limits. Part of his strategy is to claim that these "heretics" do not accept or properly interpret the scriptures. His discussion of the gospels' origins comes in this context. He is not intending primarily to supply historical information but to make a point about the reliability of the four gospels in terms of their origins. Irenaeus bolsters the authority of the gospels and seeks to guarantee their truth by emphasizing their apostolic origin:

> Matthew also issued a written gospel among the Hebrews in their own dialect, while Peter and Paul were preaching at Rome, and laying the foundations of the Church. After their departure, Mark, the disciple and interpreter of Peter, did also hand down to us in writing what had been preached by Peter. Luke also, the companion of Paul, recorded in a book the gospel preached by him. Afterwards, John . . . [3]

Irenaeus underlines that the gospels originated with the apostles who were eyewitnesses of Jesus and his work. But it seems to be especially important for him to link them with the authority of Peter and Paul. This link to Peter and Paul is important because later Irenaeus traces an unbroken line of bishops in Rome from Peter and Paul up to his own time. Irenaeus is able to make the connection with Peter and Paul more easily for Mark (the interpreter of Peter) and for Luke (companion of Paul) than for Matthew. He does not claim any contact between Matthew and Peter and Paul or that the latter influenced Matthew's writing. He does not place Matthew in Rome. Rather he simply suggests a link by dating the gospel's origin to the time when "Peter and Paul were preaching at Rome and laying the foundations of the Church."[4]

This vague link between Matthew's gospel and Peter and Paul achieves two things. (1) It suggests a relatively early date for the gospel since tradition has it that Paul and Peter were put to death by Nero in the early 60s.[5] (2) By establishing a link to the time when the famous and powerful apostles Peter and Paul were active in Rome, Irenaeus manages to associate Matthew's gospel with these authoritative church leaders. But Irenaeus wrote *Against Heresies* with larger issues in mind. So apart from claiming that Matthew wrote in Hebrew for Jews he tells us little else about the origin of the Gospel of Matthew.

Eusebius and Papias

Over a century later in *Ecclesiastical History,* Eusebius, bishop of Caesarea in Palestine (ca. 260–ca. 340), cites possible testimony about this gospel's author from Papias, a figure who lived before Irenaeus.[6] The puzzling and ambiguous words from Papias, the bishop of Hierapolis in Asia Minor between 125 and 150, have caused much debate.

Eusebius refers to and quotes from Papias' five treatises, "Interpretation of the Oracles of the Lord," a work now lost. Eusebius indicates that this work contained material that Papias learned third-hand from "the sacred apostles" including Matthew (named last on his list of apostles). Eusebius cites what Papias claims to have learned from "an elder" (or Presbyter): that Mark, the interpreter of Peter, wrote "all that he remembered, not, indeed, in order, of the things said or done by the Lord" (*Eccl. Hist.* 3.39.14–15). Almost as an afterthought Eusebius adds, "and about Matthew this was said, 'Matthew collected the oracles in the Hebrew language, and each interpreted them as best he could.' "[7]

Because this reference to Papias is potentially the earliest explicit claim about the author and origin of Matthew's gospel, scholars have scrutinized it carefully.[8] But there is much uncertainty about the meaning of this brief statement. A few examples will indicate how puzzling it is:

(1) How does the statement about Matthew relate to the statement about Mark? Missing from the translation above is a rendering of two words (μήν οὖν, *men oun,* "so," "then") which follow "Matthew" in the Greek text.[9] Does Papias use these words as general connectives adding a reference about Matthew or does he use them to suggest a particular relation-

ship, i.e. that Matthew wrote after Mark and/or that Matthew corrected Mark's order?

(2) The word translated "collected" could also suggest "arranged in an orderly manner." Is Papias/Eusebius suggesting that Matthew reordered Mark's material? It is often overlooked that Eusebius places Papias' comment on Matthew after his reference to Mark. Did Papias or Eusebius think that Mark, not Matthew, was written first?[10]

(3) Most important, what did Matthew "collect"? The meaning of the word "oracles" (or "sayings") is not clear. Some have claimed it refers to Matthew's gospel.[11] But this is not convincing. The word "oracles" would be quite inappropriate because the gospel is not just a collection of sayings but is a narrative. It seems Papias is not talking about the writing of the gospel at all. Some have suggested that Papias uses the word "oracles" to refer to Matthew's collecting or arranging Old Testament prophecies or *testimonia* which early Christians understood to apply to Jesus.[12] Or perhaps it indicates Matthew's collection of sayings of Jesus which later may have made their way into the gospel.[13]

(4) The phrase "in the Hebrew language" has caused difficulties because Matthew's gospel is in Greek and does not show signs of being a translation. The phrase might be translated "in the style of Hebrew writing."[14] This could mean that Papias knew the gospel to be in Greek but was alluding to Jewish influences (such as the Septuagint, the Greek translation of the Hebrew Bible) on its content and style.

(5) The word translated "interpreted" could also mean "translated." This may indicate that Papias knew the gospel in Greek and assumed translation from a Hebrew (or Aramaic) original.[15]

Clearly Papias is not much help. As I have suggested above, it is unlikely that Papias considered the apostle Matthew the author of Matthew's gospel. Nevertheless, early writers such as Irenaeus, Clement of Alexandria, Origen, Eusebius, and Augustine,[16] seem to think that Papias' view was that Matthew the apostle did write the First Gospel.[17]

The external evidence does not provide clear clues about the author of the Gospel of Matthew. Claims that a disciple of Jesus named Matthew wrote this gospel are undermined by the relatively late date of the evidence, its context of polemic against other groups, and its ambiguous content. Scholars turn to the gospel itself for clues about its author.[18]

INTERNAL EVIDENCE

A reading of the Gospel of Matthew reveals that at least one opinion held by ancient writers is mistaken. This is their claim that Matthew's gospel was written in Hebrew.[19] The gospel is written in Greek, not Hebrew, and does not show signs of being a translation. The claim that it was written in Hebrew was probably driven by a larger theological agenda rather than based in historical information. It conveniently served to underline the antiquity of this gospel and linked it to the apostles. Perhaps, since they were wrong about this point, these writers were also wrong in other respects.

The use of Greek raises the question of the author's ethnicity. Was he a Greek-speaking Jew or a Gentile?[20] Most scholars favor the former position although some have argued strongly for the latter view.[21] Various pieces of information adduced from the gospel's theology, vocabulary, and style have figured in the debate.[22] Important concerns and values in the author's cultural and historical world can be seen here.

Theology

Scholars have tried to identify the author's ethnicity from various themes that occur in the Gospel of Matthew. This approach is not often successful because the cultural lines between Jew and Gentile were not rigid in the ancient world. The Jewish scriptures, for instance, were translated into Greek (the Septuagint) and widely used in Diaspora synagogues. Jerusalem was influenced by Hellenistic culture and Greek was spoken in the city. It is thus difficult to conclude that a particular emphasis *must* reflect a Jewish or Gentile author. Nevertheless, several themes have figured prominently in this discussion.

For example, some scholars have seen the writer's Gentile identity in his "Gentile bias." They have suggested he saw Israel as rejected by God and Gentiles as the objects of God's favor.[23] They note the harsh treatment of the religious leaders (Matt 23) and the author's claim that Israel's scriptures are fulfilled in Jesus. But nowhere in the gospel is Israel absolutely rejected. While the kingdom is taken from Israel's leaders (21:43–45), some Jewish people do believe (the disciples and others). Access to the reign of God, the community of believers, and the task of mission are not constituted on the basis of ethnicity. They embrace Jews and Gentiles who are committed to Jesus (28:19–20). These factors point, for some scholars, to a Greek-speaking Jewish author who had an "international" vision.

Some have argued that the presentation of a virgin birth in 1:18–25 indicates a Gentile author because there are no parallels to this phenomenon in Jewish literature.[24] However, the differences between Matthew's text and Gentile parallels, and the clear Jewish features of the story (its use of the form of an annunciation story, the inclusion of a Jewish text, the role of the law, and parallels to Moses) point to a Jewish writer.

K. Clark claims that in 22:41–46 Matthew indicates that the Messiah is not a descendant of David.[25] He claims that such a view could not come from a Jewish writer. But while 22:41–46 is difficult, there is no denying that throughout the gospel the relation of Jesus to the Davidic line is emphasized (1:1; 9:27; 12:23; 15:22; 20:30–31; 21:9, 15). By Clark's own logic, this should indicate a Jewish writer.

Conversely, some say that the prominent role of the law and the emphasis on the fulfillment of Jewish scriptures indicates Jewish authorship. Such a conclusion seems reasonable. But it must be qualified. This "Jewish" material may be included because it was present in the traditions available to the (Gentile) author and was attractive to a Gentile convert. Or it may be included to support a theological agenda designed to separate a Gentile community from its Jewish heritage.

A similar argument is made about the presence of distinctive Jewish material in the gospel. Jewish authorship can be deduced from the prominent place given to Jewish traditions, institutions, and piety (David, Moses, the temple, Jerusalem [4:5; 5:34–35; 27:53], the Sabbath [24:20], the contrast with the synagogue in 6:1–18, etc.). This makes sense, but the same cautions apply.[26]

J. P. Meier claims that two examples of blatant ignorance of Jewish matters indicate a Gentile author.[27] He points to the confusion in citing Zech 9:9 in Matt 21:5 which results in the image of Jesus riding two animals. Second, Matthew impossibly links the Pharisees and the Sadducees (3:7; 16:1), ignores the vast social, theological, and political differences between them, and suggests that they share a common teaching (16:12; cf. 22:23). Meier claims that such ignorance is not possible for a Jewish author.

Yet there are other ways to account for these aspects of the gospel. The first incident attests Matthew's concern to demonstrate the fulfillment of the scriptural traditions. The second forms part of Matthew's attack on the religious leaders as a group for their refusal to follow Jesus. Whatever internal differences the Jewish groups have, Matthew's emphasis falls on that which unites them, their opposition to Jesus.

Hints from Vocabulary

A second area in which scholars look for clues about the ethnic identity of the author is the vocabulary of the gospel.[28]

One particular phrase has stimulated scholarly interest. In Mark's gospel, Jesus generally speaks of "the reign of God." In Matthew, Jesus prefers "the kingdom (or reign) of the heavens."[29] This circumlocution avoids direct reference to the divine name, perhaps indicating a Jewish author. However, the gospel refers directly to God some fifty times. It also refers four times to the "kingdom or reign of God." Not much can be concluded from this observation.

The unusual Greek word *phylaktēria* (φυλακτήρια, "phylactery") in 23:5 is not used in the Septuagint. Its use suggests a Gentile writer's misunderstanding that these sacred Jewish objects were amulets to protect against the influence of spirits or disasters. However, evidence from other Jewish writings suggests considerable flexibility in the use of and terminology for sacred objects. This observation points to a Jewish writer.

In referring to the devil, the gospel uses the Semitic form of Satan along with Greek terms, "the tempter," "the devil," or "the evil one." Some see these latter terms as evidence of a Gentile author. But since the gospel is written in Greek, such use is not surprising and does not exclude the possibility of a Greek-writing Jewish author.

Matthew omits some Semitic forms which appear in Mark's gospel.[30] He also explains the meaning of the names "Jesus" and "Emmanuel" (1:21, 23). These factors could indicate a Gentile author.[31] But this conclusion seems unsubstantiated. Both words are important for Matthew's understanding of Jesus. As the next two chapters show, Matthew frequently makes improvements to Mark.[32]

Style

The style of the Gospel of Matthew is a third area scholars investigate for clues about the identity of its author. In numerous ways Matthew improves Mark's Greek (see ch. 4).[33] This observation indicates either a Gentile or a proficient Jewish writer.

Matthew's narrative includes words and grammatical constructions which reflect Hebrew and Aramaic influences. Some of these occur in material which the author received from his sources (see chs. 3–4) and from passages cited from the Septuagint. But some seem to derive from the author himself.[34] Whether they are introduced because a Gentile, influenced by the Septuagint, wanted to imitate Hebrew style or whether they derive from the author's own (Jewish) way of thinking is difficult to decide. Compare this with the late first-century Jewish writer Josephus. He tells his readers at the beginning of *The Jewish War*[35] that he "translated" the work into Greek from his native language (probably Aramaic). Yet Josephus wrote very competent Greek which bears little evidence of Semitic influence. However, the pervasiveness of Semitic features throughout Matthew's gospel, as well as the author's apparent knowledge of the Old Testament from the Hebrew text as well as from the Greek Septuagint suggests a Jewish trilingual (Aramaic, Hebrew, Greek) writer.[36]

Comment

The ethnicity of the author of this gospel is difficult to discern. Part of that difficulty has to do with determining what constitutes "Jewish" and "Gentile." Scholars have different ideas of what might be possible or impossible for a Jewish or Gentile author to accomplish. This lack of certainty reflects the cultural complexity of the first-century world. M. Hengel, among others, demonstrates that the first-century world cannot be neatly divided into Jewish and Hellenistic spheres.[37] Hellenistic culture had spread throughout the ancient world. No part of that world, including Jewish communities within Palestine and in the Diaspora, was isolated from its influence. This makes it very difficult to determine the origin and authorship of the Gospel of Matthew on the basis of linguistic and conceptual data.

The above material, however, does not supply a convincing case for a Gentile author. The objections to Jewish authorship are not conclusive and are capable of interpretation consistent with a Jewish author. I conclude from the above data that the author was an educated Jewish Christian, and probably trilingual. He wrote competent Greek, and, it seems, knew both Aramaic and Hebrew. The last observation makes his Gentile identity unlikely, though not impossible.

The author was clearly familiar with Jewish traditions and practices. What more can be known about this author's world? Three issues need to be considered.

WHERE WAS THE GOSPEL WRITTEN?

Scholars suggest several possible places of origin for the Gospel of Matthew: Jerusalem or Palestine,[38] Alexandria in Egypt,[39] Caesarea Maritima on the coast of Palestine,[40] the Transjordan at Pella,[41] Tyre or Sidon,[42] Sepphoris or Tiberias in Galilee.[43] The most widely supported theory is that it was written in Syria, possibly in the large, culturally and ethnically diverse city of Antioch-on-the-Orontes.[44]

While no certainty is possible, several factors point to Syria and the city of Antioch. The earliest citations of Matthew's gospel are found in the letters of Ignatius, bishop of Antioch, written in the first decade of the second century,[45] and in the Didache.[46] Both were widely used throughout Syria. These references suggest widespread use of this gospel in Syria. This can be explained if a prominent Syrian center such as Antioch was the place of its origin. Further, the gospel itself provides two clues. In 4:24, after a summary of Jesus' teaching and healing ministry in Galilee, we are told that "his fame spread throughout all Syria," a reference that is missing in the parallel passages of Mark 1:28, 39, and which, given the focus on Galilee, is somewhat surprising (cf. Matt 4:12–15, 23, 25). Further, numerous scholars have noted the significant role that Peter plays in this gospel (see 10:2; 16:16–19). This emphasis may reflect Peter's prominence in the church at Antioch (see Gal 2:11–14).

Some scholars offer further support for this theory. They suggest that the gospel reflects the marks of an urban and somewhat prosperous setting.[47] Kingsbury notices Matthew's strong preference for the word "city" (twenty-six times) and almost non-use of "village" (four times) in contrast with Mark's relatively minimal use of both terms (eight and seven times respectively). His study of the numerous terms for money in the gospel suggests a familiarity with the "up-market" entities of gold, silver, and talents. But whether these observations provide information about the geographical location of the gospel's author remains debatable.

WHEN WAS THE GOSPEL WRITTEN?

Since we have no dated original manuscript of the gospel, we must try to date its time of writing in relation to (1) other documents and (2) any events to which the gospel refers. We have noted that Ignatius and the Didache provide the first evidence for the gospel's use. Their citations indicate that Matthew's gospel was written by the first decade of the second century. This is its latest possible date.

The earliest date is determined by two factors, its relation to Mark and its likely reference to the destruction of Jerusalem by the Romans in the war of 66–70 CE. In the parable of the king's wedding feast (22:1–14), verse 7 records the king's violent response to those who refuse his invitation. He sends troops to destroy them and burn their city. This verse interrupts the sequence of verses 6 and 8. It records a response that exceeds what the situation requires and is missing in Luke's version of the parable (Luke 14:15–24). Scholars have suggested that the author has added it to the parable to provide a theological interpretation of the destruction of Jerusalem in 70 CE. If this is accurate,[48] it would indicate that the gospel was written some time after 70 CE.

A further factor points to the time period between the 70s and 110 CE. Chapters 3 and 4 outline the claim that one of Matthew's sources was Mark's gospel. Though there is debate about an exact date, Mark was probably written around 70 CE. These factors indicate a window of origin of about 70–110 CE. Can we be any more precise? Many scholars prefer a date in the 80s or 90s because they see reflected in the gospel a conflict between Matthew's community and a synagogue. We will discuss this conflict further in chapter 4.

Matthew's use of Mark has several consequences for the question of authorship and for understanding the role of the authorial audience. First it reinforces a post-70 date for the Gospel of Matthew. In turn, if the gospel was written in the 80s or 90s, some sixty years have passed since the time of Jesus. This time gap makes authorship by one of Jesus' disciples most unlikely. Further, it would be improbable (though not impossible) for an eyewitness and disciple of Jesus to rely so heavily on another gospel as a source for his own account (see chs. 3–4). These factors make it most unlikely that the apostle Matthew was the author of the gospel.[49] Therefore the authorial audience is not reading an eyewitness account.

Furthermore, the Gospel of Matthew was written after the resurrection of Jesus and before his return. The story ends with his resurrection and the commission of his disciples (Matt 28). The disciples carry out their commission in the period before Jesus returns and completes God's purposes (24:3–14). This indicates that the authorial audience has the identity and life-style of disciples of Jesus. It exists in this in-between time of difficult circumstances, opposition, division, and wickedness.

WHY THE NAME "MATTHEW"?

Some scholars suggest that the use of Matthew's name in Matt 9:9 functions like a signature. It indicates authorship by the disciple Matthew and emphasizes the gospel's authority.[50] The presence of Matthew's name changes Mark's presentation of the scene narrating Jesus' call of Levi (Mark 2:14). How do we explain this change of name and the selection of "Matthew" rather than some other name? The lack of clear external evidence, the late date of origin, and reliance on Mark, all indicate the unlikelihood that this change is the signature of Matthew, Jesus' disciple.

Two possible explanations for its choice arise from the text.[51] (1) The name Matthew means "gift of God." Matthew may represent the "many tax collectors and sinners" with whom Jesus associates in the next scene (9:10–13). (2) Kiley suggests a name association between *Maththaios* (Matthew), *mathētai* ("disciples") and the verb *mathete* which means "learn" and appears at the end of the scene in 9:13. Kiley connects the words "disciples" *(mathētai)* and "learn" *(mathete)*, to propose that the concept of "learning disciples" suggested the name *Maththaios*. The character "Matthew" may be a representative disciple who portrays these realities in the scene.

But while these suggestions may explain the name Matthew in 9:9, they do not explain how "Matthew" came to be linked with the whole gospel. Neither external sources nor the gospel itself support authorship by Matthew the disciple. Matthew, moreover, has a minimal role in the narrative. Apart from 9:9, his name appears only once, eighth on the list of the twelve disciples in 10:3.

What role did the disciple Matthew play in the period before the gospel came into existence? This may account for attributing the gospel to him. Perhaps Matthew was a key teacher and/or leader in the early years (the 30s and 40s CE) of the community at Antioch. Or perhaps he contributed in a significant way to the understanding of Jesus which is presented in the gospel.[52] Maybe he assisted in reflecting on Old Testament writings and applying them to Jesus' life. Or maybe he was a source of stories and sayings of Jesus which subsequently became part of the gospel. Perhaps Papias was referring to one of these roles when he said that Matthew collected "oracles." Subsequently Papias' statement was understood as referring to the whole gospel. Or perhaps the scene involving Matthew the learning disciple (9:9) powerfully grasped people's imagination as a representative scene and the name stuck. Whatever the reason, the authorial audience understands him to be an authoritative figure.

CONCLUSION

In this chapter we have taken one step toward joining the authorial audience by considering aspects of the author's world—his identity, ethnicity, time, and place. I have discussed the claim that Matthew, the disciple of Jesus, was the gospel's author. I have concluded that this claim is not convincing because it lacks both external and internal evidence. I suggest that the gospel was probably written by an unidentifiable, educated, Jewish Christian living in Syria, possibly in the city of Antioch, sometime in the 80s in the first century CE. I suggest that the name "Matthew" was later attached to the gospel because it denotes a respected and authoritative figure who may have been associated with the gospel's traditions or a community addressed by the gospel.

The authorial audience is situated in the time after the resurrection and before the return of Jesus. This alerts us to our cultural, historical, and geographical distance from the world assumed of the authorial audience. So, to join the authorial audience is to take a cross-cultural step.

The following chapters continue to use the name "Matthew" for the gospel's author. But this does not refer to the disciple. Rather it is the conventional name in the sense outlined in this chapter. The terms "author" or "implied author" are used interchangeably to refer to the author implied or indicated by the gospel's content, structure, and style of expression.

In the next chapter we consider the gospel's genre. Thus we will take a further step to close the distance between ourselves and the world assumed by the text.

NOTES

1. Irenaeus, *Against Heresies* 3.11.7. (*The Ante-Nicene Fathers* [ed. A. Roberts and J. Donaldson; 1885 reprint; Peabody, Mass.: Hendrick-

son Publishers, 1995]). Some claim that Papias (see below) provides evidence that the titles ("The Gospel According to . . . ") were known early in the second century. But Eusebius' citation of Papias does not include the title, does not use the word "gospel," and does not indicate that he understands what Mark and Matthew write are gospels. Cf. M. Hengel, "The Titles of the Gospels and the Gospel of Mark," in *Studies in the Gospel of Mark* (Philadelphia: Fortress, 1985) 64–84, esp. 66 and note 16, p. 164.

2. Irenaeus, *Against Heresies* 3.9.1–3, 3.11.8, 3.16.2 for examples of attributed citations; see 3.13.2 for one example of unattributed allusion.

3. Irenaeus, *Against Heresies* 3.1.1.

4. In his letter to the Romans Paul is not the founder of the church. He is visiting a church that someone else has founded though he knows (of?) some of the people in the church (1:8–15; 15:22–33; 16:1–16). One possible reason for the letter may well be to introduce himself and his gospel to the congregation as well as to address difficulties between Jewish and Gentile Christians. See *The Romans Debate* (rev. and exp.; ed. Karl P. Donfried; Peabody, Mass.: Hendrickson Publishers, 1991); W. Carter, "Rome (and Jerusalem): The Contingency of Romans 3:21–26," *Irish Biblical Studies* 11 (1989) 54–68.

5. See 1 Clement 5, and the letter of Ignatius to the Romans, 4.

6. Eusebius, *Ecclesiastical History* (LCC; trans. J. Oulton with H. Lawlor; 2 vols.; Cambridge, Mass. and London: Harvard University and Heinemann, 1980). He also refers to the testimony of Origen (6.25.4), Clement of Alexandria (6.14.5) and Irenaeus (5.8.1–2), as well as citing his own account in 3.24.1–11. These figures make essentially the same claim about the gospel's author: it was written by Matthew the tax collector and disciple, in Hebrew, for Jewish believers.

7. Eusebius, *Eccl. Hist.* 3.39.1–16.

8. For discussion and bibliography, D. Hill, *The Gospel of Matthew* (NCB; Grand Rapids: Eerdmans, 1972) 22–29; W. Kümmel, *Introduction to the New Testament* (London: SCM, 1975) 49, 120–21; the articles by G. Kennedy, "Classical and Christian Source Criticism," by W. Meeks, "Hypomnēmata from an Untamed Sceptic: A Response to George Kennedy," by R. Fuller, "Classics and the Gospels: The Seminar," in *The Relationships Among the Gospels: An Interdisciplinary Approach* (ed. W. Walker; San Antonio: Trinity University, 1978) 125–92, esp. 147–52, 164–71, 176–82; R. Gundry, *Matthew: A Commentary on His Literary and Theological Art* (Grand Rapids: Eerdmans, 1982) 609–22; W. D. Davies and D. Allison, *The Gospel According to Saint Matthew* (2 vols.; Edinburgh: T. & T. Clark, 1988, 1991) 1.7–17; U. Luz, *Matthew 1–7* (Minneapolis: Fortress, 1989) 80, 94–95; also P. Sellew, "Eusebius and the Gospels," in *Eusebius, Christianity, and*

Judaism (ed. H. Attridge and G. Hata; Detroit: Wayne State University, 1992) 110–38.

9. These two words can function to supply a transition to a new sentence or topic, to indicate the conclusion of a process or to suggest a contrast with what has gone before. BAGD, 502–3; BDF, 231–32, 234–35; Liddell and Scott, *Lexicon,* 1102, 1271; J. P. Louw and E. Nida, *Greek-English Lexicon of the New Testament,* (2 vols.; New York: UBS, 1988) 2.89.50; 89.128; 91.8.

10. This possibility receives support in that after referring to Matthew writing his gospel, Eusebius comments that "Mark and Luke had *already* (ἤδη) published the Gospels according to them" (my emphasis). But this order (Mark then Matthew) would contradict his citing of Irenaeus, Origen, and Clement who place Matthew first. It is also undermined by the observation that Papias' comments refer not to Mark's writing a gospel but to making notes of Peter's preaching.

11. So B. W. Bacon, *Studies in Matthew* (London: Constable, 1930) 25–28; G. D. Kilpatrick, *The Origins of the Gospel According to St. Matthew* (Oxford: Clarendon, 1946) 3–5; C. S. Petrie, "The Authorship of 'The Gospel According to Matthew': a Reconsideration of the External Evidence," *NTS* 14 (1967–68) 15–33; Gundry, *Matthew,* 616–18.

12. F. C. Grant, *The Gospels: Their Origin and Their Growth* (London: Faber & Faber, 1957) 65, 144.

13. W. Allen, *The Gospel According to S. Matthew* (ICC; Edinburgh: T. & T. Clark, 1907) lxxx–lxxxi; T. W. Manson, *The Sayings of Jesus* (London: SCM, 1949) 18; Hill, *Gospel of Matthew,* 26; C. F. D. Moule, *The Birth of the New Testament* (3d ed.; London: A. & C. Black, 1981) 276–77.

14. J. Kürzinger, "Das Papiaszeugnis und die Erstgestalt des Matthäusevangeliums," *BZ* 4 (1960) 19–38; idem, "Irenäus und sein Zeugnis zur Sprache des Matthäusevangeliums," *NTS* 10 (1963–64) 108–15; Gundry, *Matthew,* 619–20.

15. Moule, *Birth,* 276.

16. Augustine, *De Consensu Evangelistarum,* 1.1–2.

17. In his *Apology,* written around 155 CE, Justin refers to readings from the "memoirs of the apostles" in Sunday worship services. He calls these gospels. See "First Apology of Justin," sections 66–67 (*Early Christian Fathers,* vol. 1; trans. and ed. C. C. Richardson; Philadelphia: Fortress, 1953). In his *Dialogue with Trypho* (103) he says these memoirs "were drawn up by his apostles and those who followed them." He quotes from Matthew but does not name the gospel. See, for example, "First Apology," sections 15–17. Frequently the quotes combine passages from different gospels.

18. Literary critics have talked of the implied author, the sense of the author which is revealed in the content, ordering, expression, point of view or norms and values, etc. of the text. This implied author is related to but not the same as the flesh-and-bones author.

19. A few contemporary scholars continue to argue that Matthew's gospel existed originally in Hebrew. C. C. Torrey, *Our Translated Gospels* (New York and London: Harper & Brothers, 1936) ix; B. C. Butler, *The Originality of St Matthew* (Cambridge: Cambridge University, 1951) chs. 10–11; P. Gaechter, *Das Matthäus-Evangelium: Ein Kommentar* (Innsbruck: Tyrolia, 1963) 19; W. F. Albright and C. S. Mann, *Matthew* (AB; Garden City: Doubleday, 1971) xxxvi–xlviii.

20. There has been little discussion of the gender of the author.

21. For this minority scholarly tradition, see K. W. Clark, "The Gentile Bias of Matthew," *JBL* 66 (1947) 165–72, reprinted in K. W. Clark, *The Gentile Bias and Other Essays* (Leiden: E. J. Brill, 1980) 1–8; P. Nepper-Christensen, *Das Mattäusevangelium: Ein judenchristliches Evangelium?* (ATD 1; Aarhus: Universitetsforlaget, 1954); G. Strecker, *Der Weg der Gerechtigkeit* (FRLANT 82; Göttingen: Vandenhoeck & Ruprecht, 1962); R. Walker, *Die Heilsgeschichte im ersten Evangelium* (FRLANT 91; Göttingen: Vandenhoeck & Ruprecht, 1967); S. van Tilborg, *The Jewish Leaders in Matthew* (Leiden: E. J. Brill, 1972) 171–72; H. Frankemölle, *Jahwebund und Kirche Christi* (NTA 10; Münster: Aschendorf, 1974); J. P. Meier, *The Vision of Matthew* (New York: Crossroad, 1979) 17–25; M. J. Cook, "Interpreting 'Pro-Jewish' Passages in Matthew," *HUCA* 53 (1984) 135–46.

22. I will selectively follow Clark's essay "The Gentile Bias of Matthew," and the critique by Davies and Allison, *Matthew*, 1.17–58, esp. 17–33.

23. Clark, "Gentile Bias," 165–68; Davies and Allison, *Matthew*, 1.22–24.

24. Clark, "Gentile Bias," 165; Davies and Allison, *Matthew*, 1.21–22; R. Brown, *The Birth of the Messiah* (New York: Doubleday, 1977, 1993) 143–64, 517–34, 600–603, 697–712.

25. Clark, "Gentile Bias," 167; Davies and Allison, *Matthew*, 1.22.

26. See the list in Davies and Allison, *Matthew*, 1.26–27.

27. Meier, *Vision of Matthew*, 17–25; Davies and Allison, *Matthew*, 1.31–32.

28. Clark, "Gentile Bias," 169–71; Davies and Allison, *Matthew*, 1.17–21.

29. There are four exceptions, 6:33; 12:28; 21:31, 43.

30. "Talitha koum," from Mark 5:41 (cf. Matt 9:25), "Rabbouni" from Mark 10:51 (cf. Matt 20:33), "Abba," from Mark 14:36 (cf. Matt 26:39).

31. Clark, "Gentile Bias," 171; Davies and Allison, *Matthew*, 1.19–21.

32. J. Hawkins, *Horae Synopticae: Contributions to the Study of the Synoptic Problem* (2d ed.; rev. and supp., 1909; Grand Rapids: Baker, 1968) 158–60.

33. Hawkins, *Horae Synopticae*, 117–25, 131–38, 143–53; Allen, *Matthew*, xix–xxxi.

34. Clark, "Gentile Bias," 168–69; Davies and Allison, *Matthew*, 1.80–85; M. Goulder, *Midrash and Lection in Matthew* (London: SPCK, 1974) 116–21; Moule, *Birth*, 277–80.

35. Josephus, *Jewish War* 1.3. See T. Rajak, *Josephus: The Historian and His Society* (Philadelphia: Fortress, 1984); Appendix 1, "The Native Language of Josephus," and chs. 1, 7.

36. Davies and Allison (*Matthew*, 1.32–58) marshall the evidence for Matthew's knowledge of Hebrew. See also Goulder, *Midrash and Lection*, 123–27.

37. M. Hengel, *Judaism and Hellenism* (Philadelphia: Fortress, 1974, 1981); S. Cohen, *From the Maccabees to the Mishnah* (Philadelphia: Westminster, 1987) 27–59; C. Roetzel, *The World That Shaped the New Testament* (Atlanta: John Knox, 1985).

38. D. Guthrie, *New Testament Introduction: The Gospel and Acts* (Chicago: Inter-Varsity, 1965) 26–27; Allen, *Matthew*, 310; A. Plummer, *An Exegetical Commentary on the Gospel According to St. Matthew* (London: E. Stock, 1909) xxxiii.

39. S. G. F. Brandon, *The Fall of Jerusalem and the Christian Church* (London: SPCK, 1957) ch. 12; van Tilborg, *Jewish Leaders*, 172.

40. B. Viviano, "Where was the Gospel According to St. Matthew Written?" *CBQ* 41 (1979) 533–46.

41. W. Marxsen, *Introduction to the New Testament* (Philadelphia: Fortress, 1968) 153; H. D. Slingerland, "The Transjordanian Origin of St. Matthew's Gospel," *JSNT* 3 (1979) 18–28.

42. Kilpatrick, *Origins*, 131–34.

43. J. Overman, *Matthew's Gospel and Formative Judaism: A Study of the Social World of the Matthean Community* (Minneapolis: Fortress, 1990) 159 n. 40. Both A. Segal ("Matthew's Jewish Voice," in *Social History of the Matthean Community: Cross-Disciplinary Approaches* [ed. D. Balch; Minneapolis: Fortress, 1991] 3–37) and L. M. White ("Crisis Management and Boundary Maintenance: The Social Location of Matthean Community," in *Social History* [ed. Balch], 211–47) express sympathy for a Galilean origin.

44. See G. Stanton, "The Origin and Purpose of Matthew's Gospel: Matthean Scholarship from 1945 to 1980," in *ANRW* II.25.3 (ed.

W. Haase; Berlin and New York: Walter de Gruyter, 1985) 1941–42;
For discussion of Antioch, see W. Carter, *Households and Discipleship:
A Study of Matthew 19–20* (JSNTSup 103; Sheffield: Sheffield Aca-
demic, 1994) 40–46; E. Downey, *A History of Antioch in Syria* (Prince-
ton: Princeton University, 1961); R. Stark, "Antioch as the Social
Situation for Matthew's Gospel," in *Social History* (ed. Balch),
189–210; R. Gundry, "A Responsive Evaluation of the Social History
of the Matthean Community in Roman Syria," in *Social History* (ed.
Balch), 62–67. A. J. Saldarini (*Matthew's Christian-Jewish Community*
[Chicago: University of Chicago, 1994] 11, 26) supports Syria.

45. Ignatius begins his letter to the church in Smyrna on the
Aegean Sea in Asia Minor (present-day Turkey) by listing the Smyr-
naeans' beliefs. He mentions that Jesus was "baptized by John, that 'all
righteousness might be fulfilled by him' " (1:1). This citation is found
only in Matthew's account of Jesus' baptism (Matt 3:15). Matthew's
verse includes several words that are important and distinct in this
gospel ("fulfill," "righteousness") and which also appear in Ignatius'
citation. Three other instances of Ignatius' likely use of Matthew occur
in his letters: to Polycarp (cf. 2:2 and Matt 10:16b), to the Philippians
(cf. 3:1 and Matt 15:13–14) and to the Ephesians (cf. 19:1–3 and Matt
1–2). See Richardson, *Early Christian Fathers*, 93, 108, 112–13, 118;
also J. P. Meier, "Matthew and Ignatius," in *Social History* (ed. Balch),
178–86.

46. The Didache cites Matthew's form of the Lord's Prayer (8:1–3;
cf. Matt 6:9–13). (Matthew's prayer differs from Luke's form [Luke
11:2–4] in that it has a longer address to God and includes two extra
petitions.) The Didache's anonymous use of Matthew and in combination with other gospels is typical of much second century use (2 Clement, Barnabas, 1 Clement). See E. Massaux, *The Influence of the Gospel
According to Saint Matthew on Christian Literature before Saint Irenaeus*
(3 vols.; Macon: Mercer University, 1990–93).

47. See Kilpatrick, *Origins*, 124–26; J. D. Kingsbury, *Matthew*
(Proclamation; Philadelphia: Fortress, 1986) 99–100; idem, *Matthew's
Story of Jesus*, 152–56; idem, "The Verb ἀκολουθεῖν ("To Follow") as
an Index of Matthew's View of His Community," *JBL* 97 (1978) 56–73,
esp. 66–68.

48. This view has been contested by K. Rengstorf ("Die Stadt der
Mörder [Mt 22:7]" in *Judentum, Urchristentum, Kirche: Festschrift für
Joachim Jeremias* [BZNW 26; ed. W. Eltester; Berlin: Töpelmann,
1960] 106–29) who sees the use of a widespread tradition of punitive
expeditions against resisters. R. Gundry (*Matthew*, 436–37, 600) fa-
vors a pre-70 date. He interprets 22:7 as another example of Matthew's
use of the Old Testament, in this case Isa 5:24–25.

49. A few scholars maintain that Matthew the disciple wrote the gospel. See E. J. Goodspeed, *Matthew, Apostle and Evangelist* (Philadelphia: John C. Winston, 1959) chs. 2, 3, 6, 7, 11; N. B. Stonehouse, *Origins of the Synoptic Gospels: Some Basic Questions* (Grand Rapids: Eerdmans, 1963) 19–47; Gaechter, *Matthäus-Evangelium*, 18–19; Albright and Mann, *Matthew*, clxxvii–clxxxvi; Gundry, *Matthew*, 620–22; R. T. France, *Matthew: Evangelist and Teacher* (Grand Rapids: Zondervan, 1989) 77–80.

50. Albright and Mann, *Matthew*, clxxvii–clxxix. They propose that Levi is Matthew's tribal designation.

51. See D. C. Duling, "Matthew," *ABD* (6 vols.; New York: Doubleday, 1992) 4.618–22; M. Kiley, "Why 'Matthew' in Matt 9, 9–13?" *Biblica* 65 (1984) 347–51.

52. K. Stendahl (*The School of St. Matthew* [Philadelphia: Fortress, 1954, 1968] 20–35) has argued that the gospel is a "handbook for teaching and administration within the church" derived from a "milieu of study and instruction" and issued by the leaders of a "school for teachers and church leaders." The school "preserved and expounded the doctrines and rules of its founder."

Chapter 3

Recognizing the Gospel's Genre

To join the authorial audience also requires a recognition of the gospel's genre and the roles and expectations appropriate to that genre. A genre imposes limitations on an author and creates expectations of an audience. Determining the gospel's genre, though, is a complex matter that has caused much debate among scholars. It is necessary to review this debate to learn what kind of text the authorial audience reads.

AN EYEWITNESS ACCOUNT OF JESUS' LIFE?

Various early church writers such as Irenaeus claim that this gospel was written by Matthew, one of the twelve disciples. This approach views the gospel as an eyewitness account presenting an accurate historical record of Jesus' life. To read as the authorial audience would mean treating the gospel as a historical account.

The last chapter indicates that the gospel genre is not that of an eyewitness account. The gospel was probably not written by Matthew, one of the twelve disciples. The apologetic nature and late date of these claims, the gospel's likely date of origin in the 80s, and its use of Mark as a source indicate that such a designation is inappropriate.

THE GOSPELS AS THEOLOGICAL DOCUMENTS

The eighteenth century Enlightenment prompted major changes in the way people understood the world. Reason, historical and scientific methods challenged many traditional understandings and authorities.[1] This time of questioning gave birth to several major lines of inquiry which have profoundly shaped the understanding of the gospel's genre.

The Quest for the Historical Jesus

Toward the end of the eighteenth century Hermann Samuel Reimarus, a professor of Oriental languages, argued that the gospels were documents with a theological rather than historical agenda.[2] They were written with 20/20 hindsight. They put their own theological spin on things. Reimarus claimed that after Jesus' death, his followers used the gospels to paint a portrait of Jesus which differed greatly from Jesus' own life.

Reimarus argued that Jesus believed himself to be the political Messiah of Jewish eschatological expectation whose mission was to establish a kingdom on earth. When the popular uprising of support did not happen (Reimarus finds references to this in Matt 10:23; 21:1–11), Jesus was put to death, a failure abandoned by God (27:46). After Jesus' death, his disciples, seeking to secure their own worldly position, set about reframing Jesus' life. They drew on another aspect of Jewish eschatological understanding, the expectation of a spiritual Messiah, to create a different image of Jesus. They stole his body, announced that he was risen from the dead and would return in glory and triumph. They proclaimed Jesus' death as necessary "to obtain forgiveness for humankind."[3] The gospels are written from this perspective, to proclaim Jesus as the risen and returning spiritual Messiah and redeemer of the world. Nevertheless, Reimarus argued that by careful investigation, the gospels could be and must be subjected to rational and historical inquiry to find the natural, historical origins of Christianity lying behind this proclamation.

Reimarus' work sparked considerable controversy at the time. Most scholars then and since have not agreed with his political-Messiah-turned-spiritual-Messiah analysis. Most have not agreed that radical discontinuity exists between the Jesus proclaimed in the gospels and the Jesus of history. Most have also not accepted his negative presentation of the role of the deceiving disciples in creating the gospels.

But most have accepted and developed Reimarus' insight that a gap exists between what the church taught as revealed dogma and what could be shown to have happened in history. The Jesus of history differs from the Christ of faith. Many have taken up the challenge to investigate and expose that gap.[4] Many have tried to explain how the developments in understanding Jesus took place between the time of Jesus and the time when the gospels were written. Most have also agreed with and expanded Reimarus' understanding that the gospels were not historical accounts of the life of Jesus but proclamations of the significance of Jesus produced later by his disciples and communities of faith (see further below).[5]

Reimarus' work began what has been known as the Quest for the Historical Jesus. This quest has, with a few exceptions, built on and reinforced his premise that the gospels need to be and could be investigated to discover the historical Jesus behind the Christ of faith they proclaim. Debate has continued for over two hundred years to determine how that search is to be carried out,[6] how much continuity or discontinuity exists between the historical Jesus and the Christ of faith, and what theological implications the results of the search might have for contemporary faith.[7]

The history of this quest is fascinating, but it need not concern us here. What is important is the understanding of the gospels that has emerged from this work. The premise of the work is that the gospels are documents with a theological agenda. They are proclamations about the significance of Jesus, shaped by faith and written for faith. So the authorial audience does not read for historical information but for theological edification.

In this perspective, Matthew's gospel reveals the significance of Jesus formulated in the context of a community of believers. This is not to say that it does not contain some historically reliable information about Jesus. But that is not its primary concern or focus. Rather the basic nature of the gospel is proclamation, an insight which shapes the audience's expectations.

Literary Relationships Among the Gospels

The work initiated by Johann Jakob Griesbach also contributed significantly to this understanding of the gospel's genre. In the early centuries of the church, numerous writers tried to combine the four gospels into one synthesized writing or "harmony" of the life of Jesus.[8] These attempts assumed that all four gospels contained similar content because they were eyewitness historical accounts of the life of Jesus. In 1774–76 Griesbach challenged this approach in publishing a "synopsis" of Matthew, Mark, and Luke, and some selections from John. Griesbach contributed three things of great consequence for understanding Matthew's gospel:

- He noted that among the gospels there were conflicting chronologies.[9]

- He observed that John was significantly different. He excluded John to focus on the three "synoptic" gospels.

- He stated in his introduction that his book was not a "harmony" of the life of Jesus because he did not think the conflicting chronologies could be harmonized.

In setting out the gospel material in his synopsis, Griesbach did not combine paragraphs from the various gospels to form a single narrative of Jesus' life, the usual format of the "harmonies." Instead, he set out the material in parallel columns, one per gospel. For Griesbach, the differences among the gospels were such that they could not be combined into one narrative. The extent of the differences indicated to Griesbach that the gospels were not eyewitness accounts. Yet the gospels were similar in many respects. How to explain these similarities and differences?

Griesbach explained these similarities and differences on the basis of a direct literary relationship among the three gospels.[10] He claimed that Matthew, the longest, was the first gospel written. Luke was the second and employed Matthew as a source. Mark, the third, abbreviated both gospels, sometimes following Matthew's content and order, sometimes Luke's.[11] On Griesbach's theory, the similarities among the gospels arise from the use of Matthew as a common source for both Luke and

Mark (who also used Luke); the differences arise from the involvement of different authors.[12]

Griesbach's observations identified the problem with which subsequent scholars have wrestled. This problem is known as the Synoptic Problem. It concerns the explanation of the similarities and the differences that exist among the three Synoptic Gospels. Much debate has followed and numerous proposals have been made.

The solution that currently holds most, though certainly not universal, support was proposed in 1863 by Heinrich Julius Holtzmann. Like Griesbach, Holtzmann advocated a literary dependence among the gospels. However he differed significantly from Griesbach on what those relationships looked like. Building on the work of others, he argued that Mark, not Matthew, was the earliest gospel. Both Matthew and Luke used Mark as a source, along with a second source, a collection of sayings attributed to Jesus. This solution is referred to as the "Two Document Hypothesis" because it names both Mark and another "sayings source" as the two documents used independently as sources by Matthew and Luke.[13]

Further debate followed[14] and in 1924 in a widely influential publication B. H. Streeter proposed a modification to the Holtzmann synthesis. Streeter supported the claim that Mark was the first gospel written (Markan priority) with five observations.[15]

- Matthew reproduces ninety percent of Mark, and Luke reproduces just over half of Mark.

- "In any average section," Matthew and Luke reproduce "the majority of the actual words used by Mark."

- Matthew and Luke generally support Mark's order. If one departs from that order, the other usually follows Mark.

- Mark's primacy is seen in its preservation of Aramaic words, rough style and grammar, and some offensive content which are omitted or toned down in Matthew and Luke.

- The distribution of both Markan and nonMarkan material in Matthew and Luke points to the use of Mark as a single document and the combination of this material with the other sources.

Streeter retained Mark and a sayings collection (now known as "Q"[16]) as the two basic sources for Matthew and Luke. But Streeter was aware that Holtzmann's theory did not account for all the material in Matthew and Luke. Each gospel had material that was particular to it, about twenty percent of Matthew and thirty percent of Luke. Streeter proposed that each gospel had an additional source which preserved the specific traditions of its place of origin. He called Matthew's special source "M" and Luke's source "L."

Even though debate has continued, Streeter's Four Document Hypothesis has been called the "classical statement and defence" of this position.[17] With some modification it has become the standard (though not universally accepted) "solution" to the Synoptic Problem. It accounts for the similarities and differences in the three Synoptic Gospels on the basis of the *literary* interdependence and shared sources (Matthew and Luke's use of Mark and Q) as well as material unique to each gospel (M and L).[18] Though first in the canon, Matthew was the second gospel written, some sixty or so years after the crucifixion of Jesus, and using Mark, Q, and M as sources.

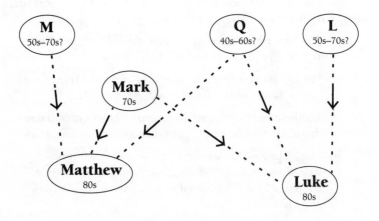

The Synoptics and Their Sources

This two-hundred-year dialogue has important implications for the understanding of the genre of Matthew's gospel. It shows that this gospel is not an eyewitness account from one of the original apostles. It does not permit such an approach for the authorial audience. Rather, by attempting to account for the similarities and differences in the three gospels' structure and content, a very different picture of each gospel's genre and origin has emerged. Matthew's gospel was created from several sources transmitted over a number of decades after the life of Jesus. They were combined to form the gospel in the late first century. While Matthew contains historical information about Jesus, it is primarily a proclamation, a testimony to the faith of early communities of faith. This latter insight has been secured by form criticism, the investigation of the processes by which the gospel traditions were formed and transmitted in the period *before* the gospels were written. This was between the death of Jesus around 30 and the writing of the first gospel, Mark, around 70.[19]

The Author of Matthew's Gospel as Pastoral Theologian

Attention to the formative role of the pre-gospel communities of faith in shaping individual units of material about Jesus leads to further reflection on the role of the authors in the composition of the gospels. This work strengthens the understanding of Matthew's gospel as a theological document and provides insight into the roles and expectations of the authorial audience.

The author of Matthew's gospel introduced diverse material and rearranged Mark's narrative. The process of assembling pericopes into a new unit shapes and interprets the material thereby impacting the audience's comprehension. Decisions to include or omit material, to locate it at a particular point in the gospel, to juxtapose it with what precedes and follows, to use particular words and style, to add to or abbreviate a section or pericope, all influence the audience's understanding. This process of composition or *redaction* (as it is commonly called) provides the gospel writers with the means to express their own theological agenda and to address the situations of their audience. *Redaction* critics have studied this process of creative reinterpretation, seeking insight into the author's theology and the audience's situation. Their work has been the dominant method of gospel study from the 1950s to the present.[20]

This approach seeks to identify the author's redactional activity by comparing pericopes across the gospels. The comparison identifies changes that Matthew makes to Mark's or Luke's (Q material) presentation. These changes are understood as clues to two things. (1) *The gospel writer's own theological understanding.* Redaction critics assume that gospel writers make consistent changes to express their own theological convictions and to shape the audience's understanding, identity, and lifestyle. Matthew emerges as a theologian in his own right, one who understands and presents the story of Jesus to express theological insights which differ from those of Mark and Luke.

(2) *The situation of the gospel writer's own community of faith.* Redaction critics contend that differences between gospels reflect not only the distinctive theological understandings of each gospel writer. They also reflect different circumstances in the communities for whom the gospels were written. So gospel writers shaped their material to impact the lifestyle and address the needs and circumstances of their own community of faith. Examination of the author's changes to the gospel material gives redaction critics a sense of the target community's situation. This helps in understanding what is required of the audience. The gospel's content and characters (for example the disciples) reveal the social and religious situation of the writer's community.

A gospel writer as pastoral theologian differs significantly from a gospel writer as eyewitness recorder. The former has a key role in shaping the gospels. So Matthew is not an eyewitness apostle. He is a pastoral theologian seeking to build up his community in its particular circumstances late in first century Antioch. Like any pastor, he presented stories about Jesus to meet the needs of his community in its particular situation. He thus strengthened their identity as disciples of Jesus and shaped their way of life. His gospel appears not primarily as an historical account of the life of Jesus but as a proclamation of the significance of Jesus for a particular community of believers. The authorial audience comprises believers who adopt the roles, identity, and lifestyle which emerge in the gospel's presentation.

An Example

Some of the earliest redaction work originates from Günther Bornkamm in a 1948 essay on Matt 8:23–27 entitled "The Stilling of the Storm in Matthew."[21] Bornkamm's work with this pericope offers an example of how the author presents material to shape the audience's understanding and lifestyle.

Bornkamm compares Matthew's version of this story with Mark's pericope (Mark 4:35–41). He assumes the "two source" hypothesis and begins his article by acknowledging his debt to form criticism for the insight that the gospels are proclamations (kerygma) not biography. They derive from and address the church's "faith in Jesus Christ, the Crucified and Resurrected." Bornkamm argues that Matthew significantly recasts Mark's story to create a different understanding for the audience. Mark presents a miracle story emphasizing Jesus' power over nature. Matthew makes changes to "give it a new meaning" as a story about "the danger and glory" of discipleship in "the little ship of the church." Matthew does not merely pass on the tradition but interprets it, directing the audience's insight.

Bornkamm's work is a good example of redaction criticism. Printed below are the texts of Mark and Matthew. I have summarized Bornkamm's observations and linked them to the text so that readers can observe him at work.

① A New Context

Bornkamm says that Matthew places the story of the stilling of the storm in a different context. For Mark the story is part of a series of miracle stories in chapters 1, 2, 4, and 5 and is included at the end of the collection of parables in chapter 4. Matthew collects these miracle stories into a different sequence in chapters 8–9 following the Sermon on the Mount in chapters 5–7. That is, after presenting the "Messiah of Word" (Matt 5–7), he presents the "Messiah of Deed" (Matt 8–9).

Mark 4:33–41		Matthew 8:18–27

Mark 4:33–41

33With many such parables he spoke the word to them, as they were able to hear it; 34he did not speak to them except in parables, but he explained everything in private to his disciples.

Matthew 8:18–27

① 18Now when Jesus saw great crowds around him, he gave orders to go over to the other side. 19A scribe then approached and said, "Teacher, I will follow you wherever you go." 20And Jesus said to him, "Foxes have holes, and birds of the air have nests; but the Son of Man has nowhere to lay his head."

② 21Another of his disciples said to him, "Lord, first let me go and bury my father." 22But Jesus said to him, "Follow me, and let the dead bury their own dead."

35On that day, when evening had come, he said to them, "Let us go across to the other side." 36And leaving the crowd behind, they took him with them in the boat, just as he was. Other boats were with him.

③ 23And when he got into the boat, his disciples followed him.

⑥

37A great windstorm arose, and the waves beat into the boat, so that the boat was already being swamped. 38But he was in the stern, asleep on the cushion; and they woke him up and said to him, "Teacher, do you not care that we are perishing?"

24A windstorm arose on the sea, so great that the boat was being swamped by the waves; but he was asleep. 25And they went and woke him up, saying, "Lord, save us! We are perishing!"

④

39He woke up and rebuked the wind, and said to the sea, "Peace! Be still!" Then the wind ceased, and there was a dead calm. 40He said to them, "Why are you afraid? Have you still no faith?"

⑤ 26And he said to them, "Why are you afraid, you of little faith?" Then he got up and rebuked the winds and the sea; and there was a dead calm.

41And they were filled with great awe and said to one another, "Who then is this, that even the wind and the sea obey him?"

⑦ 27They were amazed, saying, "What sort of man is this, that even the winds and the sea obey him?"

② Sequence (8:18-22)

Matthew places the story after a pericope which consists of two sayings. One is about discipleship and the other is about the decision to "follow" Jesus (8:18–22). The first saying addresses unconsidered discipleship (8:20) and the second "the summons to a radical decisiveness" (8:22).

③ A New Introduction (8:23)

Bornkamm notes that Matthew changes Mark's introduction to the story. In Mark Jesus invites the disciples to cross over to the other side. In Matthew Jesus goes ahead, and the disciples follow. The word *follow* is crucial. While it expresses a literal meaning, its placement after 8:18–22, in which the same verb appears twice as a metaphor for discipleship (cf. 19, 22), indicates a significant reformulation of a miracle story to one about discipleship. This "new meaning" is confirmed and elaborated for Bornkamm in subsequent changes.

④ A Changed Word

The disciples' cry in 8:25 is significant. Bornkamm notes that Mark's disciples address Jesus as "Teacher" but Matthew's disciples use "Lord." In Matthew this title is used for Jesus by those seeking help from one of power (8:2) and authority (8:6–8), and always by disciples (8:21, contrast the scribe's address in 8:19). Bornkamm notes other uses of this "divine predicate of majesty" (7:21; 14:28, 30; 16:22; 17:4, 18:21; 24:42; 25:37, 44; 26:22) and concludes that the disciples' address "contains a confession of discipleship."

⑤ Rearranged Order of Material

In Mark the miracle of calming the storm precedes Jesus' "accusing" words (4:39). Matthew reverses the order; in the midst of the storm Jesus speaks first to the disciples (8:26a). Mark's accusation of "no faith" is rendered "little faith" (8:26), an expression which appears only in Matthew (6:30; 14:31; 16:8; 17:20) except for one use in Luke (12:28). Matthew uses the term to denote weak, anxious, and paralyzed faith rather than "no faith." The scene presents a "typical situation of discipleship."

⑥ A Changed Word

Bornkamm returns to verse 24 to note that Matthew changes Mark's words to denote the storm. Matthew's choice is significant for Bornkamm. He argues that the word "storm" (σεισμός; *seismos*) denotes "apocalyptic horrors," the distress of the end of the age, the time in which disciples live.[22] The "disciples on the sea become a symbol of the distresses involved in discipleship of Jesus." Jesus' word to the storm addresses the situation of the disciples, reassuring them of rescue in trial, security in the midst of storm.

⑦ Different Characters

In Mark the disciples wonder who has calmed the storm. But in the Greek text of Matthew it is people, not the disciples who ask this question. Bornkamm explains the change by saying that these people "represent those who are encountered by the story through preaching." The story functions as a "call to imitation and discipleship."

Bornkamm concludes from his observations that these changes create for the audience an understanding that differs significantly from Mark's presentation. In Matthew's hands the storm scene is

> a description of the dangers against which Jesus warns anyone who over-thoughtlessly presses to become a disciple: . . . the story shows him [Jesus] as the one who subdues the demonic powers and brings the βασιλεία (kingdom, reign) of God and who therefore can also demand and is able to reward the sacrifice of abandoning earthly ties such as stand in the way of the second follower.[23]

It is clear that Bornkamm's work as a redaction critic recognizes that the text assumes a situation of struggle and hardship for the authorial audience. The audience encounters instruction and correction for a life of following Jesus. The passage strengthens its identity as disciples and shapes its way of life.

THE GOSPEL AS ANCIENT BIOGRAPHY

Much form and redaction work insists that the gospels were, because of their theological content and pastoral orientation, a unique genre in the ancient world.[24] But other scholars have argued that their content, form of writing, and function as accounts about Jesus resemble an ancient biography (a *bios*).[25] This larger genre embraces their theological and pastoral content and functions, creating certain expectations and roles for the authorial audience.

It should be noted that ancient biographies had somewhat different conventions about content and function than modern biographies. Ancient biographies do not attempt a comprehensively detailed presentation. They do not engage in psychological analysis of inner motivations. Instead actions reveal character. They focus on the typical and have a clear didactic function.

Readers of ancient biography expected to find a narrative account of the career and public contribution of a notable public figure (king, military commander, statesman, philosopher, holy sage).[26] The work focused on this person. A general chronological outline spanned birth to death. The opening verse of Matthew names Jesus as the character of focus, as well as initiating the record of his origin (1:1). The opening two chapters of Matthew present the audience with a genealogy (1:1–17) and accounts of Jesus' origin and early childhood (1:18–2:23). His death receives considerable attention, being foreshadowed in God's address of 3:17 and predicted explicitly in 12:14 and 16:21. The second half of the narrative indicates how it happens. It provides various declarations of its significance (see ch. 14 below).

In between, an audience would expect an ancient biography to use episodic and topical organization. Similar material appeared together. In Matthew a collection of miracle stories is found in chapters 8–9. Jesus' teaching is largely though not exclusively grouped into five collections (Matt 5–7; 10; 13; 18; 24–25), which are thematically organized (discipleship in Matt 5–7; the mission teaching of ch. 10; the community instruction of ch. 18; the eschatological material of chs. 24–25). Anecdotes (brief and instructive actions or sayings called *chreia*,[27] miracle and conflict stories) and speeches reveal the person's character and virtues (or vices). The life of the main character intertwines with other characters. The audience determines good and bad characters from their actions, comparisons, and the consistencies (or inconsistencies) between a character's words and actions.

In addition to expectations about content, the audience of an ancient biography had certain expectations about the biography's functions. C. Talbert identifies five functions of biography which an audience would expect to experience: (1) to provide readers with a pattern to copy; (2) to dispel a false image of the teacher and provide a true model to follow; (3) to expose a false teacher; (4) to legitimate authentic tradition and teaching after the time of the founder; (5) to show the key to interpreting the teacher's teaching.[28] Burridge identifies seven possible functions: eliciting praise, providing a model, informing, entertaining, preserving memory, instructing, and providing material for debate and argument (apologetic and polemic). For gospels he particularly emphasizes the last two, along with providing a model.[29] Biographies functioned to shape identity and guide the audience's way of life.

The audience thus expects a biography to present the figure's teaching and life as a possible model for its own living. The paradigmatic actions and words of the hero legitimate or discredit important cultural or community values and practices. In reading Matthew's gospel, the authorial audience expects to find legitimation for its identity and way of life, its past and future in relation to Jesus. Frequently, it experiences Jesus' words and actions exemplifying and commending values which are contrary to conventional social values. Sometimes the contrast is made explicit as in the rejection of anxious greed and lust for power (6:25–34; 20:20–28). Sometimes the audience's knowledge of social conventions and structures is assumed as in chapters 19–20. These chapters assume certain knowledge of hierarchical, patriarchal household patterns which are rejected in favor of more egalitarian patterns.

The recognition of the gospel's genre as a biography unlocks a set of expectations and roles for the authorial audience. Naming the genre and identifying some of the text's expected features and functions assist us in taking another step toward joining the authorial audience. In Part Two we will discuss further expectations concerning plot and character presentation.

CONCLUSION

This chapter sketches the emergence over the last two hundred years of important understandings about the genre of the gospels in general and Matthew's gospel in particular. This understanding is significant as another step toward joining the authorial audience and reading "as the author intended."

It is no longer possible to see the gospel's genre as an eyewitness account of the life of Jesus. Rather, Matthew is an ancient biography or story which functions as a vehicle for proclamation about Jesus. Though it contains historically accurate material, this gospel proclaims the significance of Jesus for the purpose of shaping the identity and lifestyle of a particular community of faith. Its sources are Mark (the first gospel), material known to us as "Q" (sayings of Jesus common to Matthew and Luke), and "M" (material unique to Matthew's gospel). An unknown pastoral theologian shaped these traditions about Jesus to address the particular circumstances of his community or communities of faith, existing perhaps in the Syrian city of Antioch in the eighth decade of the first century. The author uses the genre of an ancient biography to express his theological and pastoral concerns. The recognition of this genre denotes a set of expectations and roles which guide the authorial audience in its reading. The audience in turn expects a biography to portray its hero's life in a way that shapes its own identity and lifestyle.

NOTES

1. W. Walker and R. Norris, D. Lotz, R. Handy, *A History of the Christian Church* (4th ed.; New York: Charles Scribner's Sons, 1985) 567–72, 579–85, 622–39; J. González, *The Story of Christianity* (San Francisco: Harper & Row, 1985) vol. 2, chs. 21, 28. For discussion, W. Kümmel, *The New Testament: The History of the Investigation of its Problems* (Nashville: Abingdon, 1972) Parts 2–4; S. Neill and N. T. Wright, *The Interpretation of the New Testament* (2d ed.; Oxford: Oxford University, 1988) ch. 1; W. Baird, *History of New Testament Research: Volume One: From Deism to Tübingen* (Minneapolis: Fortress, 1992); A. Schweitzer, *The Quest of the Historical Jesus* (3d ed.; London:

A. & C. Black, 1906, 1954); W. Farmer, *The Synoptic Problem: A Critical Analysis* (New York: Macmillan, 1964) chs. 1–5. For more general discussions, K. F. Nickle, *The Synoptic Gospels* (Atlanta: John Knox, 1980); W. Barnes Tatum, *In Quest of Jesus* (Atlanta: John Knox, 1982); J. D. G. Dunn, *The Evidence for Jesus* (Philadelphia: Westminster, 1985); G. Stanton, *The Gospels and Jesus* (Oxford: Oxford University, 1989).

2. Reimarus opposed the church's exalted claims about the divine Christ. He believed (with numerous others in the eighteenth century Enlightenment) that claims of revelation and dogma must be subjected to reason. He found the gospels unreasonable and contradictory. Reimarus investigated the gospels with rational and historical inquiry to find the natural, historical origins of Christianity. Some of Reimarus' work was published after his death (1768) in 1774–78 by Lessing. One selection (or "fragment") was entitled "The Aims of Jesus and His Disciples." For discussion and text, *Reimarus: Fragments* (ed. C. H. Talbert; Philadelphia: Fortress, 1970); Schweitzer, *Quest,* 13–25; Kümmel, *New Testament,* 89–90; Baird, *History,* 170–73.

3. *Reimarus: Fragments,* 151.

4. In his 1835 book *The Life of Jesus Critically Examined* (and its subsequent editions), D. F. Strauss analyzed the gospels section by section. For text and introduction, D. F. Strauss, *The Life of Jesus Critically Examined* (ed. P. Hodgson; Philadelphia: Fortress, 1973). Also W. Wrede, *The Messianic Secret* (reprint, 1901; Greenwood: Attic, 1971). Also *The Messianic Secret* (Issues in Religion and Theology 1; ed. C. Tuckett; Philadelphia: Fortress, 1983). In contemporary scholarship, the Jesus Seminar has set about a minute examination of the gospels. See R. Funk and R. Hoover, *The Five Gospels* (New York: Macmillan, 1993).

5. M. Kähler, *The So-Called Historical Jesus and the Historic Biblical Christ* (trans. C. Braaten; Philadelphia: Fortress, 1964, 1892); R. Bultmann, *Jesus and the Word* (New York: Charles Scribner's Sons, 1934); idem, *Theology of the New Testament* (London: SCM, 1952) 3–53; idem, "The Primitive Christian Kerygma and the Historical Jesus" in C. Braaten and R. Harrisville, *The Historical Jesus and the Kerygmatic Christ* (New York: Abingdon, 1964) 15–42. In emphasizing the eschatological identity and context of Jesus, Bultmann extends the influence of Reimarus and J. Weiss, *Jesus' Proclamation of the Kingdom of God* (reprint, 1892; Philadelphia: Fortress, 1971); Schweitzer, *Quest,* ch. 19.

6. For discussion of possible criteria, see D. Harrington, "The Jewishness of Jesus: Facing Some Problems," *CBQ* 49 (1987) 1–13; M. E. Boring, "The Historical-Critical Method's 'Criteria of Authen-

ticity': The Beatitudes in Q and Thomas as a Test Case," *Semeia* 44 (1988) 9–44; R. Stein, "The 'Criteria' for Authenticity," in *Gospel Perspectives* (ed. R. T. France and D. Wenham; Sheffield: JSOT, 1980) 225–63; also Stanton, *Jesus and the Gospels,* 160–63; Tatum, *In Quest of Jesus,* 76–77; Nickle, *Synoptic Gospels,* 160–66. In contrast to the mid-twentieth century when the prevailing view was that we could know only a little about Jesus, more recent scholarship is much more optimistic. E. P. Sanders (*Jesus and Judaism* [Philadelphia: Fortress, 1985] 2) comments, "The dominant view today seems to be that we can know pretty well what Jesus was out to accomplish, that we can know a lot about what he said, and that these two things make sense within the worlds of first-century Judaism."

7. For example, Bultmann claimed that the quest was historically impossible because of the theological nature of the gospels as sources, and theologically illegitimate because faith, the response to proclamation, does not depend on historical certainty. Since Käsemann inaugurated the "new quest" in 1953, many scholars are convinced that the investigation of the historical Jesus is theologically legitimate, necessary, and historically possible because the gospel proclamation or kerygma assumes continuity between the historical Jesus and the risen Christ. The proclamation about Jesus includes material from the life of Jesus, such as Jesus' death on a cross, his loving and inclusive friendship with outcasts and sinners, his authority. For discussion, E. Käsemann, "The Problem of the Historical Jesus," *Essays on New Testament Themes* (Philadelphia: Fortress, 1964, 1982) 15–47; idem, "Blind Alleys in the 'Jesus of History' Controversy," in E. Käsemann, *New Testament Questions of Today* (Philadelphia: Fortress, 1969) 23–65; G. Bornkamm, *Jesus of Nazareth* (London and New York: Hodder & Stoughton, 1960) 53–63, 179–86; E. Schweizer, *Jesus* (London: SCM, 1971).

8. See Tatian's *Diatessaron* in *Ante-Nicene Fathers* (ed. A. Menzies; reprint, 1896; Peabody, Mass.: Hendrickson, 1995) 9.43–129.

9. John places the cleansing of the temple at the beginning of Jesus' ministry (2:13–22). The synoptic writers locate it near the end when Jesus enters Jerusalem. The synoptics present Jesus moving from a Galilean ministry to Jerusalem (Mark 11; Matt 21; Luke 19) while John's Jesus moves back and forth. He is in Jerusalem in John 2, 5:1, 7:14.

10. Much earlier, Augustine seems to have recognized some literary interdependence. Matthew is the first gospel. "Mark follows him closely, and looks like his attendant and epitomizer." See Augustine, "The Harmony of the Gospels," in *Nicene and Post-Nicene Fathers,* First Series (ed. P. Schaff; reprint, 1899; Peabody, Mass.:

Hendrickson, 1995) 6.78. Griesbach's proposal also placed Matthew first, but proposed that Mark worked with Matthew and Luke.

11. Farmer, *Synoptic Problem*, 5–9; Kümmel, *History*, 74–75; Baird (*History*, 143–48) notes that Griesbach's suggestion had been made earlier in 1764 by English cleric Henry Owen.

12. Griesbach's explanation was immediately challenged. In 1784 Gotthold Ephraim Lessing proposed a second explanation for the similarities and differences among the three gospels. Instead of appealing to literary relationships among the three gospels as Griesbach did, he suggested a single common source for them, one original gospel, an Aramaic Ur-gospel. Lessing's proposal has suffered because no one has been able to locate the common source he proposed. On Lessing, Farmer, *Synoptic Problem*, 4–5; Kümmel, *History*, 76–77; for subsequent discussion, Kümmel, *Introduction to the New Testament*, 45–48.

13. See Kümmel, *History*, 146–55; Farmer, *Synoptic Problem*, 22–47.

14. See Farmer, *Synoptic Problem*, 48–117.

15. B. H. Streeter, *The Four Gospels: A Study of Origins* (New York: Macmillan, 1925) summary, 151–52; discussion, 155–360.

16. The designation Q probably originated from the German word "Quelle" which means "source." Though there is some debate, J. Weiss' 1890 work seems the earliest. See H. K. McArthur, "The Origin of the 'Q' Symbol," *ExpT* 88 (1977) 119–20; J. Schmitt, "In Search of the Origin of the Siglum Q," *JBL* 100 (1981) 609–11; F. Neirynck, "The Symbol Q (= Quelle)," *ETL* 54 (1978) 119–25.

17. G. M. Styler, "The Priority of Mark," in Moule, *Birth*, 285–316, esp. 285.

18. For the continuing debate, *The Two Source Hypothesis* (ed. A. J. Bellinzoni; Macon: Mercer University, 1985). Areas of debate include (i) Streeter's notion of "Proto-Luke," an earlier version of Luke consisting of Q and L material; (ii) the existence of Q; (iii) the nature of Q (oral or written? an expanding tradition?); (iv) the relationship of Luke and Matthew; (v) the nature (written or oral?), places and circumstances of origin, and extent of both M and L; (vi) Griesbach's hypothesis with proposed Matthean not Markan priority. For evaluation, C. Tuckett, *The Revival of the Griesbach Hypothesis* (Cambridge: Cambridge University, 1983).

19. On form criticism, K. Schmidt, *Der Rahmen der Geschichte Jesu* (Berlin: Trowitzsch, 1919); M. Dibelius, *Die Formgeschichte des Evangeliums* (Tübingen: J. C. B. Mohr, 1919); ET, *From Tradition to Gospel* (London: Ivor Nicholson and Watson, 1934); R. Bultmann, *The History of the Synoptic Tradition* (rev. ed., reprint, 1963; Peabody, Mass.:

Hendrickson, 1994). See E. McKnight, *What Is Form Criticism?* (Philadelphia: Fortress, 1969); C. Tuckett, *Reading the New Testament: Methods of Interpretation* (Philadelphia: Fortress, 1987) ch. 7, "Form Criticism"; S. Travis, "Form Criticism," in *New Testament Interpretation* (ed. I. H. Marshall; Exeter: Paternoster, 1979) 153–64.

20. See N. Perrin, *What Is Redaction Criticism?* (Philadelphia: Fortress, 1969); Tuckett, *Reading the New Testament,* "Redaction Criticism," 116–35; S. Smalley, "Redaction Criticism," in *New Testament Interpretation* (ed. Marshall), 181–95.

21. G. Bornkamm, "The Stilling of the Storm in Matthew," in *Tradition and Interpretation in Matthew* (ed. G. Bornkamm, G. Barth, H. J. Held; Philadelphia: Westminster, 1963) 52–57. G. Stanton (*A Gospel for a New People: Studies in Matthew* [Edinburgh: T. & T. Clark, 1992] 24–28) discusses the emergence of Matthean redaction criticism. Also J. Rohde, *Rediscovering the Teaching of the Evangelists* (London: SCM, 1968) 1–46; for Matthean studies, 47–112.

22. He cites Matt 24:7; 27:54; 28:2; Mark 13:8; Luke 21:11; Rev 6:12; 8:5; 11:13, 19; 16:18.

23. Bornkamm, "Stilling of the Storm," *Tradition and Interpretation,* 57.

24. For example, Bultmann, *History of the Synoptic Tradition,* 371–74.

25. For further discussion of the genre(s) of Matthew, A. Momigliano, *The Development of Greek Biography* (Cambridge: Harvard University, 1971); M. Gerhart, "Generic Studies: Their Renewed Importance in Religious and Literary Interpretation," *JAAR* 45 (1977) 309–22; P. Cox, *Biography in Late Antiquity: A Quest for the Holy Man* (Berkeley: University of California, 1983); D. Aune, *The New Testament in Its Literary Environment* (Philadelphia: Westminster, 1987) 11–76; D. Aune, "Greco-Roman Biography," in *Greco-Roman Literature and the New Testament: Selected Forms and Genres* (ed. D. Aune; SBLSBS 21; Atlanta: Scholars, 1988) 107–26; S. Saunders, *"No One Dared Ask Him Anything More:" Contextual Readings of the Controversy Stories in Matthew* (Ph.D. diss., Princeton Theological Seminary, 1990) 59–114. Saunders argues for the notion of mixed genre which includes features of Jewish historiography. R. A. Burridge, *What Are the Gospels? A Comparison with Graeco-Roman Biography* (SNTSMS 70; Cambridge: Cambridge University, 1992); J. L. Bailey and L. D. Vander Broek, *Literary Forms in the New Testament* (Louisville: Westminster/John Knox, 1992) 91–98.

26. For the "cluster of defining traits" that defines ancient biography, see Cox, *Biography in Late Antiquity,* 54–65; Burridge, *What Are the Gospels?* 109–27.

27. See V. K. Robbins, "The Chreia," in *Greco-Roman Literature and the New Testament* (ed. Aune) 1–23; Cox, *Biography in Late Antiquity,* 58.

28. C. Talbert, *What Is a Gospel? The Genre of the Canonical Gospels* (Philadelphia: Fortress, 1977) 92–98.

29. Burridge, *What Are the Gospels?* 149–52, 214–17.

Chapter 4

The Audience's Religious Traditions

To join Matthew's authorial audience the reader must know certain religious traditions and experiences. We saw in the last chapter that the author's sources are traditions about Jesus, known to us as Q (material common to Matthew and Luke but not to Mark), the Gospel of Mark, and M (material unique to Matthew). It seems unlikely that the author knows these traditions but his community does not. It is more likely that these traditions were familiar to his community and had functioned before Matthew's gospel was written. Thus the authorial audience comprises followers of Jesus who are familiar with these traditions.[1]

This chapter sketches some of this assumed knowledge and experience. We will use redaction criticism to examine some ways in which the author shapes these sources to address the followers of Jesus.[2] This will reveal the audience's assumed knowledge as well as the beliefs and perspectives that are important to the author as he interprets the traditions for the audience. I suggest that Matthew creatively shapes the traditions to present a distinct theological agenda and addresses his community's situation. At the same time he carefully conserves the traditions. That is, his gospel both confirms and reconfigures the authorial audience's knowledge, experience, identity, and lifestyle as disciples of Jesus.[3] It is helpful to consult a gospel synopsis while reading this chapter.[4]

MATTHEW AND MARK[5]

Matthew includes all but approximately fifty-five verses of Mark's 661 verses. He uses about 8,555 of Mark's 11,078 words.[6] While Matthew is dependent on Mark's gospel, he is not slavishly bound to it as we saw from Bornkamm's example in the last chapter. If he were, there would be no need to write his gospel. Matthew transmits, reinterprets, and reformulates Mark in five ways: (1) omissions, (2) additions and expansions, (3) reordering, (4) abbreviating, and (5) improving style. In each instance I discuss several examples to illustrate what is typical throughout the gospel. Some distinctive gospel themes and content emerge as well as an understanding of how the author adjusts and affirms the audience's religious knowledge, experiences, identity, and lifestyle.

Omissions

Omissions of Larger Units

Most of the verses omitted from Mark are found in eight pericopes or text-segments:

- Mark 1:23–28—The healing of the demoniac in the synagogue

- Mark 1:35–38—Jesus departs from Capernaum

- Mark 4:26–29—The parable of the seed growing secretly

- Mark 7:31–37—Jesus heals a deaf mute

- Mark 8:22–26—A blind man is healed at Bethsaida

- Mark 9:38–40—The strange exorcist

- Mark 12:41–44—The widow's mite

- Mark 14:51–52—The flight of the naked young man

Redaction scholars try to identify theological and literary reasons for each omission. In most instances the pericope either does not fit Matthew's agenda or the omitted story's content or point has already been adequately covered. This seems to be the case with the miracle stories. More difficult is the omission of Mark 4:26–29 (the parable of the seed growing secretly) from Matt 13:24. One reason for this may be a focus in 13:1–30 on the rejection of Jesus and his "word of the kingdom" (13:19). The explanation of the parable of the sower (13:18–23) accounts for some human responses to God's action. At this point in Matthew, Mark's parable of the seed growing secretly would occur. But this parable would move the reader's attention to God's secretive action. At 13:24 there appear to be further responses to God that Matthew wishes to include. So he omits this material at 13:24 and replaces it with the parable of the weeds and wheat (13:24–30) which describes the coexistence of positive and negative responses to God, and the certainty of judgment at the end of the age. It encourages perseverance and true discipleship in the midst of the evil of the present age. But it is not clear why Matthew does not use Mark's parable in relation to the parables of the mustard seed and leaven in 13:31–33 which pick up this emphasis of God's secret action. Perhaps the author thought that these parables were sufficient for the audience's understanding.

Omissions of References to Jesus' Emotions and Limitations

The Jesus of the Gospel of Mark experiences human emotions, weakness, and limitations in knowledge and actions. Matthew, however, removes many references to Jesus' emotions, particularly "unfavorable" indications of Jesus' impatience or frustration.[7]

> Mark 3:5 (3:1–6, healing the man with the withered hand on the Sabbath) describes Jesus' response, "He looked around at them with anger; he was grieved at their hardness of heart." Matthew omits this emotion from 12:12, especially since Jesus has stressed mercy at 12:7.

> Mark 8:12 (8:11–13, the Pharisees seek a sign) narrates that Jesus "sighed deeply in his spirit" in response to the Pharisees' request. Matthew 12:39 and 16:2 omit this expression of frustration and introduce Jesus' response with a bland "He answered them."[8]

Matthew generally omits references to Jesus' inability to do something or to circumstances that seem to limit him.[9]

Mark 6:5 (6:1–6, Jesus is rejected at Nazareth) explains that Jesus "was not able to" (lit.) do any miracle or "mighty work" because of their unbelief. Matthew 13:58 changes Mark's "was not able to" to a more descriptive "And he did not do." Mark's "no mighty work" becomes "not . . . many mighty works."

Mark 6:48 (6:45–52, walking on the water) narrates that Jesus notices the disciples "making headway painfully" (lit.) but "meant to pass by them." Matthew 14:25 omits this apparent reference to Jesus' unwillingness to help.

Mark 8:23–25 (8:22–26, a blind man is healed at Bethsaida) narrates a double attempt to heal the man after the first effort does not effect full healing. Matthew omits the scene totally.

Mark's Jesus displays ignorance by asking questions to elicit knowledge. Matthew omits these questions. He presents Jesus as already possessing knowledge or being sufficiently in control to have no need to know.[10]

Mark 5:30 (5:25–34, healing the woman with a hemorrhage) presents Jesus as knowing that "power had gone forth" but not knowing to whom. Matthew removes this aspect to focus on Jesus' direct address to the woman (Matt 9:21–22).

Mark 8:12 (8:11–13, the Pharisees seek a sign) has Jesus ask, "Why does this generation ask for a sign?" Matthew's Jesus does not need to ask. He already knows why, declaring, "An evil and adulterous generation asks for a sign" (Matt 16:4; 12:39).

Mark 9:16 (9:14–29, Jesus heals a boy possessed with a spirit) has Jesus ask the disciples what they were discussing with the crowds. Matthew omits the question (Matt 17:14) as well as Jesus' subsequent inquiry as to how long the child has been possessed (Mark 9:21; cf. Matt 17:17–18). A similar reference to Jesus asking the disciples what they were discussing in Mark 9:33 is omitted from Matt 18:1.

Matthew's changes to Mark's material recast the audience's knowledge. Matthew's more exalted presentation of Jesus guides the audience to greater reverence for and trust in Jesus. It decreases his human qualities and emphasizes those which show his control of circumstances. Jesus is Emmanuel, "God with us," a description not found in Mark (Matt 1:23). Markan material which suggests Jesus' limitations or ignorance detracts from the audience's acceptance of this more uplifted presentation.

Redaction critics explain these changes as necessary to address the difficult circumstances and experiences which the author assumes of his audience. The next two chapters discuss the situation Matthew's community faced. It probably involved debate and controversy with a synagogue. At issue are claims about the revelation and presence of God. This gospel claims Jesus as the revealer of God's presence and will (1:23; 5:17–48; 11:25–27). To set its story in a context of dispute requires exalted claims about Jesus. This secures the community's identity and understanding. Mark's recognition of revelation in the midst of and by means of Jesus' weakness and vulnerability is a liability in this context. The omission of less flattering or ambiguous material from Mark ensures the exalted presentation of Jesus in Matthew's gospel. Matthew uses this method to address the needs of his community and modify the identity and understanding of his audience.

Omissions of Smaller References to the Disciples' Failings

A further set of omissions reformulates the audience's knowledge of what it means to be a disciple of Jesus. Matthew recasts the presentation of the disciples found in Mark. Mark's disciples are frequently uncomprehending, self-seeking, and faithless.[11] Matthew's disciples, while not ideal figures, more often model the faithful, understanding, and obedient discipleship required of his audience.

> Mark 4:13 (4:13–20, interpretation of the parable of the sower) rebukes the disciples for not understanding. Matthew omits the rebuke (Matt 13:18). Jesus blesses the disciples for their understanding (13:16–17).[12]

> Mark 9:6 (9:2–10, the transfiguration) indicates Peter does not "know what to say for they were terrified." Matthew (17:4) omits Peter's fear and lack of comprehension. In 17:6 (cf. Mark 9:7), after the disciples hear God speak, Matthew appropriately adds to Mark, "they fell to the ground, and were overcome with fear." Mark's account ends with the disciples "questioning what this rising from the dead could mean" (9:10), a reference Matthew omits (Matt 17:9).

Mark 10:35–37 (10:35–45, the disciples' ambition) presents James and John seeking positions of honor. Matt 20:20–21 allocates the question to their mother, who is not present in Mark's scene. An earlier dispute among the disciples about who is the greatest (Mark 9:33–34) is omitted in Matt 18:1.

Additions and Expansions

Matthew adds to and expands Mark's material. Redaction critics try to discern theological, pastoral, or literary reasons for these additions. They also examine them to discover the community situation being addressed.

Additions of Larger Blocks of Material

Matthew adds a birth narrative to Mark's opening (Matt 1–2). This narrative includes key statements about Jesus' commission to save from sin and manifest God's presence (1:21, 23). This material supplies the audience with a central understanding about Jesus at the outset of the gospel. This influences the understanding of all subsequent material. Matthew includes five major sections of Jesus' teaching (chs. 5–7, 10, 13, 18, 23–25). Several of these sections expand on Mark's material (compare Matt 13 with Mark 4; Matt 23–25 with Mark 13) while the others add to Mark's narrative (Matt 5–7; 10; 18). This supplies the audience with important teaching about discipleship, the church, and the coming judgment (eschatology).

In chapter 18, for instance, the first nine verses follow Mark 9:33–50, though with abbreviation (compare Matt 18:6–9 with Mark 9:42–50), omission (Mark 9:38–40), and relocation (Mark 9:41 with Matt 10:42). At verse 10, however, Matthew departs from Mark to provide further instruction about relationships among disciples. The next twenty-five verses have no parallel in Mark. He picks up Mark 10 again in chapter 19.

Matthew's Sermon on the Mount (Matt 5–7) has no Markan parallel in form or content. Matthew creates this section by interrupting and reformulating Mark's narrative at 1:21:

". . . and immediately on the Sabbath he entered the synagogue and taught" (lit.).

Matthew changes the synagogue location to a mountain and replaces the synagogue audience with the newly-called disciples (5:1–2). Many have explained the change to a mountain as an explicit echo of Moses' receiving the Ten Commandments on Mount Sinai. The new setting enables the audience to understand Jesus as an authoritative figure who in the tradition of Moses reveals God's will.

After adding three chapters of teaching not found in Mark, Matthew picks up Mark 1:22 in Matt 7:28–29 to describe the response to Jesus' teaching:

> "The crowds were astonished at his teaching, for he taught them as one who had authority, and not as their scribes."

Matthew cites this verse word for word, except for two additions. (1) He adds "the crowds" to clarify Mark's unspecified "they."[13] (2) At the beginning of the verse he adds a clause, "When Jesus had finished these sayings" (7:28). He uses this same clause to close each of Jesus' five major teaching blocks (see 11:1; 13:53; 19:1; 26:1). The last use, 26:1, repeats the first use in 7:28 word for word, except for the addition of the adjective "all," ("when Jesus had finished *all* these sayings" [lit.]). For the audience, the repeated clause and added adjective connect the five teaching sections together and establish the close of Jesus' teaching ministry before the passion. Matthew's expanded teaching alters Mark's presentation and provides the audience with much more instruction about the identity and lifestyle of disciples.

Addition of Biblical Citations

Matthew adds Old Testament scriptures to the sayings of Jesus to strengthen Mark's text and to reinforce or expand the audience's knowledge.[14] In Matt 9:12–13, for example, Jesus responds to criticism that he eats with "tax collectors and sinners": "Those who are well have no need of a physician, but those who are sick." At this point Mark 2:17 continues, "I have come to call not the righteous but sinners." Matthew, however, interrupts this sequence in 9:13. He adds Jesus' instruction and citation from Hos 6:6, "Go and learn what this means, 'I desire mercy, not sacrifice.' "[15] This addition "strengthens the reply of

Jesus by appealing to scripture: Jesus can associate freely with sinners because God is gracious and merciful."[16] Matthew's expansion underlines for the audience that Jesus, as "Emmanuel, God with us" (1:23), is carrying out God's merciful commission to save sinners (1:21).

Matthew adds other scriptural references, particularly those which indicate that Jesus "fulfills" the prophets' predictions (1:22; 2:5–6, 15, 17, 23; 4:14; 8:17; 12:17; 21:4; 26:54; 27:9). The audience understands from these additions that Jesus' words and actions manifest God's previously disclosed will.

Addition of Words and Phrases

Redaction critics also see Matthew's theological interests and perspectives in particular words and phrases which he adds. While Matthew retains many words or phrases from Mark which are familiar to the audience,[17] he also expands on these words and phrases.

Mark uses the name "Jesus" about eighty times while Matthew uses it at least 154 times. Matthew's increased use emphasizes for the audience the Matthean explanation of the meaning of Jesus' name in 1:21, "save his people from their sins." The continual use of his name assists the audience to recall Jesus' mission and understand a central element of Matthew's christological presentation.

Another change in christological understanding results from Matthew's altered use of "Son of God." In Mark's gospel no *human* calls Jesus "Son of God" until the centurion's confession at the cross (Mark 15:39).[18] Demons address Jesus by this title (Mark 3:11; 5:7), but it remains a "demonic" title without reference to the cross. Part of Mark's point seems to be that any confession of Jesus' identity which focuses only on his power and does not recognize God's will in his suffering and death is inadequate.

Matthew, however, applies the term to all of Jesus' ministry. In 14:33 and 16:16, before any teaching about the cross, Matthew's responsive and insightful disciples confess Jesus to be Son of God. Both instances are Matthew's additions to Mark (compare Matt 14:33 with Mark 6:51–52; Matt 16:16

with Mark 8:29). Matthew inserts the title two further times into Mark's passion narrative (compare Matt 27:40, 43 with Mark 15:29–30, 32), underlining its significance for all of Jesus' ministry.[19]

Matthew also changes the meanings of Markan words. Mark uses the verb προσκυνέω (*proskyneō,* "to worship") twice with negative connotations. Mark 5:6 speaks of a demoniac who worships Jesus, and in 15:19 soldiers mock Jesus. Matthew omits both Markan references (compare Matt 8:29 and 27:30) and uses προσκυνέω in his upgraded presentation of Jesus and the disciples. He adds the verb seven times to Markan passages to signal the appropriate, genuine, and reverential way a disciple should approach Jesus (not just the twelve, Matt 2:2, 8, 11).[20]

Expansion of Markan Themes

Matthew expands themes familiar to the audience from Mark. (1) He strengthens the audience's understanding of the end of the age (Mark's eschatological orientation). In Matt 24–25, he extends Mark's eschatological discourse (Mark 13) by adding parables. Several of these come from Q (Matt 24:37–44, 45–51; 25:1–13, 14–30, 31–46). He adds four references to the future coming of Jesus, Son of Man, by using the word παρουσία (*parousia,* "coming," "advent"). At 24:3 he rephrases Mark's material to include this word while in 24:27, 37, 39 (cf. Mark 13:23, 27) he adds it to Q material (Luke 17:24, 26, 30).

(2) Matthew strengthens instruction for the audience about discipleship with the added and expanded teaching discourses. He also makes numerous other smaller additions through adding key words like "little faith," "hypocrite," and "lawlessness." These additions contribute to the presentation of the identity and expected lifestyle of disciples and indicate Matthew's particular interest in ethical and faith-full behavior.[21]

(3) Matthew also adds terms for the community of disciples. These terms ("church," "little ones," "the righteous") underline the communal identity and context of discipleship, and are in contrast to other groups such as the synagogue and "the Gentiles."[22]

One scholar has identified ninety-five words and phrases
which are characteristic of Matthew. Other scholars add over
a hundred more to the list.[23] Not all of these terms are added
to Mark's material; some derive from Matthew's other sources.
But the number of such terms indicates Matthew's extensive
efforts to affirm and reconfigure the audience's understanding. Davies and Allison note that Matthew's characteristic
language is evidence of the importance of christology, eschatology, ethics, ecclesiology, and the role of the Hebrew Bible
in this gospel.[24]

Reordering

Matthew reorganizes the order of scenes in Mark's narrative. This reordering, accomplished by omissions, additions,
and reorganization, is particularly pronounced in Matt 3:1–
13:58 (Mark 1–6). After this Matthew follows Mark's order
more closely.

Chapters 8–9, a collection of mainly miracle stories, provide an interesting example of Matthew's extensive reorganization, abbreviation, omission of and addition to material from
Mark 1, 2, 4, and 5.

- Matthew 7:28–29 closes the Sermon on the Mount with
  a redacted Mark 1:22.

- Matt 8:1–4 (healing the leper) abbreviates Mark
  1:40–45. Matthew omits Mark 1:23–28, reorders
  1:29–31, 32–34 (Matt 8:14–17), and omits 1:35–39.

- Matt 8:5–13 (healing the centurion's servant) adds Q
  material not in Mark (Luke 7:1–10).

- Matt 8:14–15 (healing Peter's mother-in-law) abbreviates Mark 1:29–31.

- Matt 8:16–17 (summary of healing) abbreviates Mark
  1:32–34 while adding a scripture citation from Isa 53:4
  in verse 17.

- Matt 8:18–22 (would-be followers) adds material not in
  Mark (Q; Luke 7:57–62).

- Matt 8:23–27 (stilling the storm) abbreviates Mark
  4:35–41.

- Matt 8:28–34 (the Gadarene demoniacs) follows Mark's
  order but abbreviates Mark 5:1–20 (325 words in Mark,
  136 in Matt).

- Matt 9:1–8 (healing the paralytic) departs from Mark's
  order to abbreviate Mark 2:1–12 (196 words in Mark,
  126 in Matt).

By examining the changes made to each scene in chapters 8–9
and by noting the new combination of pericopes, redaction critics
can identify what Matthew wants to affirm or alter in the audience's understanding. For instance, we have noted that Matthew
redacts Mark 1:22 to conclude the Sermon on the Mount (Matt
7:28–29). He then follows the three chapters of teaching with two
chapters of Jesus' actions. To begin chapters 8–9, Matthew rear-
ranges Mark's order in Mark 1:23–45 to give prominence to the
story of the leper's healing as the opening story in 8:1–4 (Mark
1:40–45). To achieve this he omits Mark 1:23–28 and 35–39,
placing 1:40–45 ahead of the healing stories in 1:29–31 and
32–34.

The redaction critic D. J. Harrington sees several reasons
for setting the story of the healing of the leper first.[25] Jesus
commands the healed leper to show himself to the priest (8:4)
in accord with Leviticus 14. This command demonstrates Jesus'
teaching in the Sermon on the Mount (5:17–48) that he came
to fulfill, not abolish, the Law and the Prophets. So his followers
must do the same. Matthew's account also highlights the
prayerful and faithful attitude of the leper (8:2) as the context
for his experience of Jesus' power. Through these changes the
audience's knowledge from Mark's gospel is confirmed and
reconfigured.

Throughout the rest of these chapters, the identity of Jesus
(including the origin of his power) and the requirements of
discipleship, are in the forefront as Matthew abbreviates, reorders, and supplements Mark's material. For example, the addition of Isa 53:4 to 8:17 (Mark 1:32–34) presents Jesus' miracles
as the carrying out of the divine will and as part of his merciful
ministry which culminates in his death and resurrection. The

reordering of Mark's material emphasizes that Jesus has God-like power over all things, including diseases (8:1–17), nature (8:18–27), demons (8:28–34), and sin (9:1–8). God is the one who controls the created world (compare Ps 107:23–30) and who forgives sins. The audience witnesses Jesus faithfully carrying out the mission given him in 1:21, 23, to save from sin and manifest God's presence.

Jesus' actions raise the question of his identity (8:27, 29) and the source of his power (9:3, 34) thereby focusing attention on the issue of discipleship. Disciples and Gentiles (indicated by the Q story of the centurion [8:5–13]) seek his cleansing (8:2), his healing (8:6), his deliverance and salvation (8:25), his forgiveness (9:2), his resurrecting power (9:18), his mercy (9:28). In faith they hear his call (9:9; 10:1) and recognize both their unworthiness and dependence on his merciful power (8:2, 8–10, 13, 26; 9:2, 22, 28–29). The emphasis on faith is heightened by Matthew's added material in 8:8–13 about the Gentile's faith in contrast to Israel's lack of faith. He also changes the wording in 9:28. The question to the blind man in Mark 10:51, "What do you want me to do for you?" becomes in Matt 9:28, "Do you believe [lit., have faith] that I am able to do this?" These characters display for the audience desirable attitudes and actions.

Matthew's reordered material demonstrates and contrasts other responses to Jesus' actions. Some want to follow but are unwilling to make the commitment (8:18–22; cf. 9:9). Others find the way of discipleship hard and dangerous and receive reassurance of his merciful and powerful presence (8:23–27). Some respond to his power by asking him to leave the neighborhood (8:34), by glorifying God (9:8), by marveling (9:33), by expressing hostile opposition (9:3–4, 10–13), and by attributing God's power to the devil (9:34).

Clearly, Matt 8 and 9 do not collect miracle stories for the sake of displays of power. Rather, they express christological and ecclesiological (discipleship) concerns, reflecting the insights of the evangelist and his understanding of the needs and circumstances of his community. One important issue is the community's relationship to Jewish traditions and heritage (8:4; 9:13, 14–17). The stories emphasize for the audience that this tradition continues but as defined by Jesus. Another issue is the acceptance of Gentiles and the Gentile mission as part of the community's identity (8:5–13; 9:36–38). The community must extend mercy to all who are open to the call of Jesus (8:18–22; 9:9, 10–13, 35–38). The last section of chapter 9 is explicit about the theme of mission work as it leads into the missionary instructions of chapter 10. In commissioning his disciples, Jesus entrusts his power and preaching to them (10:7–8). Material in chapters 8–9 reminds the community that it lives and works in a demonic and dangerous world (8:23–27, 28–34). Often it is the religious authorities who exhibit the most opposition (9:3, 34). The chapters reassure the audience of Jesus' presence in the midst of such a world.

Abbreviation

A further feature of Matthew's use of Mark involves abbreviating Mark's material. Mark's ninety-seven-word account of the leper's healing (Mark 1:40–45) becomes sixty-one words in Matt 8:1–4. Whereas Mark takes 196 words to tell the story of the healing of the paralytic (Mark 2:1–12), Matthew (9:1–8) employs 126 words.[26] Matthew omits Mark's material for theological reasons as we have noted. In other places Matthew abbreviates Mark by omitting unnecessary details[27] and redundancies. In Mark 4:3, Mark writes (in a literal translation):

"And he was teaching them in parables many things and he was saying to them in his teaching . . ."

Matthew improves Mark with a much more economical statement (a literal translation of 13:3):

"And he told them many things in parables saying . . ."

Matthew's different theological agenda and more economical style are also evident in comparing the abbreviations of major sections such as Mark 5:1–43 (699 words) and Matt 8:28–34, 9:18–26 (271 words); Mark 6:14–29 and Matt 14:1–12; Mark 9:14–29 and Matt 17:14–20.

Style

Finally, Matthew makes numerous improvements to Mark's style. Identifying these detailed changes requires knowledge of the Greek text. Lists and examples can be found in several commentaries.[28] Two examples indicate the nature of some of these changes:

(1) Some forty times Mark joins pericopes together by using the phrase "and immediately" (καί εὐθύς, *kai euthys*). While the phrase provides urgency and energy, its continual use becomes repetitive and imprecise. Matthew finds other ways to introduce and connect material.[29]

(2) Mark often switches between the past (aorist) tense and the historic present tense. His use of the historic present (about 150 times) allows him to tell his story vividly as though it was happening in the audience's presence. Mark especially uses the historic present with verbs of movement (comes, goes up/out) and speaking (says) to suggest this effect. For example (in a literal translation)

> Mark 1:40—And a leper *comes* to him, saying . . .

> Mark 2:5—And when Jesus saw their faith, he *says* to the paralytic . . .

> Mark 5:38—And he allowed no one to follow him except Peter and James and John . . . And they *come* to the house of the ruler of the synagogue and he *sees* a tumult . . . [30]

Matthew changes all but twenty of Mark's 150 uses of the historic present tense. Most often he changes the present tense back to the past (aorist) tense (compare Mark 2:5 with Matt 9:2), frequently using an aorist participle to replace the present tense form.[31] He also omits clauses with this construction (compare Mark 3:3–4 with Matt 12:11–12).

Conclusion

This discussion of five ways Matthew uses Mark's material indicates that Matthew creatively interprets Mark as well as conserves this source. In doing so he both confirms and reinterprets the audience's knowledge of traditions about Jesus. Matthew continues important Markan emphases familiar to the audience concerning Christology, discipleship, and eschatology. Yet Matthew shapes this material to present some different perspectives.

MATTHEW'S USE OF Q

Matthew's second source is Q, a collection of the sayings of Jesus common to Matthew and Luke. These were also familiar to the audience. While space precludes a detailed discussion of Matthew's use of Q, the same paradox is evident. In places Matthew carefully and faithfully preserves Q material, its wording,[32] literary forms,[33] and order.[34] Yet Matthew also interprets and reshapes Q material. In this way he both confirms and reconfigures the audience's understanding and identity.

For example, Matthew takes the phrase "the law and the prophets" from one Q saying (Luke 16:16; Matt 5:17) and adds it to another Q saying (Luke 6:31; Matt 7:12). This forms a frame around the middle section of the Sermon on the Mount (5:17; 7:12), and emphasizes the relationship between Jesus' teaching and Jewish traditions.

Stanton notes other instances in which Matthew expands familiar Q sayings to convey his own perspective or emphasize a point.[35] First, Matt 10:8 expands the Q saying about sending disciples to preach and heal (Luke 9:2) by adding references to raising the dead and cleansing lepers. These are activities Jesus performs (8:1–4; 9:18–19, 23–26). This addition presents discipleship as the imitation of Jesus. Second, Matthew's expansion of a Q saying (Luke 6:40) in 10:24–25 presents discipleship as involving rejection like Jesus experienced and makes the former Q saying closer to Mark's view (cf. Mark 6:1–6). This emphasis on imitating Jesus recasts the Q view of mission work. In Q Gentile faith is seen as rebuking Israel into repentance. If Israel does not repent, Q announces judgment.[36]

Matthew also reinterprets Q material and reconfigures the audience's knowledge by placing material in different contexts. In Q, the parable of the lost sheep (Luke 15:3–7) is used against the Jewish leaders who criticize Jesus for associating with tax collectors and sinners. Matthew 18 gives it a new context: community discourse. With the help of a new introduction (18:10a) and conclusion (18:14) which contain some of his favorite phrases,[37] Matthew turns this parable into a lesson about the Christian community's responsibility to care for every disciple.

Matthew borrows and adapts Q's technique of ending sections with an emphasis on judgment.[38] He takes over Q's language for "judging" (κρίνω, *krinō*) and "judgment" or "justice" (κρίσις, *krisis*) and increases its usage.[39] This future judgment will be carried out by Jesus the Son of Man. Matthew retains Q's title for Jesus and increases its frequency by adding it to Markan material (16:28; 24:30) as well as using it in his own material (13:41; 25:31). Yet Matthew does something new with this theme of judgment. The audience knows from Q that judgment will come on Israel. But Matthew refocuses the material, warning the church of the consequences of unfaithful discipleship (see 7:15–27; 23:1; 24:3).

Several brief observations can be made about Matthew's use of the Q source. (1) Matthew uses material from Q as he does that of Mark. He creatively reinterprets and preserves the original material. We have noted several ways in which aspects of discipleship (including mission, community relationships, observance of the traditions of the law and the prophets, judgment) are elaborated or reframed by Matthew's changes.

(2) Matthew reworks Q and Mark similarly. He especially employs addition and reordering.[40] But a major difference exists in his use of the two sources. Matthew inserts Q into his narrative whereas Mark is already a narrative. Luz notes the transforming effect of this narrative context. Q material presents some demanding sayings of Jesus. But Matthew inserts these sayings into a narrative of God's previous gracious dealings with Israel (1:1–17) and of God's gracious initiative with Jesus, Emmanuel, "God with us" (1:23). This new narrative and theological context transforms the impact of the Q material so that grace and demand, the indicative and imperative exist together.[41]

(3) Q is useful to Matthew because apart from the stories of Jesus' temptation (Matt 4:1–11; Luke 4:1–13) and his healing of the centurion's son/slave (Matt 8:5–13; Luke 7:1–10), it consists wholly of sayings and parables of Jesus. This collection of sayings enables Matthew to overcome Mark's deficiency of not supplying the content of Jesus' teaching.

MATTHEW'S USE OF M

Determining Matthew's use of "M" raises difficult questions about the nature of this source and about how Matthew may have used it. Earlier scholars generally saw M as a coherent written source. They held that it comprised the material in Matthew not deriving from Mark or Q. As to a time and place of origin, they name the decade of the 50s or 60s and Jerusalem as the prime candidates. Central to its purpose was instruction in obeying the law.[42]

More recently, the view of a coherent written source has been questioned, as has the basis for constituting the source. Stephenson Brooks argues that the old way of determining M (what does not derive from Mark or Q) is a good start but must be developed further to investigate Matthean redaction of this material. He argues that by examining the style (especially aporias or grammatical and conceptual disjunctions in the material), the vocabulary, and the content of this material, Matthean additions can be separated and M material isolated.[43] Without examining the parable material, he uses this method to identify nineteen M sayings (forty-nine verses). He finds in this material three attitudes concerning the relationship of Matthew's community to the synagogue and concludes that M is not a written coherent source. Rather, it is a tradition which indicates three stages of the community's pre-gospel experience with the synagogue spanning inclusion, conflict, and separation. This aspect of the audience's experience is taken up in Matthew's use of this material in the new narrative and social context of his gospel and the situation it addresses.

Davies and Allison also reject the notion of M as a unified composition. Rather, it is a "symbol for the plurality of sources . . . which cannot be identified with Mark, Q, or Matthean redaction." These traditions include the infancy stories, some isolated sayings, ten parables, some passion traditions, and cult instruction (6:1–18) which along with some material in chapter 23 may have formed an anti–Pharisaic source reinforcing the differences between the synagogue and Matthew's community.[44]

Because of the uncertainty about the origin and nature of this material, it is difficult to discuss its use in the way that we have done with Mark and Q. We can, though, on the basis of our discussion of Mark and Q, hypothesize that Matthew has used it in the same fashion, creatively interpreting and conserving material familiar to the audience. Matthew inserts this material to strengthen the themes and instruction of his other sources and to address the needs of his community.

CONCLUSION

In this chapter we have taken a third step toward joining the authorial audience. We have identified some of the traditions about Jesus with which the authorial audience is assumed to be familiar and have examined some of the ways in which the author has shaped these traditions to address the followers of Jesus. His use of the material indicates that he both confirms and reconfigures the audience's knowledge and experiences, affirming and shaping its identity and lifestyle. The discussion has alerted us to some of the beliefs and perspectives that are important to both the audience and the author as he interprets familiar traditions.

NOTES

1. Luz, *Matthew 1–7*, 73–78.

2. For Matthew's treatment of the sources of the Sermon on the Mount, see W. Carter, *What Are They Saying About Matthew's Sermon on the Mount?* (Mahwah: Paulist, 1994) ch. 1.

3. Luz (*Matthew 1–7*, 73–78) emphasizes that Matthean redaction is also probably rooted in the reflection and worship of his community. In reconfiguring Mark, Q, and M, Matthew may be largely confirming and representing what the community has already done. In this chapter our emphasis must fall, for reasons of space, on the use of Mark, Q, and M.

4. For the sense in which I am referring to "the author" or to "Matthew," see the conclusion of ch. 2.

5. For discussion of Matthew's use of Mark, see Allen, *Matthew*, xii–xl; Bacon, *Studies in Matthew*, ch. 6; Luz, *Matthew 1–7*, 52–76; Davies and Allison, *Matthew*, 1.73–74; Stanton, *Gospel for a New People*, 326–45.

6. Kümmel, *Introduction,* 57, n. 32a.

7. I am generally drawing from Allen, *Matthew,* xxxi–xxxii, and Hawkins, *Horae Synopticae,* 117–59.

8. Cf. Mark 6:6 with Matt 13:58; Mark 10:14, 21 with Matt 19:14, 21.

9. For further examples of Jesus' inability to control circumstances, compare Mark 1:45 with Matt 8:4; Mark 7:24 with Matt 15:21; Mark 9:30 with Matt 17:22; Mark 11:13 ("to see if he could find anything on it") with Matt 21:19.

10. For further examples compare Mark 5:9 with Matt 8:29–30; Mark 6:38 with Matt 14:16–17; Mark 14:14 with Matt 26:18.

11. See L. T. Johnson, *The Writings of the New Testament* (Philadelphia: Fortress, 1986) 147–71.

12. For other Matthean changes to Markan references to the disciples' lack of understanding compare Mark 4:35–41 with Matt 8:23–27; Mark 6:51–52 with Matt 14:33; Mark 8:17–18 with Matt 16:9–12; Mark 8:29 with Matt 16:17–19; Mark 9:13 with Matt 17:13; Mark 9:32 with Matt 17:23.

13. The addition, though, creates a problem with Matt 5:1–2. There the disciples compose the audience for Jesus' teaching.

14. Stanton, *Gospel for a New People,* 328–33.

15. Note that the author adds other references to mercy throughout Matthew (5:7; 12:7; 23:23).

16. Stanton, *Gospel for a New People,* 328–29. He notes other additions in Matt 12:5–7 (Mark 2:26–27), 10:5–6 (Mark 6:6a), 15:24 (Mark 7:25), 21:41c, 43 (Mark 12:9, 11), 24:10–12, 26 (Mark 13:13, 23), 26:52–54 (Mark 14:47). Stanton (333) finds similar additions to Markan *narratives;* see Matt 14:28–31; 16:12; 17:6–7, 13.

17. For example, Jesus, disciples, follow, teach, preach, gospel, understand, Pharisees, scribes, Sadducees, Galilee.

18. The point here is that no *human* uses the term. God uses it in Mark 1:11 and 9:7 to establish it as the definitive perspective of the gospel. The rest of the gospel indicates that the term embraces both the suffering and the power of Jesus. Hence no human can adequately make this confession until they see God's will carried out in the weakness of Jesus' death.

19. Compare Matthew's expanded use of "Son of David." Matthew retains Mark's use of it by people seeking healing (Matt 9:27; 20:30, 31) and as a reference to Jesus the Messiah (Matt 22:42). He adds the title to other Markan healing accounts (compare Matt 12:23 with Mark 9:33; Matt 15:22 with Mark 7:25–26) and expands its messianic use (compare Matt 1:1; 21:9, 15 with Mark 11:9, 11).

20. Compare Matt 8:2 with Mark 1:40; Matt 9:18 with Mark 5:22; Matt 14:33 with Mark 6:51; Matt 15:25 with Mark 7:25; Matt 20:20 with Mark 10:35; Matt 28:9, 17 with Mark 16:8, 14.

21. Matt 8:26 identifies disciples as having "little faith" rather than "no faith" in Mark 4:40. Matthew adds this same word (ὀλιγόπιστος *oligopistos*) two more times (compare Matt 14:31 with Mark 6:50–51; Matt 16:8 with Mark 8:17). He adds references to humility or meekness from his own material (Matt 5:5; 11:29) to Mark 11:3–4 in Matt 21:5. The undesirable quality of "lawlessness" (ἀνομία, *anomia*) appears three times in Matthew's unique material (7:23 [maybe Q]; 13:41; 23:28). He adds it to Mark 13:13 in Matt 24:12. Mark refers to the Pharisees and scribes once as "hypocrite" (ὑποκριτής, *hypocritēs*, Mark 7:6). Matthew (fifteen times) retains Mark's one usage (Matt 15:7) and adds it to other Markan passages (compare Matt 22:18 with Mark 12:15; Matt 23:14 with Mark 12:40). The rest appear mostly in material unique to Matthew.

22. Matthew uses "church" (ἐκκλησία, *ekklēsia*) twice in his own material (18:17) and adds it to Mark 8:29 in Matt 16:18. Matthew finds the phrase "one of these little ones" in Mark 9:42 (cf. Matt 18:6) and uses it three more times (10:42; 18:10, 14). He adds "righteous" (used once by Mark in 2:17 [= Matt 9:13]) in 5:45; 10:41; 13:43, 49; 25:37, 46 as an ecclesiological reference.

23. Davies and Allison, *Matthew,* 1.75–79. On 75–76, they list the ninety-five words from Hawkins, *Horae Synopticae,* 4–8. Hawkins (*Horae Synopticae,* 3) defines "characteristic" as vocabulary which occurs at least four times in Matthew, which is either not found in Mark or Luke, or which appears in Matthew twice as often as in Mark and Luke together. Davies and Allison (*Matthew,* 1.77–79) add 143 words. For similar lists, see Luz, *Matthew 1–7,* 52–73; Gundry, *Matthew,* 1–5, 641–49.

24. Davies and Allison, *Matthew,* 1.79–80; Luz, *Matthew 1–7,* 73–74.

25. D. Harrington, *The Gospel of Matthew* (Sacra Pagina; Collegeville: Liturgical, 1991) 112–44. Harrington's redaction-critical discussion pays attention to Matthew's redaction of Mark and to the situation of the community being addressed. In addition to the commentaries, see H. J. Held, "Matthew as Interpreter of the Miracle Stories," in *Tradition and Interpretation,* 165–299; W. G. Thompson, "Reflections on the Composition of Matt 8:1–9:34," *CBQ* 33 (1971) 365–88; J. D. Kingsbury, "Observations on the 'Miracle Chapters' of Matthew 8–9," *CBQ* 40 (1978) 559–73.

26. Word totals are taken from Hawkins, *Horae Synopticae,* 159.

27. See Allen, *Matthew*, xvii–xix, xxiv–xxvi. As one example, in the feeding of the five thousand, Mark (6:39–40) describes Jesus ordering "all to sit down *by companies* on the *green* grass. *So they sat down in groups, by hundreds and by fifties.* And taking the five loaves . . . " Matthew (14:19) omits the italicized words.

28. Allen, *Matthew*, xix–xxxi; Hawkins, *Horae Synopticae*, 117–59. Davies and Allison (*Matthew*, 1.74) provide a succinct summary. The discussions provide examples of Matthew's frequent omission of Mark's use of πάλιν ("again"), the adverbial πολλαί ("many things"), ὅτι ("that") with verbs of saying, ἄρχω with infinitive ("began to"), εἶναι with participle ("was/were —ing"). Matthew tends to replace the imperfect with the aorist. He also reduces the frequency of redundancies, double negatives, the use of a compound verb with the same preposition, unusual vocabulary, and various awkward grammatical constructions.

29. Matthew's changes to the ten appearances of this phrase in Mark 1 indicate five ways in which Matthew improves and varies Mark's style in connecting scenes.

(1) He omits the phrase (Mark 1:21b, 23, 28; cf. Matt 8:14 with Mark 1:30).

(2) He replaces the phrase with another connective (cf. Matt 4:1 τότε [*tote*, "then"] with Mark 1:12).

(3) He omits καί (*kai*, "and," cf. Mark 1:10 with Matt 3:16) while retaining εὐθύς.

(4) He replaces καί with the connective δέ (*de*, "and," cf. Mark 1:18, 20 with Matt 4:20, 22).

(5) He retains the phrase, though sometimes changing Mark's εὐθύς to εὐθέως (cf. Mark 1:42 with Matt 8:3).

30. See also Mark 3:3–4; 8:22.

31. Compare Mark 1:40 with Matt 8:2; Mark 5:38 with Matt 9:23.

32. Fitzmyer lists ten passages in which Matthew incorporates Q material almost word for word. See J. Fitzmyer, "The Priority of Mark and the 'Q' Source in Luke," in *Jesus and Man's Hope* (ed. D. Miller; Pittsburgh: Perspective, 1970) 1.131–70, esp. 151. He lists Matt 3:7b–10 and Luke 3:7b–9; Matt 6:24 and Luke 16:13; Matt 7:3–5 and Luke 6:41–42; Matt 7:7–11 and Luke 11:9–13; Matt 11:4–6, 7b–11 and Luke 7:22–23, 24b–28; Matt 11:21–23 and Luke 10:13–15; Matt 11:25–27 and Luke 10:21–22; Matt 12:43–45 and Luke 11:24–25; Matt 23:37–38 and Luke 13:34–35; Matt 24:45–51 and Luke 12:42–46.

33. A. Jacobson, "The Literary Unity of Q," *JBL* 101 (1982) 365–89. Jacobson identifies blessings or macarisms (7 in Q, 2 in Mark,

13 in Matt), woes (9, 0, 14), eschatological correlatives (Matt uses four from Q at Matt 12:40; 24:27, 37, 38–39), and prophetic threats of judgment (12 in Q and Matt, 2 in Mark).

34. Davies and Allison (*Matthew*, 1.118–119) argue that Matthew retains and reflects the basic order in Q: a programmatic sermon, missionary discourse, anti–Pharisaic denunciations, and eschatological prophecies and warnings. (Compare Luke 6:17–35 with Matt 5; Luke 6:36–49 with Matt 7; Luke 11:39–52 with Matt 23; Luke 17:23–37 with Matt 24.)

35. Stanton, *Gospel for a New People*, 333–39. Stanton discusses Matt 6:9–13; 7:12, 15–20; 7:21; 10:8, 24–25, 41; 18:10a, 14; 5:13a, 14a, 16; 23:28, 32–34.

36. See P. D. Meyer, "The Gentile Mission in Q," *JBL* 89 (1970) 405–17. He examines Luke 11:29–32 = Matt 12:38–42; Luke 7:1–10 = Matt 8:5–10; Luke 13:28–29 = Matt 8:11–12; Luke 14:15–24 = Matt 22:1–10; Luke 13:34–35 = Matt 23:37–39. Also Jacobson, "Literary Unity," 379–80.

37. For example, "one of these little ones" (18:10, 14), "your Father in heaven" (18:10, 14), "the will of your Father" (18:14).

38. Luz (*Matthew 1–7*, 74 n. 105) identifies Luke 3:16–17; 6:16–19; 7:31–35; 10:12–16; 11:31–32; 11:49–51; 12:39–46, 57–59; 13:28–35; 17:23–37. For Matthew's use of this technique, see Bornkamm, "End-Expectation and Church," in *Tradition and Interpretation*, 15–51.

39. Neither word appears in Mark. Κρίνω (*krinō*) appears in Q at Luke 6:37 = Matt 7:1 (2x), Luke 18:30b = Matt 19:28. Matthew reinforces its usage by creating 7:2a (2x) and adding it to another Q saying in Matt 5:40 (= Luke 6:29b). Matthew takes over four Q usages of κρίσις (*krisis*), but uses the word another eight times, four of which heighten the theme of eschatological warning (10:15; 11:24; 12:36; 23:33). See Jacobson, "Literary Unity," 375–76.

40. See Carter, *Sermon on the Mount*, ch. 1.

41. Luz, *Matthew 1–7*, 75–76. Luz sees the influence of Matthew's community in this presentation.

42. For example Streeter, *Four Gospels*, 150, 231–32, 249–70; Manson, *Sayings of Jesus*, 21–26; Kilpatrick, *Origins*, 14–36; for a useful summary chart of their reconstructions, S. H. Brooks, *Matthew's Community: The Evidence of His Special Sayings Source* (JSNTSup 16; Sheffield: JSOT, 1987) 159; W. D. Davies, *The Setting of the Sermon on the Mount* (Cambridge: Cambridge University, 1966) 387–401.

43. Brooks, *Matthew's Community*, 12–19.

44. Davies and Allison, *Matthew*, 1.121–27.

Chapter 5

The Audience's Social and Religious Experiences: Part 1

We have now taken three steps toward joining the authorial audience by investigating (1) the identity, time, place, and cultural world of the gospel's author (ch. 1), (2) its genre (ch. 2), and (3) the religious traditions about Jesus with which the audience is assumed to be familiar (ch. 3). In this and the next chapter we take a fourth step toward joining the authorial audience. The author assumes that his readers have certain religious, social, and cultural experiences as followers of Jesus. He has an image of the challenges and difficulties, the strengths and weaknesses of the circumstances in which they live. In this regard the authorial audience approximates the gospel's actual audience. In places the text seems to allude to and address this experience as the context for hearing the author's presentation of the story of Jesus. Using redaction criticism, we will pay particular attention to the author's reworking of the traditions as clues to the circumstances and situation of the community or communities[1] which the author is addressing.[2]

I indicated in chapter 1 that the community for which Matthew writes may have existed in Syria, possibly the city of Antioch, toward the end of the first century. We have three possible ways of finding out about its circumstances. One way involves using other writings from near the time of the gospel's writing which describe Matthew's community. But no such writings exist.[3] A second approach involves learning about life in first-century Antioch. This approach would identify possible issues confronting Matthew's community in this environment.

A third approach, which can be coupled with the second one, views the gospel as a source of information about its own situation. It regards the text as a window into the situation behind the gospel. This third approach assumes that a text reflects the circumstances it addresses.

This approach is difficult to employ, though, because the gospel sets the story of Jesus in Palestine, not Antioch. As we have seen, it uses traditions that had existed previously in different contexts. Aware of these difficulties, redaction critics have paid particular attention to the *changes* which Matthew makes to his sources. They assume that these changes express Matthew's own theological understanding as well as his understanding of the particular community which he addresses. Attention to these changes indicates some contours of the circumstances of Matthew's audience and assists us in understanding the experiences and knowledge, identity, and lifestyle assumed of the authorial audience.

Implicit in this approach is a circular movement described by one redaction critic: "In order to read the text responsibly, we need to know about the circumstances that elicited it, but in our quest for its setting we have only the text of the Gospel itself."[4] Such an approach requires careful reading in order to formulate an understanding of the aspects of Matthew's community assumed of the audience. Subsequent rereadings test and modify these understandings. As in the last chapter, a synopsis of the Gospel of Matthew is a useful companion to this and the next chapter.

A MINORITY COMMUNITY

Josephus, a first-century Jewish historian, identifies Antioch[5] as the third largest city in the Roman empire.[6] Estimates place Antioch's population anywhere between 150 thousand and 300 to 400 thousand.[7] About forty percent of the city's area consisted of public buildings and monuments. Living areas were densely populated.[8] A small wealthy elite controlled the political and economic systems, particularly the use of land and raw materials. Apart from the impressive mansions of the elite, most people lived in crowded multi-storied tenement buildings. Streets were narrow, functioning as both the communal living room and open waste disposal areas. Where a piped water supply was absent, water was carried in jars and stored. Disease, filth, and foul smells from decaying matter were pervasive.

The population was diverse with various ethnic groups settled within the city.[9] Newcomers were attracted by the city's various roles. Antioch, the administrative center of the province of Syria, was home to sizable numbers of civic and military personnel. It was also a commercial, manufacturing, and farming center at the intersection of important trading routes, both road and river. Ethnic groups brought diverse customs and religious observance. Temples dedicated to Zeus, Apollo, Dionysius, Artemis, Aphrodite, Ares, Herakles, Asclepius, and Isis existed as did a sizable Jewish population with perhaps three synagogues.[10] Social and ethnic divisions were rigidly maintained.

Not surprisingly, social order was frequently threatened by personal, social, economic, religious, and ethnic conflicts. Natural catastrophes such as fire, flooding, famine, and epidemics caused social havoc.[11] Stark summarizes his discussion of Antioch in the first century by saying it was

> . . . a city filled with misery, danger, fear, despair and hatred. Antioch was a city where the average family lived a squalid life in filthy and cramped quarters . . . The city was filled with hatred and fear rooted in intense ethnic antagonisms and exacerbated by a constant stream of strangers. This city was so lacking in stable networks of attachments that petty incidents could prompt mob violence . . . . Antioch was repeatedly smashed by cataclysmic catastrophes. A resident could expect literally to be homeless from time to time providing that he or she was among the survivors.[12]

Evidence for a Christian group in the city derives from Christian writings such as Galatians 2 (early 50s CE) and Acts 11:19–30 (80s CE). The general information about Antioch, however, points to a basic fact about this Christian community's existence. It was a minority community in a large and diverse city.

It is impossible to put any total on the number of Christians in Matthew's community at Antioch. There is no doubt, though, that this new religious movement was very small. On the basis of other New Testament writings such as Romans 16:5 and 1 Corinthians 16:19, Matthew's community probably met in a house or houses, or perhaps a rented hall. It has been estimated that the large house of a wealthy patron could accommodate about forty to fifty people for a meeting.[13] This small community comprising one or several house groups faced the huge task of defining its identity and way of life in a large city which did not share its particular orientation and commitment, nor its new patterns of social relationship.

Matthew's images of disciples emphasize this minority status. Matthew retains Mark's striking designation of disciples as "little ones" (18:6 = Mark 9:42). But several verses later he uses the term twice more. He adds it at the beginning (18:10) and end (18:14) of the Q parable of the ninety-nine sheep underlining the value of the "little ones" (18:10–14; cf. Luke 15:3–7). He also adds it to Markan material in 10:42 (Mark 9:41). At 11:25 he retains Q's designation of disciples, the recipients of Jesus' revelation, as "infants" (Luke 10:21). He also retains and expands Mark's image of disciples as "children."[14] These images present the Matthean community as, among other things, small and powerless.

The authorial audience is assumed to be familiar with the difficult issue of how this tiny group of followers of Jesus might participate in the daily life and structures of this city while maintaining their identity and allegiance to the God whose presence they encounter in Jesus.

A COMMUNITY RECENTLY SEPARATED FROM A SYNAGOGUE

Redaction critics have observed that in his redaction of his sources Matthew increases negative references to the synagogue and the religious leaders. Six types of changes can be noted.

(1) Five times Matthew uses the phrase "their synagogues" (4:23; 9:35; 10:17; 12:9; 13:54) and one time "your synagogue"

(23:34, referring to the Jewish leaders). Only one of these six references is borrowed from Mark (Matt 4:23 = Mark 1:39).[15] Matthew adds the other five, three to Mark and two to Q.[16] The effect of Matthew's expanded use of "their synagogue" is to underline the distance of Jesus and his followers from the synagogue.

Several of these passages emphasize alienation and hostility between the synagogue and Jesus' disciples. In 10:17 Jesus warns disciples that they will be flogged in *their* synagogues. In 13:54–58 a synagogue rejects Jesus. Alienation is present even when Matthew refers to "*the* (not their) synagogue." In 6:2 and 5 and 23:6 the behavior of "the hypocrites in the synagogues" is condemned and contrasted with that of the "you" of the Christian communities.

(2) Matthew omits favorable references to the synagogue. (a) In Mark 5:21–43 Jairus is a "ruler of the synagogue" (ἀρχισυνάγωγος, *archisynagōgos*, 5:22, 35, 36, 38) who asks Jesus to heal his daughter. Matthew removes any reference to the synagogue by abbreviating the title "ruler of the synagogue" to "ruler" or "official" (Matt 9:18, 23). Matthew's only other use of the term "official" appears in 20:25 in a negative reference to Gentile officials. (b) Luke's version of the Q tradition about the healing of the centurion's servant presents the centurion as a lover of the Jewish people and builder of a synagogue (Luke 7:5). Jewish elders appeal to Jesus on the centurion's behalf (Luke 7:3). Matthew omits these references but retains praise for the man's faith (Matt 8:5–13).

(3) Matthew takes over from Mark the familiar references to the role of the religious leaders in opposing and killing Jesus[17] but presents a more negative picture. He adds "scribes" to Mark's one reference to the Pharisees as hypocrites (Mark 7:1, 6; Matt 15:1, 7). He also adds seven references to hypocritical Pharisees, six of which appear in chapter 23.[18] Four times he replaces Mark's references to "scribes" with references to Pharisees.[19] Unique to Matthew are his descriptions of them as "blind guides" and "blind fools" (23:16, 17, 19, 24, 26; cf. 15:14).

(4) Matthew recasts the use of the term "rabbi." Twice in Mark Peter addresses Jesus as "Rabbi." Matthew substitutes "Lord" in one instance, a term used in Matthew only by

disciples (compare Mark 9:5 with Matt 17:4) and omits the other (Mark 11:21 with Matt 21:20).

Matthew retains Mark's third use of "rabbi," by the traitor Judas (Mark 14:45; Matt 26:49). Two additional references reinforce its negative associations with betrayal and false discipleship. In 26:21–25 when Jesus announces that one of the disciples will betray him, the disciples ask one by one, "Is it I, Lord?" Matthew adds "Lord" to Mark's account (26:22; Mark 14:19). Matthew adds a verse to Mark in which Judas asks Jesus the same question. But instead of addressing Jesus as "Lord" Judas calls him "rabbi" (26:25). Second, in 23:7 "rabbi" is a title that the self-seeking and hypocritical scribes and Pharisees prefer (23:2–7). Matthew's Jesus forbids its use in the Christian community (23:8).

(5) Some similar dimensions are evident in Matthew's heightened negative portrayal of the term "scribes" (γραμμα-τεύς, grammateus). (a) Mark comments on the contrast between the authority present in Jesus' teaching but absent from the teaching of "*the* scribes" (Mark 1:22). Matthew intensifies the distance between Jesus and the scribes by changing "*the* scribes" to "*their* scribes" (Matt 7:29). (b) Matthew changes the Q tradition of the *person* who volunteers to follow Jesus (Luke 9:57) into an account of the *scribe* who is rejected by Jesus (Matt 8:19). The rejected scribe addresses Jesus as "teacher" while the disciple addresses him as "Lord" (8:21).[20] (c) In chapter 2 (material unique to Matthew), the scribes exemplify condemned behavior. They interpret the scriptures correctly but do not act on their knowledge (2:4–6) to pay homage to Jesus. "Knowing," but not "doing," God's will is not the way of discipleship (7:24–27; 12:46–50). (d) Matthew significantly recasts Mark's sympathetic account of the scribe whom Jesus declares to be "not far from the kingdom of God" (Mark 12:28–34). Matthew's account (22:34–40) turns the scribe into a Pharisee (22:34), removes Mark's double reference to the scribe's appreciation for Jesus' answers (Mark 12:28, 32), and removes Jesus' commendation of the scribe (Mark 12:34). (e) Overall, Matthew adds eleven references to "scribes," ten of which are negative.[21]

(6) Some further instances in which Matthew intensifies the polemic against the synagogue and its leaders include:[22]

(a) Matthew receives from Q Jesus' blessing on those who are persecuted "on my account" (5:11–12). Matthew underlines this theme by adding his own blessing on those persecuted "for righteousness' sake" (5:10). He then contrasts the lifestyle of his readers with the righteousness of the "scribes and the Pharisees" (5:20). In this context the contrast between disciples and the unspecified members of the synagogue who give alms, pray, and fast falsely (6:1–18) presents the scribes and the Pharisees as hypocrites.

(b) In 8:5–13 (cf. Luke 7:1–10) Matthew takes over the Q tradition's account of the Roman centurion whose faith is presented as being superior to any found in Israel (cf. 8:10). Matthew adds to this story material found in another context in Q (cf. Luke 13:28–29) in which Gentiles enter God's reign. In so doing he reorients the Q material. Q's call to repentance functions in its new context to reinforce the more general theme of Israel's lack of faith. In two other contexts (21:43; 22:7) Matthew adds verses to parables from Mark (12:1–12 esp. v. 11) and Q (Luke 14:15–24, esp. v. 21) to underline the punishment of Israel's leaders. And the final woe announced against the hypocritical scribes and Pharisees in chapter 23 (23:29–36) identifies them more explicitly than in Q as murderers of followers of Jesus (cf. 23:34 with Luke 11:49).

How do we explain Matthew's heightened negative presentation of the synagogue and the religious leaders? Most redaction critics argue that it reflects the community's experiences of bitter conflict with and separation from at least one of the synagogues in Antioch. Matthew's largely Jewish community had belonged to a synagogue but was either expelled or withdrew voluntarily. Their situation shows distance, hostility, and alienation in relation to this community in Antioch. The intensity of the hostility in the gospel suggests a recent as well as bitter separation from a synagogue.[23] It is important for our purposes to note that the authorial audience is assumed to be familiar with this experience.

Stanton suggests that this intensified polemic is not addressed directly to the "scribes and Pharisees." Rather it is "in-house," existing for the benefit of Matthew's audience. In the context of conflict and persecution, Matthew's community struggles to make sense of the pain and hostility of its rejection.

It seeks to secure distance between itself and the synagogue and to articulate its own place as a beleaguered but special group in God's scheme of things. The words of Jesus provide insight, comfort, and direction, reinforcing its identity and guiding its lifestyle.[24]

Scholars have connected this conflict with the devastating circumstances resulting from the Romans' destruction of the Jerusalem temple and priesthood in 70 CE (Matt 23:38; 24:2; 26:61). The following decades were a time of much anguish and debate as various groups wrestled with what had happened and with what the future would be like.[25] Significant for the gradual reformulation of Judaism was the emergence of Pharisaic leadership to provide new focus, new theological understanding, and patterns of worship centered on synagogues.[26] Their emergence as leaders may explain Matthew's increased negative references to them.

Issues Involved in the Recent Bitter Separation

Given that Matthew's community had recently separated from the synagogue, there are some clues in the gospel about the dispute and separation. Rome's destruction of the Jerusalem temple in 70 required significant reformulation of important theological ideas and religious practices. Prior to the year 70 the temple was seen as a sacred place of God's presence and of atonement for sin. It was the place where the sacred story of the people's past experiences with Israel's faithful God was told and sacred time maintained through the celebration of the festivals. Festivals such as Yom Kippur (Day of Atonement) and Sukkoth (Booths) were occasions for retelling the story, reinforcing identity, and securing faithful living.[27]

The temple's destruction by the Romans in 70 CE shattered both a way of worship and the understanding of a life lived in relation to God. Questions arose about God's faithfulness and power, about how and where one encounters God's presence, about how and where one experiences atonement and God's forgiving mercy, about how one knows God's revealed will. In this debate communities such as Matthew's made claims about Jesus. Eventually, it was no longer possible for them to make claims about Jesus and remain a part of the synagogue community. At least three likely claims can be identified from heightened emphases in Matthew's gospel.[28]

Jesus Forgives Sin

Matthew takes over the Markan stories about the controversy of Jesus forgiving sin.[29] But he also heightens the claim that Jesus forgives sin.

(1) The gospel opens with a passage that has no parallel in Matthew's sources. An "angel of the Lord" names Mary's baby Jesus, "for he will save his people from their sins" (1:21). The scene presents Jesus as the one whose divine mission is to save from sin. (2) Matthew removes from Mark a reference to John preaching a baptism of repentance *for the forgiveness of sins* (cf. 3:1; Mark 1:4). Matthew recognizes that John calls for repentance (3:2) and for people to "confess their sin" (3:6; Mark 1:5) but he restricts forgiveness of sin to Jesus. (3) In Matthew's version of the last supper Jesus gives thanks for the cup and describes it as "my blood of the covenant, which is poured out for many *for the forgiveness of sins*" (26:28, italics added). Matthew adds the words "for the forgiveness of sins" to Mark 14:24. The cross and Jesus' death (as well as Jesus' life, 9:1–8) are a means of forgiveness. (4) Matthew adds several sections which remind the community that God's forgiving mercy in Jesus leads to forgiveness within the community (5:23–24; 18:23–35; cf. 6:12, 14–15).

In claiming that God's saving forgiving work is experienced in Jesus, Matthew reinterprets Jewish traditions and contemporary debates. For example, Matthew claims that Jesus is "greater than the temple" (12:6). Twice Matthew adds Hosea 6:6 to Markan traditions, "I desire mercy not sacrifice."[30] Rabbi Yohanan ben Zakkai also saw the Hosea text as providing a new way of atoning and of living in post-temple Judaism through deeds of lovingkindness.[31] But Matthew maintains a focus on Jesus as the one commissioned by God to save from sin and make forgiveness available. Only in commitment to him, "following" him (4:18–22), "acknowledging" him (10:32–33), "receiving" him (10:40), "believing" in him (18:6), is forgiveness encountered. In the post-70 period of rethinking religious practices and understanding, Matthew's community holds that forgiveness is encountered in Jesus. This understanding is portrayed in and reinforced by the Gospel of Matthew.

Jesus Manifests God's Presence

The task of saving from sin forms one part of Jesus' divinely commissioned work (1:21). In 1:23, Matthew presents Jesus with a further role. He is to manifest God's presence among human beings. This theme is woven through the narrative in sections that are unique to Matthew. The presence of God is encountered among the community which gathers in Jesus' name for worship (18:20), in its mission of mercy among the dispossessed (25:31–46), and in its teaching and preaching mission (28:18–20). This claim that God's forgiving presence is encountered in Jesus shapes the identity and lifestyle of Matthew's post-70 community.

Jesus Interprets God's Will

Matthew also presents Jesus as the one who brings the definitive interpretation of God's will. In a section unique to Matthew (5:21–48), Jesus quotes Jewish traditions six times in order to present their definitive interpretation. The interpretations support the claim made in 5:17 that Jesus has come not "to abolish the law and the prophets . . . but to fulfil [them]." Jesus interprets the scriptural traditions (found in the Septuagint—the Greek translation of the Hebrew Bible) to indicate their "true" meaning (9:13; 11:10; 12:1–8; 12:9–14; 13:14–17; 15:1–20; 19:3–12; 22:34–40; 22:41–46). The words of Moses, David, Isaiah, and Jeremiah, properly understood in the light of Jesus' interpretation, are presented as endorsements of his divine authority. Jesus' life also demonstrates a complete consistency with the scriptures: his birth (1:23; 2:6, 15, 18), where he lives (2:23; 4:15–16); his healing (8:17), his teaching methods (parables, 13:35), his actions of going to Jerusalem (21:5), his arrest (26:56), and betrayal (27:9–10). The authorial audience is assumed to be familiar with the authority of the scriptural traditions which Jesus fulfills.

Matthew closes the Sermon on the Mount with a scene of the final judgment. The criterion of this judgment is people's response to Jesus' words. Whoever "hears these words of mine and acts on them" will survive the judgment, but it will be otherwise for whoever "hears these words of mine and does not act on them" (7:24–27). Jesus' words are eternal (24:35) and continue as authoritative teaching for the community (28:20). In the post-70 era the Matthean community understands that in Jesus, not in Moses or in Jewish traditions or in the claims of other revealer figures, is the definitive and authoritative manifestation of God's will.[32]

Post-70 Debates

It is not difficult to imagine Matthew's community making claims that God's forgiveness, presence, and definitive will are encountered in Jesus in the context of debates about the experience of these realities in post-temple Judaism. In a situation of crisis and reformulation, numerous documents in the names of such authoritative figures as Abraham, Enoch, Moses, Baruch, Ezra, and Solomon present definitive revelations and teaching. The Mosaic tradition was a central concern among Pharisaic circles. Within this matrix Matthew's community makes claims about encountering God's forgiving, saving presence in Jesus and in the community committed to him. Hence Matthew explicitly identifies Jesus as being greater than the temple (12:6), Jonah (12:41), and Solomon (12:42). Commitment to him and not claims of privilege based on descent from Abraham (3:7) provides the basis of membership in the people of God (cf. 12:50; 21:43; 22:7).

But the leaders of the synagogue are presented in the gospel as finding such claims to be unacceptable. The religious leaders declare Jesus' forgiveness of sin to be "blasphemy" (9:3). They attribute his manifestations of the reign of God to the working of the devil (9:34; 10:25; 12:24). They say his association with "tax collectors and sinners" indicate he is a "glutton and a drunkard" (11:19). They view his breaking of Sabbath traditions as deserving of death (12:14). They question his authority and its source (21:23–27). In turn, Matthew's Jesus cited the religious leaders for rejecting God's work (21:33–46), for knowing "neither the scriptures nor the power of God" (22:29), and for being "hypocrites" who "shut up" the reign of God (23:13). This describes a situation of rising antagonism and hostility.

Each group refuses to recognize the legitimacy of the other. This leads to the separation of Matthew's group from the synagogue. The authorial audience is assumed to be familiar with this bitter and disruptive separation, with the issues involved in it, and with the theological claims about Jesus emerging from it and confirmed in the gospel.

CONCLUSION

In this chapter, using redaction criticism, we have noted two likely aspects of the situation of Matthew's community. This knowledge is assumed of the authorial audience as it reads this gospel. (1) It is a small, minority community facing the challenges and difficulties of living in a large and diverse society. (2) It has experienced separation from the synagogue in a recent bitter dispute. A number of issues probably figured in this debate including claims about Jesus' God-given roles to forgive sin, manifest God's presence, and interpret God's will. The author of the Gospel of Matthew assumes the authorial audience understands these experiences and issues.

NOTES

1. Stanton (*Gospel for a New People,* 50–51; idem, "The Communities of Matthew," *Int* 46 [1992] 379–91) argues for Matthew's address to *communities* since Matthew would not have "composed such an elaborate gospel for one relatively small group." I use the term "community" to refer to several groups meeting in different houses.

2. See D. Senior, *What Are They Saying About Matthew?* (New York: Paulist, 1983) 5–15; J. D. Kingsbury, "Conclusion: Analysis of a Conversation," in *Social History* (ed. Balch) 259–69; Stanton, *Gospel for a New People,* 113–281; Carter, *Sermon on the Mount,* ch. 3; Saldarini, *Matthew's Christian-Jewish Community.*

3. Some have tried to trace a trajectory from Matthew's gospel to later groups who found his gospel useful. On Ignatius and Matthew, W. Schoedel, "Ignatius and the Reception of the Gospel of Matthew in Antioch," in *Social History* (ed. Balch) 129–77, and the response by J. P. Meier, 178–86; on Matthew and 5 Ezra and the Apocalypse of Peter, see Stanton, "5 Ezra and Matthean Christianity in the Second Century," in *Gospel for a New People,* 256–77, and E. Schweizer,

"Matthew's Church," in *Interpretation of Matthew* (ed. Stanton) 129–55; also idem, "The 'Matthean' Church," *NTS* 20 (1974) 216; on Matthew and the Didache, see Schweizer, "Matthew's Church."

4. Stanton, "Communities of Matthew," 381.

5. For what follows, see the discussions and bibliography of Stark, "Antioch," in *Social History* (ed. Balch) 189–210; F. W. Norris, "Artifacts from Antioch," in *Social History* (ed. Balch) 248–58; R. Rohrbaugh, "The Pre-Industrial City in Luke–Acts," in *The Social World of Luke–Acts: Models for Interpretation* (ed. J. Neyrey; Peabody: Hendrickson, 1991) 125–49; D. E. Oakman, "The Countryside in Luke–Acts," in *Social World* (ed. Neyrey) 151–79; Carter, *Households and Discipleship*, 35–42; Downey, *History of Antioch*.

6. Josephus, *Jewish War* 3.29. Rome and Alexandria were probably the two largest cities.

7. Downey, *History of Antioch*, Excursus 2, 582–83; F. M. Heichelheim ("Roman Syria," in *An Economic Survey of Ancient Rome* [ed. T. Frank; Baltimore: Johns Hopkins, 1938] 121–257, esp. 158) estimates between 300,000 and 450,000. C. Kraeling, "The Jewish Community at Antioch," *JBL* 51 (1932) 130–60. Stark ("Antioch," in *Social History* [ed. Balch] 192) estimates about 150,000.

8. R. MacMullen (*Roman Social Relations* [New Haven: Yale University, 1974] 62–64, 168 n. 16) estimates a density of about two hundred per acre, comparable to or surpassing the worst overcrowding in modern cities.

9. Stark ("Antioch," in *Social History* [ed. Balch] 196–97) cites one estimate of at least "eighteen identifiable ethnic quarters within Antioch."

10. Josephus, *Ant.* 12.119; Kraeling, "Jewish Community," 143.

11. Stark ("Antioch," in *Social History* [ed. Balch] 206) notes destruction of property and life from major fires in 24 and 70 CE, from earthquakes in 37, 42 and 115, from anti-Jewish riots in 40 and 66–70, from famine in 46–47. Life was precarious for many.

12. Stark, "Antioch," in *Social History* (ed. Balch) 198.

13. J. Murphy-O'Connor (*St. Paul's Corinth* [Good News Studies 6; Wilmington: Michael Glazier, 1983] 153–61, esp. 156) identifies the average size of a triclinium (dining room) as thirty-six square meters and of an atrium as fifty-five square meters. In discussing houses excavated at Antioch, R. Stillwell ("Houses of Antioch," *Dumbarton Oaks Papers* 15 [1961] 47–57, esp. 49–50, 55) notes dining rooms ranging from twenty-five to ninety square meters, rendering an average size of about fifty square meters.

14. Compare Matt 18:2 (retained), 3 (expanded), 4 (expanded), 5 (retained), with Mark 9:36, 37; 10:15; Matt 19:13–15 with Mark 10:13–16.

15. Matthew omits Mark 1:23–28, the other pericope in which the phrase appears. The distinctiveness of Matthew's use can be seen in comparing it with Mark's "the synagogues" (Mark 1:21, 29; 3:1; 6:2; 12:39; 13:9). Luke (not a source for Matthew) uses "synagogue" fifteen times and only once refers to it as "their synagogue" (Luke 4:15). John (also not a source) uses the noun just twice (John 6:59; 18:20) but without using "their."

16. Compare Matt 9:35 with Mark 6:6a; Matt 12:9 with Mark 3:1; Matt 13:54 with Mark 6:2. For Q, compare Matt 10:17 with Luke 12:11; Matt 23:34 with Luke 11:49.

17. Compare Matt 12:14 with Mark 3:6. Matthew's omission of Mark's "Herodians" intensifies the focus on the Pharisees. Compare Matt 16:21 with Mark 8:31; Matt 20:18–19 with Mark 10:33–34; Matt 26:2–4 with Mark 14:1.

18. Matt 23:13, 15, 23, 25, 27, 29; cf. Matt 22:18 with Mark 12:15.

19. Compare Matt 9:11 with Mark 2:16; Matt 9:34, 12:24 with Mark 3:22; Matt 22:41 with Mark 12:35.

20. For Matthew's use of "teacher" by non-disciples, 12:38, 19:16; 22:16, 24, 36.

21. The one positive image appears in 13:52 and seems to refer to disciples who have entered into the kingdom of heaven (cf. 4:17).

22. Stanton, *Gospel for a New People,* 146–68, esp. 154–57.

23. The possible role of the group of rabbis led by rabbi Yohanan ben Zakkai (and later by Gamaliel II) who met at the town of Yavneh (or Jamnia) northwest of Jerusalem has caused much debate. Davies (*Setting,* 259–72, 315) argues that Matthew's Sermon on the Mount was "the Christian answer to Jamnia," and that the *Birkath ha Minim,* a curse on heretics composed around 85 CE, was responsible for the exclusion of Matthew's community from the synagogue. Most scholars have not been persuaded by such a direct link with Yavneh. The deliberations at Yavneh are considered more a process than an event; there is no evidence that it functioned as a central council issuing decrees to all synagogues to obey. The role of Christian groups as a primary target seems overstated, and the *Birkath* prays for God's destruction of the heretics, not for their exclusion from the synagogue. For discussion, see R. Kimelman, "*Birkat Ha-Minim* and the Lack of Evidence for an Anti–Christian Jewish Prayer in Late Antiquity" in *Jewish and Christian Self-Definition* vol. 2 (ed. E. P. Sanders, A. Baumgarten, A. Mendelson; Philadelphia: Fortress, 1981) 226–44; S. Katz, "Issues in the Separation of Judaism and Christianity after 70 CE; A Reconsideration," *JBL* 103 (1984) 43–76, esp. 63–75.

24. Two other views of the relationship between the synagogue and Matthew's community should be noted. (1) Matthew's community

exists as a sub-group within a synagogue with considerable conflict and dispute between the group committed to Jesus and the rest of the synagogue (an internal or *intra-muros* conflict). See Kilpatrick, *Origin*, 122; Bornkamm, "End-Expectation and Church in Matthew," in *Tradition and Interpretation*, 39; G. Barth, "Matthew's Understanding of the Law," in *Tradition and Interpretation*, 58–164; Davies, *Setting*, 290, 332. The pericope upholding the payment of the tax on diaspora synagogues (17:24–27), the opening verses of chapter 23 urging obedience to the teaching of the scribes and Pharisees, the carrying out of synagogue discipline (10:17; 23:34), and respect for the Sabbath (24:20) are frequently cited in support. For discussion, Stanton, *Gospel for a New People*, 118–24, 192–206. (2) A second view sees the dispute with Judaism as belonging to the past of a now predominantly Gentile community. See van Tilborg, *Jewish Leaders*, 171; Strecker, *Der Weg*, 34; Meier, *Vision of Matthew*, 17–23. This view focuses on Matthean redaction of traditions, his interest in Gentiles, his hostility to and rejection of Israel and the religious leaders, his ignorance of Jewish customs and groups (such as linking the Pharisees and Sadducees in 16:1, 6, 11). For discussion, Stanton, *Gospel for a New People*, 131–39.

25. Harrington's discussion (*Matthew*, 10–19) of rabbinic and apocalyptic strands of Judaism (4 Ezra and 2 Baruch) in the post-70 era is helpful.

26. J. Neusner, *From Politics to Piety: The Emergence of Pharisaic Judaism* (Englewood Cliffs: Prentice-Hall, 1973) ch. 6; Cohen, *From the Maccabees to the Mishnah*, ch. 7.

27. Roetzel, *World of the New Testament*, 54–64; Neusner, *Politics to Piety*, ch. 6.

28. The importance of claims about Jesus as the interpreter of God's will have often been recognized. See Bornkamm, "End-Expectation and Church," *Tradition and Interpretation*, 25. There has been less discussion of the other christological issues identified here. See Stanton, *Gospel for a New People*, 169–91. He considers claims about Jesus as a magician and deceiver, and about the meaning of the title "Son of David."

29. Compare Matt 9:1–8 with Mark 2:1–12; Matt 12:31–37 with Mark 3:28–30.

30. Compare Matt 9:13 with Mark 2:17; Matt 12:7 with Mark 2:26.

31. Neusner, *Politics to Piety*, ch. 6.

32. For discussion of other claims to authoritative revelation in relation to John, see W. Carter, "The Prologue and John's Gospel: Function, Symbol and the Definitive Word," *JSNT* 39 (1990) 35–58.

Chapter 6

The Audience's Social and Religious Experiences: Part 2

The fourth step toward joining the authorial audience is to identify clues from the gospel about the circumstances of Matthew's community. In chapter 5 we identified two aspects of its experience and lifestyle: (1) its minority status in the large city of Antioch, and (2) its recent bitter separation from the synagogue. In this chapter we will identify two further aspects.

A COMMUNITY IN TRANSITION, BUILDING A NEW IDENTITY

In transition out of the synagogue, Matthew's community must build a new identity. At the center is Jesus; his merciful presence and authoritative teaching of the will of God constitute the central focus of the community.[1] In circumstances of hostility, relationships among members of the new family are crucial (5:21–48; 12:46–50; 18:1–35). This struggle to secure a new identity, to understand the present in relation to the past and future, comprises part of the experience assumed of the authorial audience.

One important issue for the community is its relationship to its Jewish heritage. What place does it have in the history of God's dealings with Israel? Some scholars see in this gospel evidence of a debate about the role of Jewish traditions and laws in the Christian community.[2] They suggest that some wanted to abandon the law and emphasize miracle-working and prophetic gifts. Others, including Matthew, wanted to maintain observance of the law. The pervasive references to Jesus' interpretation of Jewish traditions (5:21–48; 22:37–39), the emphasis on the abiding validity of the law (5:17–20; 24:20), Matthew's condemnation of "lawlessness" (ἀνομία, anomia),[3] and his warnings against miracle workers and false prophets (7:15–23; 24:11–13) indicate Matthew's position.

While the proposal that the text reflects this internal community dispute has been strongly advocated, others have not been convinced. With good reason they prefer to see these warnings and emphases not as polemic directed against a specific group within the community but as general warnings intended to maintain the faithful living of all the community.[4]

With regard to the role of its Jewish heritage, Matthew's redaction indicates continuity and discontinuity.[5] The opening genealogy, material unique to Matthew, places Jesus' coming in continuity with Israel's past but as a new phase in that history (1:1–17). Like the synagogue his community is to pray, fast, and gives alms or charity. But there is an important difference. Unlike what he deems to be the hypocritical practice of the synagogue, this community must do these tasks with integrity (6:1–18). Likewise, Matthew's community keeps the same scriptures, but Jesus' teaching provides their definitive interpretation (5:17–48, the fulfillment citations). Love of God and neighbor unlocks them (22:34–40; 9:13; 12:7).

The community's identity is expressed by the term "church" (ἐκκλησία, ekklēsia), a term used three times in Matthew (16:17; 18:17). Matthew has added this term to his sources. Redaction critics see this as a significant statement about the identity and self-understanding of Matthew's community. In nonbiblical Greek the term ekklēsia denotes the assembly of citizens, called together by a herald to consider civic matters. In the Septuagint it is usually used to translate the Hebrew term qahal. This term designates Israel as a people in covenant relationship with God, summoned by God to live a particular way of life.[6] In using ekklēsia, the gospel recognizes its audience as continuing Israel's special place in the history of God's saving work. Such a claim was not restricted to Matthew's community. Other Christian groups were already claiming to be the "assembly of God" (lit.; 1 Cor 1:2; 1 Thess 1:1; Rom 16:5) as were non-Christian Jewish groups such as the Qumran community (11QM 4:10).

It is significant that Matthew says that the church is based on the confession that Jesus is "the Christ, the son of the living God" (16:16).[7] Peter repeats the earlier confession of all the disciples (14:33). Commitment to Jesus provides the center for this community's identity, not social, ethnic, or economic homogeneity.

Matthew's redaction of Mark's version of this scene (Mark 8:29–30) changes the nature of the exchange between Jesus and Peter. After Peter's confession, Mark's Jesus charges them to tell no one (Mark 8:29–30). Matthew, though, follows Peter's confession (16:16) with a significant addition of three verses (16:17–19). In these additional verses Matthew's Jesus blesses Peter for his receptiveness to divine revelation (16:17). His confession results not from his own insight but from God's work through Jesus (cf. 11:25–27; 13:35). Peter's confession provides the foundation for Jesus' building of the church (16:18, "*I* will build) which is accountable to Jesus ("*my* church"), and is guaranteed divine protection against all destructive powers ("the gates of Hades will not prevail," 16:18b).

Jesus recognizes Peter's important role in the church's establishment: "You are Peter and on this rock I will build my church" (16:18).[8] Peter also has a vital role in its ongoing life (16:19). Jesus gives to him "the keys of the kingdom of heaven" (16:19a). The image of the "keys of the kingdom" probably derives from the prophecy of Isaiah that Eliakim would replace Shebna as master of king Hezekiah's household (Isa 22:22). Just as Eliakim would control entrance to the king, so Peter would control access to the reign of God. The image also appears in several works which date from around the same time as Matthew's gospel. The keys are offered to God as a symbol of the unfaithfulness of the priests and religious leaders and of their failure to interpret God's will (2 Bar 10:18; 4 Bar 4:4). By giving them to Peter and to the community of disciples, Jesus recognizes this community as a place of worship and as agents of God's will. Jesus also commits to Peter the role of "binding and loosing." This phrase is variously interpreted as the authority to preach "the gospel of God's reign" (4:23; 9:35), to admit and excommunicate members, to regulate the community life, and to forgive sin.

Two chapters later in 18:17–18, the second passage in which Matthew adds *ekklēsia*,[9] Peter's function of "binding and loosing" is extended to the whole community. This extension suggests that Peter's primacy in 16:16–19 is to be understood in terms of his temporal place in salvation history rather than in terms of a role exclusive to him.[10]

Consistent with this community's identity as a community called into being by Jesus is the claim that his teaching defines its lifestyle (5:21–48; 7:24–27; 12:46–50; 24:35). The community is sustained in worship by the Eucharist (26:26–29) in which it celebrates the covenant of the forgiveness of sin (Exod 24:8; Jer 31:31–34) and keeps alive the hope of the fullness of God's coming reign (26:29). Entry into this community is through baptism "in the name of the Father and of the Son and of the Holy Spirit" (28:19). To be baptized "in the name of" denotes allegiance and identification. Leadership is not carried out through rabbis as in the synagogue (23:8) but there seem to be Christian scribes (13:53) and perhaps prophets (24:24). Generally, though, there is suspicion of hierarchy (20:20–28).

A lifestyle in which each member cares for the others is emphasized throughout the gospel. Mercy and forgiveness are hallmarks (5:21–26; 9:13; 12:7; 18:21–35). The community has an active role in effecting and maintaining reconciliation among all members (18:15–18). The emphases on the reconciled family of God, brothers and sisters of Jesus who do the will of God (12:46–50), results from two emphases: (1) To treat others with mercy and forgiveness is a consequence of and continuing condition for the experience of God's mercy and forgiveness (6:14–15; 18:21–35). (2) The lifestyle of discipleship, the doing of the will of God, requires the support of other members of the community. To be a minority community, faithful to its allegiance to Jesus in the large city of Antioch, is a difficult challenge. The community needs the resources of each individual. It is also reassured that God's presence is among them in its prayerful worship (18:19–20; 12:6) and mission work (25:31–46; 28:18–20).

The authorial audience is assumed to be part of a community in transition. This *ekklēsia* is establishing its identity and way of life in relation to a stormy and sacred past, a challenging present, and an accountable future.

AN ALTERNATIVE COMMUNITY ON THE MARGINS OF SOCIETY

The authorial audience is not only distinct from the synagogue but from the surrounding society. Its orientation and center are not shared by that society. How, then, does it live "against the grain" in the large diverse city of Antioch?

One response is, of course, to withdraw and separate itself from the rest of the city. But unlike the Qumran community, withdrawal does not seem to be an option. Faithfulness to Jesus in the midst of daily city life is required (5:14–16). It seems that figures like Peter, James, and John have abandoned their family and economic means of existence to follow Jesus (4:18–22). But the gospel sometimes indicates otherwise.[11] Matthew retains Mark's story of Jesus' visit to Peter's house and family to heal his mother-in-law (8:14–15). James' and John's family connections continue to be obvious through the gospel (10:2, 20:20; 26:37; 27:56). Jesus has a house (9:10, 28; 13:1, 36).

The ambivalence of a distinctive focus on Jesus but continued participation in society is evident in the way that Gentiles (non-Jews) are presented in the gospel. Matthew adds references to Gentiles that frequently are negative.

(1) In 5:47 Matthew adds to Q material (Luke 6:27–28, 32–36) a reference to the Gentile's everyday custom of greeting friends. This practice contrasts with Jesus' instruction that his followers extend love beyond friends even to enemies and persecutors. Contrary to contemporary social practices, the community of disciples is an inclusive, not exclusive, community with a variety of patterns for social interaction.

(2) In M material (6:7), Matthew condemns Gentile religious practices of praying to many gods to ensure some divine favor and protection in the harsh realities of everyday life. He contrasts this practice with the certainty of praying to a merciful God who already knows what the praying one needs.

(3) In a slight modification to Q material in 6:32[12] Matthew condemns the Gentile world for its wrong priorities. It is too concerned with acquiring the material necessities of everyday life. By contrast, Matthew's community is to seek the reign and righteousness of God (6:33).

(4) In 10:18 (cf. 20:19) Matthew adds a reference to "the Gentiles" to Q material (cf. Luke 12:11; 21:12–13) to specify that they oppose the community's mission and inflict hardship on it. (5) He makes a similar addition in 24:9 to Mark 13:13 to emphasize that "the nations"[13] hate disciples and put them to death. (6) In Matthew's own material in 18:17, a member of the Matthean community who sins and refuses to be reconciled is to be treated as a Gentile. This may mean excommunication, but since Gentiles also exhibit faith (8:5–13) and are the objects of mission (28:18–20), it may also be a command to make extra efforts to reconcile the offending party.

(7) In 20:25 the hierarchical nature of Gentile society in exercising power over others is attacked. "It shall not be so among you." This attack comes in the context of a two-chapter section (chs. 19–20) that proposes an egalitarian household structure in contrast to the traditional hierarchical and patriarchal household structure which pervaded the ancient world.[14]

Matthew is suspicious of Gentile society. He does not approve of its values and practices. In summarizing Jesus' mission to the Gentiles he describes them as living in death and darkness (4:16). He is very aware that disciples live "against the grain." They contrast the commitments and priorities of their society. They have a different center, identity, lifestyle. At times the community's faithful commitment to Jesus is under threat of persecution. At other times, it is threatened daily by the "ways of the world," the "cares of the world and the lure of wealth" (13:22), its values, commitments, and social practices. Continually Matthew's Jesus calls the community to live vigilantly an alternative reality.

Yet along with these negative references are some positive statements about Gentiles. (1) The gospel's opening genealogy, unique to Matthew, includes four Gentile women. This indicates that God's purposes extend beyond Israel and include male and female.[15] (2) Chapter 2 is also unique to Matthew. Here Gentile visitors from the East come to worship Jesus. In contrast to Herod and the Jerusalem leaders, they exhibit the proper response to his birth. (3) Matthew 4:15 is an addition to Mark 1:21. Here the starting place for Jesus' mission is "Galilee of the Gentiles," into which comes the light of salvation (4:16). (4) We have noted that Matthew edits the Q material concerning the Gentile centurion's faith in 8:5–13 so that it anticipates the "many" who will enter the kingdom (8:11). (5) Also noteworthy are repeated references to the community's mission to both Israel and all the nations (4:19; 10:5–23; 15:21–28; 24:9–14; 26:13; 28:18–20[16]). (6) In 12:17–21 (cf. Mark 3:12) Matthew adds a citation from Isaiah chapters 11 and 42 which, with a double reference to the Gentiles, underlines Jesus' divinely ordained mission to proclaim justice to the Gentiles.

The combination of these favorable and suspicious references sets Matthew's community on the margins of society. They are in an ambivalent place. They do not withdraw, but because of their commitment to Jesus and his teaching they cannot embrace the values and conventional practices of their society. They are an alternative marginal community.[17]

The Gospel of Matthew suggests that this alternative community oppose conventional values and identify with marginal and despised outsiders. For example in chapters 19–20 Matthew overturns the conventional wisdom about how households are ordered. Disciples are to form marriages of "one flesh." The image connotes a marriage of mutuality rather than one of dominant male power as expressed in privileged divorce practices (19:3–9). Those unable to live this way should be eunuchs for the kingdom (19:10–12). This image powerfully expresses marginal existence. Eunuchs were despised and excluded from traditional households because they could not contribute to the future of the society. Jesus blesses the comparison.

Disciples are referred to as children not parents (19:13–15; cf. 23:8b–9). Children were among the lowly outsiders, the humbled, until they became adults and citizens (cf. 18:1–6). Also, contemporary social conventions maintained social and economic boundaries between rich and poor. But according to Matthew disciples are to be in solidarity with the poor and not define their identity by their wealth (19:16–30, esp. 23, 24; cf. 6:19–34). Disciples are servants and slaves not masters (20:20–28; cf. 23:10–12). They use power not to dominate but to seek the good of others (20:26–28). Disciples are blind beggars (20:29–34) who despite the crowds' opposition (20:31) cry out for God's saving mercy manifested in Jesus. Disciples are learners not teachers (23:8). Such is the marginal identity of Matthean disciples.

Yet this community is also a mission community. As intimidating as it is to be a small, alternative, marginal, community in large, urban Antioch, the gospel requires it to be in mission. Scholars have seen a dispute within the community about the nature of what Matthew alone calls the "gospel of the kingdom" (4:23; 9:35; 24:14; cf. Mark 1:39; 6:6; 13:13). Does the gospel extend to Jews and Gentiles? Does the identity of the *ekklēsia* include both Jews and Gentiles? Some have interpreted the references to Gentile faith and Gentile mission as legitimizing the community's decision to conduct mission to the Gentiles and to include believing Gentiles within the community.[18] The references indicate the outcome of the debate: Within ethnically diverse and tense Antioch, the Christian community will include members of any nationality.

This mission is not just a preaching mission. In material unique to Matthew, the gospel requires that community members respond to God's love and mercy with practical mercy to the sick, homeless, hungry, naked, and imprisoned (25:31–46). Among the marginal Christian community Emmanuel is encountered (25:37–40, 44–45).

Stark suggests that such a message had profound implications for the community's survival and experience in a city like Antioch. The community offered hope because its members helped one another survive the misery and hardships of sustaining daily life.[19] In a context of ethnic diversity and social tensions, such a community of practical and relational mercy offered an appealing alternative social reality. Matthew's gospel legitimates an all-inclusive community which transcends ethnic, social, and economic boundaries.

Whether this is the actual identity and lifestyle of the community, a vision for it, or a bit of both, is a difficult question. A number of scholars have seen the gospel as addressing problems in the community which threatened such faithful discipleship. J. D. Kingsbury concludes his redaction critical study of Matt 13 by claiming that Matthew's shaping of the chapter reflects and addresses moral laxity in the church community:

> As a relatively wealthy congregation in a heathen environment, materialism and secularism are immediate problems . . . there is spiritual slothfulness . . . hatred among Christians . . . lovelessness . . . cases of apostasy . . . a certain prevalence of lawlessness.[20]

From his study of 17:22–18:35, W. Thompson identifies division as a problem for the community.[21] The division results from external forces such as Gentile persecution and miracle-working false prophets who advocate lawlessness. These forces cause scandal, betrayal, and hatred. Through his shaping of the gospel, Matthew urges humility and reconciliation (5:21–26), forgiveness (18:21–35), and merciful treatment of each of the little ones (9:13; 12:7; 18:1–14). Constantly he holds out the responsibility of the community of disciples to do the will of God (7:24–27; 12:46–50) in order that the community might live the reality to which it is called. The authorial audience is assumed to be familiar with the challenges and opportunities of this situation.

CONCLUSION

The discussion in these last two chapters has suggested several features of the authorial audience's experience. Using redaction criticism to examine Matthew's use of his sources we have identified some likely aspects of the situation of Matthew's community in later first-century Antioch. (1) It is a minority community in a large and diverse city. (2) A recent and bitter dispute with a synagogue has resulted in Matthew's community separating from the synagogue. (3) In its situation of transition, the gospel seeks to secure the community's identity and lifestyle with words of legitimation, explanation, and direction. (4) The community has a marginal existence. Its ambivalent attitude toward society involves being set apart (because of its commitment to Jesus) but being a participant in its daily life with a command to carry out missionary activity. It is an alternative, inclusive community reconciling its own divisions and the divisions of its society. The authorial audience is assumed to be familiar with these social and religious experiences as it reads or hears Matthew's gospel.

NOTES

1. This emphasis on the center, rather than the boundaries of the community derives from Saunders, *"No One Dared Ask Him Anything More,"* 472–77.

2. G. Barth, "Matthew's Interpretation of the Law," *Tradition and Interpretation,* 75–76, 159–64; J. Zumstein, *La condition du croyant dans l'évangile selon Matthieu* (OBO 16; Göttingen: Vandenhoeck & Ruprecht, 1977) 171–81.

3. Matthew adds this word to his sources in 7:23; 13:41; 23:28 24:12.

4. For instance Strecker (*Der Weg,* 276) noted that the phrase in 5:17 "Do not think" appears in 10:34 where a theoretical possibility, not an actual situation, is considered. The absence from the text of indicators that a specific subgroup is being addressed should also be noted.

5. Most of the passages cited in this paragraph are either unique to Matthew or reflect Matthean redaction of Mark or Q. Exceptions include the Q material of the Lord's Prayer in Matt 6:9–15 and Luke 11:1–4, 25–26, and the saying in Matt 5:17–18a (Luke 16:16–17). Matt 22:34–40 derives from Mark 12:28–34 with important redaction (for instance, the omission of the scribe's comment about burnt offerings in 12:33b, and Jesus' commendation of him in 12:34).

6. See Deut 9:10; 31:30; 1 Kgs 8:14; 1 Chron 29:1, 10, 20; Ezra 10:1, 8; Neh 5:7, 13.

7. Recall Matthew's redaction of Peter's confession in Mark 8:29. In Mark Peter confesses "You are the Christ." The confession "Son of God" is not possible until the cross for Mark (15:39).

8. Just what this refers to is not clear. It may refer to Peter's ministry in Antioch in the 40s CE (cf. Gal 2:11–14) or it may indicate a claim to connect the community with a significant disciple of Jesus.

9. Matt 18:15–18 presents some Q material (Luke 17:3; 20:23) as well as exclusive Matthean content.

10. J. D. Kingsbury, "The Figure of Peter in Matthew's Gospel as a Theological Problem," *JBL* 98 (1979) 67–83.

11. W. Carter, "Matthew 4:18–22 and Matthean Discipleship: An Audience-Oriented Perspective," *CBQ;* forthcoming. See also S. Barton, *Discipleship and Family Ties in Mark and Matthew* (SNTSMS 80; Cambridge: Cambridge University, 1994).

12. Matthew changes Q's reference to "all the nations" (Luke 12:30) to "Gentiles."

13. It should be noted that the same Greek word (ἔθνη, *ethnē*) appears in 10:18 and 24:9.

14. See Carter, *Households and Discipleship*, 15–203.

15. So Tamar 1:3; Rahab and Ruth 1:5; the wife of Uriah (Bathsheba) 1:6. See M. Johnson, *The Purpose of Biblical Genealogies* (SNTSMS 8; Cambridge: Cambridge University, 1969) 152–69; Brown, *Birth of the Messiah*, 71–74, 32–37, 590–96; E. D. Freed, "The Women in Matthew's Genealogy," *JSNT* 29 (1987) 3–19.

16. Some have argued (D. R. A. Hare, *The Theme of Jewish Persecution of Christians in the Gospel According to St. Matthew* [SNTSMS 6; Cambridge: Cambridge University, 1967] 80–145) unconvincingly that the mission to the Jews has finished. See the exchange between J. P. Meier ("Nations or Gentiles in Matthew 28:19?" *CBQ* 39 [1977] 94–102) who argues for mission to Jew and Gentile, and D. Hare and D. Harrington (" 'Make Disciples of All the Gentiles' [Mt 28:19]," *CBQ* 37 [1975] 359–69).

17. D. Duling ("Matthew and Marginality," in *1993 SBLSP* [ed. E. H. Lovering; Atlanta: Scholars, 1993] 642–71, esp. 648, 663) says Matthew has an "ideology of 'voluntary marginality,' " which Duling defines as "individuals or groups who consciously and by choice live outside the normative statuses, roles and offices of society because they reject hierarchical social structures."

18. Luz, *Matthew 1–7*, 84–87.

19. Stark, "Antioch," in *Social History* (ed. Balch), 198–205; See B. F. Harris, "The Idea of Mercy and its Graeco-Roman Context," and E. A. Judge, "The Quest for Mercy in Late Antiquity," in *God Who Is Rich In Mercy: Essays Presented to D. B. Knox* (ed. P. T. O'Brien and D. G. Peterson; Sydney: Macquarie University, 1986) 89–121.

20. J. D. Kingsbury, *The Parables of Jesus in Matthew 13* (Richmond: John Knox, 1969) 135. See also L. White, "Grid and Group in Matthew's Community: The Righteousness/Honor Code in the Sermon on the Mount," *Semeia* 35 (1986) 61–90. D. Garland (*The Intention of Matthew 23* [NovTSup 52; Leiden: E. J. Brill, 1979]) argues that ch. 23 warns the church (23:1) and its leaders of the consequences of unfaithfulness. Such a warning is necessary because the church "is a mixture of weeds and wheat, good and rotten fish, good and evil wedding guests, faithful and evil servants" (214–15).

21. W. G. Thompson, *Matthew's Advice to a Divided Community* (AnBib 44; Rome: Biblical Institute, 1970) summary 258–64.

Chapter 7

Competent to Read: Utilizing Narrative Conventions

So far in Part One we have taken four steps toward joining the authorial audience. (1) We have recognized its first-century world by examining the possible identity, ethnicity, historical, and geographical location of the gospel's author (ch. 2). (2) We have explored the gospel's genre as a biography, noting that this creates limitations for the author and expectations for the audience (ch. 3). (3) We have identified some of the audience's religious traditions which the author confirms and reconfigures in writing the gospel (ch. 4). (4) We have discussed four aspects of the audience's assumed social experience, identity, and life-style as participants in a minority, separated, transitional, and marginal community of disciples of Jesus (chs. 5–6). In this chapter we will take a fifth step toward joining the authorial audience. To read as the authorial audience means being competent to recognize and utilize the narrative conventions which the author employs to guide the audience in its reading.

In reading or hearing the gospel "as the author intends," the authorial audience faces the obstacle of interpreting the extensive amount of data which it encounters in the text. The audience must make sense of this potentially overwhelming material if it is to redescribe or restate what the gospel is about. The author employs narrative conventions or signals to help the audience identify important material. He assumes the authorial audience will notice these conventions and utilize them in connecting elements into a coherent and unified reading. Reading or hearing requires this competency and active participation from the authorial audience. In this chapter we will look at two aspects of the reading/hearing experience: the audience's use of the author's conventions in guiding its interpretation, and ways in which the audience deals with "gaps" in the text.

RECOGNIZING THE AUTHOR'S CONVENTIONS

The author guides the audience's interpretation of the text by employing a variety of conventions to tell the story.[1] These conventions are "rules" or "practices" or "literary devices" which facilitate communication between author and audience and signal important dimensions of the text. They enable the audience to notice and attribute significance to important aspects of the text and to recognize a hierarchy of details and events. They are linked to the work's genre and its historical and cultural settings, though they can be shared across a number of genres and contexts. The author assumes the audience has adequate skills to make appropriate use of these conventions. Here we will identify a few of the conventions which Matthew employs. We will discuss other conventions in Part Two.

The author of Matthew assumes that the position of an event in the gospel underlines its importance. M. Perry has discussed the *primacy effect*.[2] That is, material at the beginning of the gospel has a strong impact on the audience's understanding of the whole of the gospel. In Matthew the opening chapters establish the point of view from which the whole story is told and the values by which the audience must evaluate subsequent events, sayings, and characters. The opening phrase "The record of the origin of Jesus Christ" (1:1), the use of the genealogy (1:2–17), the presence of angels (1:20–21; 2:13, 19) and dreams (1:20; 2:13, 19, 22) emphasize God's initiative and purposes. The conception and naming of Jesus in 1:18–25 indicate the mission which Jesus will carry out through the gospel's plot. The audience is assumed to be competent enough to notice that the use of an "angel of the Lord" to convey information (1:20) and the provision of an explanation for the meaning of the name "Jesus" (1:21) emphasize the importance of this material.

The audience is also assumed to be attentive to the *latency effect,* the impact of the gospel's ending. In chapter 28 the account of Jesus' post-resurrection activity leaves the audience with important statements about God's purposes, about God's abiding presence in Jesus, and about the mission of the community of disciples (28:19–20). The author also employs sequences of similar material. Chapters 8–9 group together a number of miracle stories. Chapter 12 accumulates conflict stories. Chapter 13 uses a sequence of seven parables while further sequences of three parables appear in chapters 21–22 and 24–25. These sequences of repeated material signal important aspects of the text for the audience.

The author uses other conventions to assist the audience's interpretation. The gospel's controlling point of view is expressed, for instance, through different speakers. God (3:17; 17:5) and Jesus authoritatively maintain it while the religious leaders challenge it. The frequently used scripture citations ("This happened so that what was spoken by the Lord through the prophet might be fulfilled, saying . . .") confirm for the audience that God's will is manifest in every aspect of Jesus' life and death.

The author assumes that the audience will note frequent use of repetition to underline significant aspects. For example, the theme of God's presence in the person of Jesus is asserted at the beginning, underlined with a citation of scripture and direct explanation of "Emmanuel" (1:22–23), repeated in the middle of the gospel as Jesus instructs the believing community (18:20), and restated at the end when the risen Jesus commissions the disciples for mission ("I am with you always," 28:19–20). The audience utilizes repetition, the primacy and latency effects, the citation of scripture, direct explanation, and the authoritative speaker Jesus to understand the importance of this theme.

With regard to plot, the author uses a range of conventions to enable the audience to unify events as well as determine the more important ones. Events are repeated; summaries underline typical events (4:23; 9:35). The audience looks for connections among events whether of cause, consequence, contrast, or sequence. The author signals important developments in the plot by repeated formula ("From that time Jesus began to . . . ," 4:17; 16:21), new actions (the conception of Jesus, 1:18–25; Jesus' arrival in Jerusalem, 21:1–27; Jesus' resurrection, 28:1–10), and by new focus (response to Jesus, 11:2–6). He also uses predictions such as the fourfold predictions about Jesus' death (16:21; 17:22–23; 20:17–19; 26:2) to emphasize significant events.

The audience encounters little direct description of characters in the gospel. Appropriate to the genre of an ancient biography, the author uses actions to reveal key characteristics or traits of characters. Repeated actions underline these traits. Jesus is established as the central character in the opening verse ("The account of the origin of Jesus Christ," 1:1) and chapter as the goal of the genealogy (1:17) and as the one commissioned by God to carry out God's purposes (1:18–25). The ways in which other characters interact with Jesus disclose their traits. The comparisons and contrasts among characters (Jesus and disciples, Jesus and the religious leaders) are shaped by the gospel's point of view and are worked out in the plot. The religious leaders' negative reaction to Jesus, for instance, leads to their putting him to death.

Throughout the gospel the author interweaves narrative sections with long speeches by Jesus (chs. 5–7, 10, 13, 18, 23–25). In this way the author draws the audience's attention to important aspects of Jesus' teaching. This interspersing provides the audience with the means to observe whether Jesus consistently lives his own teaching and to assess the actions of other characters in relation to his teaching.

The author uses such conventions to guide the audience. He assumes the audience is competent to notice these conventions and utilize them to interpret the gospel's message.

THE AUDIENCE AND GAPS IN THE TEXT

Central to the audience's role in making sense of Matthew's gospel are the text's "gaps" or "blanks," a notion derived from Wolfgang Iser.[3] Iser argues that the audience encounters "gaps of indeterminacy" which it fills in, expands, and connects with other parts of the text to form a coherent reading. These gaps take various forms. For example, the audience must:

- Make sense of the grammatical connections between words.

- Supply pronouns with content.

- Connect clauses.

- Recognize literal or metaphorical speech.

- Supply appropriate content for an image.

- Recognize an allusion to another reality or story.

- Supply connections between larger sections of the text.

- Fit the material into a coherent framework.

The author assumes his audience is competent to undertake these tasks.

Frequently, despite the author's conventions, a number of possibilities for filling the gaps exist. The audience reads on looking for further data to determine which option to choose or to confirm its choice. Sometimes new developments require a revision of a previous decision. Reading requires rereading. Like a crowd at a tennis match, the audience looks in two directions, forward in anticipation and backward in retrospection. That is, reading is an ongoing process in which the sequence of the text is crucial.

Gaps draw the audience into a process of connecting various segments of the text, its words, clauses, sentences, paragraphs, or sections into a framework which makes sense of the whole work. Blanks open up possibilities as well as limit the options available to the audience. The author's conventions enable the authorial audience to construct a framework that organizes the disparate material into a coherent whole. They provide a foundation for connecting the parts and organizing the data of the text. Multiple (but not unlimited) readings are possible because an audience may construe the material in different ways. But as the audience moves through the text some readings will become impossible because they cannot embrace new aspects of the text.

Iser is aware not only of the role of the audience in this process but also its impact on the audience. He argues that through the process of formulating the connections, of playing the role of the authorial audience, readers become aware of ways in which they have unconsciously perceived the world, or norms by which they live. This new awareness, this insight into the inadequacies of the familiar and normal, "disconfirms" them. More than this, it causes an openness to new possibilities and insights which emerge from engaging what is unfamiliar in the text.[4] Reading is an educative process which dismantles the familiar and creates new understandings.

Though Iser emphasizes the transformative nature of this interaction, it should be noted that the process of insight and restatement might confirm and strengthen existing commitments, identities, worldviews, and lifestyles rather than transform them.[5] This is especially true when reading Matthew since the authorial audience is assumed to belong to the community of disciples of Jesus. The possibility exists, though, that a reader might resist rather than embrace the insights and framework emerging in the interaction between the authorial audience and the text.[6]

Umberto Eco helpfully identifies seven specific dimensions of the audience's assumed competency to fill the gaps which Iser identifies as being so central to the interaction of text and audience.[7] Eco's seven categories can be illustrated by using Matthew 8:1–2a.

Jesus has just completed the teaching which comprises the Sermon on the Mount. He impressed the crowds with his authority which surpassed that of "their scribes" (7:29).

> When Jesus had come down from the mountain, great crowds followed him; and there was a leper who came to him and knelt before him saying, "Lord if you choose" (Matt 8:1–2a).

1. Basic Dictionary

The audience must supply content for the words encountered in a text. At times this seems easy. The first line and a half of 8:1–2a ("come down," "mountain," "great crowds," "followed") present little problem (or so it seems). "Leper" though is more complex. Because this is a masculine noun in Greek, the audience assumes that the leper is a man rather than a woman. While this information about his gender would be crucial in some contexts (for instance, the women in the gene-alogy, 1:1–17) here it is subordinated to another piece of information. In being called a leper, he is characterized by a disease. If the reader does not know the significance of being a "leper" in the world from which the text originates, the rest of the scene will be difficult.

2. Rules of Co-reference

The audience uses the rest of a sentence or larger section of text to establish meaning. In 8:1 we have two pronouns "he" and "him" (the latter appears twice). The identity of the he/him is central to the meaning of the verse. By attending to this verse alone, the audience determines that the "him" whom the crowds follow and the leper approaches is the same as the "he" who comes down from the mountain. But who is this "he/him?" Since 8:1–2a follows chapters 1–7, the audience uses the pre-vious material to identify the he/him as Jesus (7:28).

3. Contextual Selections

Contextual selections refer to using the larger context of the text and its world of origin to supply meanings for words. While the audience knows from 7:28 that the "he/him" is Jesus, all of chapters 1–7 supply information about the importance of Jesus. The audience recalls, for instance, that he is the one whom God has commissioned to save from sin and manifest God's presence (1:21, 23). The reference to "mountain" recalls 5:1, the place in which Jesus delivers the sermon of chapters 5–7. The verb used to name the leper's "coming" to Jesus consistently denotes respectful, humble approach to Jesus by people who recognize his special authority.[8]

4. Circumstantial Selections

These require the audience to supply information assumed by the text but not made explicit by it. So, for instance, we noted above that the significance of the one who approaches Jesus in 8:1–2a lies in his disease more than his gender. The authorial audience makes explicit the significance of his disease since the text does not tell us anything about it. It is important to know that leprosy in the ancient world is not the same as modern day Hansen's disease.

It is assumed that the audience is familiar with the regulations concerning skin diseases in Leviticus 13–14. Most significant in these regulations is the provision that such a person be isolated from the community, distinguished by wearing torn clothes, disheveled hair, and crying out "unclean" (Lev 13:45–46). The person's house can also be destroyed (Lev 14:34–47). A leper was considered to be under God's punishment and was excluded from the worshiping congregation (2 Chron 26:20–21).

The approach of a *leper* to Jesus raises questions about how Jesus will respond. The audience knows that Jesus is Emmanuel, God with us, commissioned to manifest God's presence (1:23). He has already blessed the merciful (5:7). In the context of cultural conventions and Matthew's larger text, the audience understands Jesus' response of touch in 8:3 to be most significant. It expresses God's mercy for this traditionally excluded person. Jesus practices what he preaches. Also, the recall of the Levitical material helps the audience interpret Jesus' instruction (8:4) that the leper go to see the priest. Because this action is consistent with and upholds the Mosaic law, Jesus is demonstrating what he taught in 5:17 (contextual selection).

5. Rhetorical and Stylistic Overcoding

This concept refers to the audience's ability to understand the genre or type of the literature and the nature of its language. We discussed in chapter 3 that the choice of a genre creates limits for an author and expectations for the audience. Eco cites as an example the phrase which begins some works: "Once upon a time." In recognizing a fairy tale, an audience formulates certain expectations about its content, form of writing, and function. Reading a fairy tale differs from reading a recipe or an encyclopedia article. By chapter 8 of Matthew the audience knows that it is a biography.

The audience is assumed to be competent to recognize different types of language within the work. This recognition involves, for example, hyperbole (cutting off one's hand or foot,

18:8–9) and the difference between literal and metaphorical language (the light of the world; the salt of the earth, 5:13–16). The reader must know John the Baptist's command to "prepare the way of the Lord" (3:3) does not involve earth-moving machinery.

Sometimes discerning a type of language is difficult. In 8:1 the crowds "follow him." Using rules of co-reference (number 2 above), the audience already knows from 4:18–22 that the verb "following" denotes not just a literal accompanying of Jesus but the way of discipleship. Is the audience to understand that the crowds follow in 8:1 as disciples (metaphorical) or as interested spectators (literal)? Given the absence from 8:1 of two vital aspects of the encounter between Jesus and the fishermen in 4:18–22, his call and their active commitment to him, the verb here probably indicates a literal, rather than metaphorical, sense.[9]

6. Inferences from Common Frames

Common frames refer to cultural practices (social, economic, domestic, religious, etc.) which may be assumed or referred to explicitly by a text. The audience invokes a cultural practice to make sense of the text. The discussion of leprosy above (number 3, Circumstantial Selections) provides one example of this category.

Another example appears in 8:1. The language used to refer to the leper's reverent approach to Jesus—his kneeling before Jesus, his address to him as Lord, and his petition for help invokes the religious practice of worship. The audience knows that the verb for "approach" is used in the Septuagint and in the Hellenistic world for worshippers "who approach God or bring sacrifices to an altar."[10] In using this verb to indicate "approaching" Jesus, Matthew leads the audience to understand Jesus to be the temple. Matthew 1:23 has already revealed that Jesus is Emmanuel, the one in whom God's presence is encountered. The audience, though, will need to read on for more confirmation of this fact. It is important that in later chapters Jesus claims to be greater than the temple (12:1–6), to be present when disciples pray (18:20), and to know that the temple will be destroyed (24:1–2).

7. Inferences by Intertextual Frames

This term refers to the audience's familiarity with other literary traditions and texts. The authorial audience of Matthew is assumed to know the traditions of the Old Testament. We have previously seen this in the discussion of leprosy and the reference to temple worship.

Another example occurs in the opening phrase of 8:1, "When he came down from the mountain." This phrase is almost identical with the description of Moses' descent from Sinai in the Septuagint text of Exod 34:29. This connection, which builds on a similar echo in 5:1 to "going up the mountain," links Jesus and Moses. The mountain becomes a place of revelation with Jesus the revealer. But there are further complications. Some scholars suggest that these references invoke not Sinai but traditions about Zion as the mountain on which the fullness of the new age is inaugurated (cf. 4:17) to which the people of God gather and on which Jesus is enthroned. In this view the mountain becomes the place to encounter the fullness of the new age.[11] In this instance reading as the authorial audience is very difficult. Several Old Testament traditions may be being invoked. Or an audience may hear something not intended by the author. The audience must recall previous clues and read on to clarify, if possible, whether one or both are valid.

8. Ideological Overcoding

This term refers to the values and commitments of the audience as well as to those of the text. A reader may accept or reject the commitments or point of view of the text. For instance, the authorial audience understands that 8:1–4 depicts a scene in which the leper is transformed by the healing power and presence of God manifested in Jesus. As the actual audience we may find such an action absolutely impossible, we may be open to the possibility, or we may actively seek it for ourselves.

CONCLUSION

In this chapter we have taken a fifth step toward joining the authorial audience. We have discussed the importance of the narrative conventions which the author employs in telling the story of Jesus. In using these conventions the author assumes the authorial audience to be competent in its reading or listening skills to notice and interpret these conventions, and to fill in the gaps it encounters in the text. Using Eco's analysis we have identified seven dimensions of this task.

We have now concluded Part One and the five steps toward joining the authorial audience. We have sought to narrow the distance between our world and that of this ancient text and its authorial audience by investigating five areas. (1) We began by inquiring into the author's world, his possible identity, ethnicity, time and place of living. (2) We discussed the genre of the gospel, concluding that it was an ancient biography narrating the life of an important religious teacher. Determining its genre identifies the limitations and expectations which author and audience share. (3) By investigating the author's use (redaction) of traditions about Jesus familiar to the audience, we sought to identify some of the authorial audience's assumed knowledge and experiences of Jesus. The author affirms, expands, and reconfigures this knowledge. We also noted some of the perspectives important to the author. (4) By employing knowledge about life in Antioch and investigating changes to the traditions about Jesus as reflected in the gospel, we sought to delineate four aspects of the social location and religious experiences assumed of the authorial audience. (5) We identified some of the narrative conventions which the author employs in telling the story of Jesus. The author assumes that the authorial audience notices and interprets these conventions, and fills in the gaps it encounters in the text.

From our discussion in Part One we can identify the following important features of the authorial audience:

- It understands Greek, the language of the gospel.

- It probably lives in Syria, perhaps Antioch, late in the first century.

- It recognizes the genre of the gospel as a biography.

- It consists of a community of disciples of Jesus, familiar with stories about and the teaching of Jesus (from traditions known to us as Mark, Q, and M). It lives in the

time after the resurrection and before the return of
Jesus (24:15; 27:8; 28:15).

• It is a minority, separated, transitional, and marginal
community.

• It is familiar with the Septuagint, the Jewish scriptures
in Greek.

• It is able to notice and utilize the narrative conventions
employed by the author.

The term "audience" indicates that Matthew's gospel was written
to be read out loud, to be heard by a group whose members did
not have individual copies to study.[12]

In Part Two, *Reading Matthew,* we will look at four important aspects of the authorial audience's task in interpreting
Matthew's gospel: The construction of the gospel's point of view
(chs. 8–9), its formulation of a coherent understanding of the
plot (chs. 10–11), its determination of the significance of various settings for the plot's actions (ch. 12), and its building of
characters through attention to their traits (chs. 13–16).

NOTES

1. Rabinowitz, *Before Reading,* 42–169. Rabinowitz discusses four
general conventions, those of notice, signification, configuration, and
coherence. Material identified in this chapter will be expanded in
chapters 8–16.

2. M. Perry, "Literary Dynamics: How the Order of a Text Creates
its Meaning," *Poetics Today* 1 (1979–80) 35–64, 311–64, esp. 53–58.

3. W. Iser, *The Act of Reading: A Theory of Aesthetic Response*
(Baltimore: Johns Hopkins University, 1978) 163–231; W. Iser, "Interaction between Text and Reader," in *The Reader in the Text: Essays
on Audience and Interpretation* (ed. S. Suleiman and I. Crosman; Princeton: Princeton University, 1980) 106–19.

4. Iser (*Act of Reading,* 212–31) uses two terms "negation" and
"negativity" to describe aspects of this process.

5. T. Eagleton, *Literary Theory: An Introduction* (Minneapolis:
University of Minnesota, 1983) 78–82.

6. J. Fetterley, *The Resisting Reader: A Feminist Approach to American Fiction* (Bloomington: Indiana University, 1978) xi–xxvi.

7. U. Eco, *The Role of the Reader* (Bloomington: University of Indiana, 1979) 18–23. M. A. Powell ("Expected and Unexpected Readings in Matthew: What the Reader Knows," *Asbury Theological Journal* 48 [1993] 31–52) approaches the question in terms of the implied reader's knowledge, identifying four areas: (1) universal (or common) knowledge (five loaves and two fish will not feed five thousand people); (2) knowledge revealed within the narrative, especially that which is recurrent and coherent; (3) knowledge presupposed by the spatial, temporal, and social setting of the narrative; (4) knowledge of other literature cited or alluded to in the narrative. Several points of overlap with Eco's seven categories will be evident. I particularly utilize numbers 2–4 in Carter, *Households and Discipleship.*

8. See J. R. Edwards, "The Use of προσέρχεσθαι in the Gospel of Matthew," *JBL* 106 (1987) 65–74.

9. Kingsbury, "ἀκολουθεῖν," 56–73.

10. Edwards, "Use of προσέρχεσθαι," 65–67.

11. This setting will be discussed further in ch. 12. See D. Allison, *The New Moses: A Matthean Typology* (Minneapolis: Fortress, 1993); T. Donaldson, *Jesus and the Mountain: A Study in Matthean Theology* (JSNTSup 8; Sheffield: JSOT, 1985).

12. B. Knox, "Silent Reading in Antiquity," *GRBS* 9 (1968) 421–35; S. Moore, *Literary Criticism and the Gospels: The Theoretical Challenge* (New Haven: Yale University, 1989) 84–98.

PART TWO: READING MATTHEW

Chapter 8

The Audience and God's Point of View

In hearing Matthew's gospel, the authorial audience must make sense of the world which the author presents. This world includes perspectives on reality and human identity. It consists of actions, characters, and settings. But the author does not want the audience to value all perspectives, actions, and characters equally. Some ways of looking at the world are advocated while others are criticized. Some points of view and values are to be accepted while others are rejected. Some characters are more significant than others. Some actions are good and noble while others are not.

In 26:1–16, for instance, four short scenes offer four perspectives on Jesus' imminent death. (1) Jesus reminds the disciples that his death will occur "after two days" (26:1–2); (2) the hostile religious leaders plot to kill him (26:3–5); (3) an unnamed woman anoints Jesus "for burial" (26:6–13, 12); (4) Judas, one of the twelve disciples, offers to betray him (26:14–16). These four actions comprise a sequence of sixteen verses. Yet the audience has no difficulty in knowing that Jesus is right, the woman does a wonderful thing, while the religious leaders and Judas do not. In some stories, betrayal and plotting the death of a key figure would be commendable actions, but not in this gospel. How does the audience know to reach these evaluations of the four actions? How does it know which attitudes, values, actions, and characters are upheld and which are not?

The point of view from which the implied author tells the story is central to evaluating the actions, words, relationships, and values of the gospel's plot and characters.[1] Through a variety of conventions the authorial audience learns *the* perspective or point of view by which the implied author selects and evaluates the actions, characters, and setting of the story world. An actual audience has to decide to accept or reject this point of view.

USPENSKY'S FIVE ASPECTS OF POINT OF VIEW

In his classic study, Boris Uspensky has identified five "planes" or aspects of point of view.[2] An author uses these five dimensions to express the story's points of view. An audience uses these conventions to understand those points of view.

(1) The *phraseological* plane concerns the choice of the words used in telling the story. We have already noted some examples: the use of "Lord" as a form of address for Jesus denotes disciples while "teacher" or "rabbi" indicates non-disciples. The verb "approach/come" (προσέρχομαι, *proserchomai*) expresses reverence in approaching Jesus. We will note phraseological examples throughout this section.

(2) and (3) The *spatial* and *temporal* planes denote the place and time from which actions and characters are described. We will see that the author is privileged to know everything that needs to be known for telling his story. The author is able to be anywhere (omnipresent) and knows about the past, present, and future. We will particularly consider the contribution of this plane in chapter 12.

(4) The *psychological* plane concerns knowledge of the characters' inner feelings, motives, thoughts, and perceptions which the "omniscient"[3] author includes in the narrative. Chapters 13–16 discuss the presentation of characters in Matthew's gospel.

(5) The *evaluative* or *ideological* plane is, in a sense, the sum of the four named above. It concerns the overriding perspective or way of looking at the world to which the previous four aspects contribute, and which shapes the author's selection and evaluation of material in those areas.

This chapter focuses primarily on this last aspect, the evaluative or ideological point of view. We will particularly notice the contributions of the phraseological, temporal, and psychological planes. Here I suggest that the audience of Matthew's gospel quickly learns, and is frequently reminded through a variety of conventions, that the author tells the story from God's point of view. This point of view evaluates all actions, characters, and perspectives. We will discuss the conventions which the author uses to establish this point of view in Matthew chapters 1–3.

MATTHEW 1:1–17: ESTABLISHING GOD'S POINT OF VIEW

The gospel's opening section involves the temporal plane. It looks back to review God's previous dealings with Israel. The author places the coming of the Christ, Jesus, in this context as another stage in God's activity.

The opening phrase names the origin of Jesus the Messiah as its subject (1:1). It then identifies Jesus as "Son of David, Son of Abraham."[4] This reference invokes the audience's knowledge of Abraham and David as leading figures in God's history with Israel. But it is not clear in what sense Jesus is their descendent. Abraham is the Gentile whom God called, promising him descendants and land as well as blessing on all the families of the earth (Gen 12:1–3). God called David to be king of Israel, promising him a line, kingdom, and throne that would last forever (2 Sam 7:8–17). But both characters had checkered relationships with God including fear, deception, and adultery. At most the gospel's opening verse connects Jesus with these two figures who had played important roles in God's purpose. It leaves open, though, the question of exactly how Jesus is their descendant.

The genealogy in verses 2–17 answers this question. Jesus is their descendent in that, like them, he is called to a major role in God's purposes (1:17). The repetition of the references to Abraham (1:1, 2), to David (1:1, 6), and to the Babylonian exile (1:11, 12) underlines God's involvement with these figures and events. Verse 17 reinforces their central role by highlighting the genealogy's three-part structure. In establishing this connection, the genealogy demonstrates the reliability of the opening assertion and the trustworthiness of the author.[5]

In addition to focusing on these central figures, the genealogy elaborates the active presence and intervention of God throughout Israel's history. Its content, while appearing to narrate descent from one generation to the next, is not strictly based on birth or natural descent. Random choices appear. Descent follows the line of Perez not Zerah (1:3). It omits three kings between Joram and Uzziah in verse 8 (cf. 1 Chron 3:11–12). It omits Jehoiachim, the actual father of Jechoniah and his brothers in verse 11 (Josiah was his grandfather).

The selective list of names, organized on the basis of three groups of fourteen, clearly serves a purpose other than a strict biological record.[6] The names invoke stories of Israel's experiences with God. In the context God, unnamed but assumed throughout, emerges as the main character. God is the one controling the events and bringing Israel's history to the point of the appearance of Jesus.

In recalling stories of Abraham, David, and the exile (to name but three), the audience learns something of the nature of God. This God constantly intervenes in human affairs. God took initiative in calling Abraham and selecting David. God promised Abraham land and descendants and David an eternal kingdom. God remained faithful to these promises even when both men failed. Abraham and Sarah's age threatened the promise, as did the offering of Isaac as a sacrifice (Gen 18–22) and the devastating experience of God's judgment in exile. Yet God remained faithful and powerfully active to deliver on the promises. Continually God guided Israel forward into a new future.

This God knows what is right and wrong, what is expected of human beings. The double references to exile in verses 11–12 are a reminder of the various interpretations of this event in the scriptures. For the Deuteronomist historian and for Jeremiah the exile was God's punishment for people who had broken covenant (1 Kings 9:1–9). For Deutero-Isaiah it was the occasion for God's merciful deliverance, for a new exodus and new creation (Isa 40–55). For Ezekiel God had not abandoned the people but was with them even in exile (Ezek 1) mercifully bringing them back from death to life and a new future (Ezek 37).

This God worked in irregular ways to achieve these lifegiving purposes. God selected the younger rather than the older brother (Isaac, not Ishmael, 1:2), but then selected the older rather than the younger brother, Perez not Zerah (1:3; cf. Gen. 38:27–30) and Jechoniah not Zedekiah (Matt 1:11; 1 Chron 3:16). God chose the fourth brother Judah, not the first (1:2b) although the other eleven rate a collective mention. God's workings also include the sinful kings David (1:6) and Manasseh (1:10)[7] as well as righteous kings like Hezekiah (1:9–10). They include male and female (Tamar [1:3], Rahab, Ruth [1:5], and Uriah's wife Bathsheba [1:6]). They embrace Jews and Gentiles (Abraham and the above four women).

From the genealogy the authorial audience becomes aware that through these events God is at work. It gains some understanding of the lifegiving purposes, the inclusive and unusual ways of working, and the faithful and merciful nature of the God who has actively guided events up to the coming of Jesus the Christ. These opening verses establish God's point of view as the fundamental perspective of the gospel by which all characters, actions, words, and values are assessed.

MATTHEW 1:18–25: GOD'S INITIATIVE AND JESUS' MISSION

1:18–25 elaborates the references to "Jesus Christ" and the origin and coming of the Christ in 1:1 and 1:16 by narrating the "origin" (lit.) of Jesus.[8] The central perspective here is that God's will and action bring forth Jesus so that he may carry out God's purposes. God through the Holy Spirit takes the initiative and intervenes directly in the sinful human realm to bring about Jesus' birth, commissioning Jesus as the agent of God's will.

Verse 18 informs the audience (but not Joseph) that Mary is pregnant (1) after her betrothal to Joseph, (2) before they have had sex, and (3) because of the actions of the Spirit. Verse 19 goes inside Joseph's thoughts (the psychological plane) to narrate the betrothed Joseph's response to her pregnancy. Joseph decides to divorce her. The audience is not told explicitly why he makes this decision. There is a gap in the text. The description of Joseph as a "righteous" man but one who does not want to shame Mary offers the authorial audience a clue to explain Joseph's actions. The opening seventeen verses have invoked God's previous dealings with Israel, so the authorial audience knows that Israel's law is an appropriate context in which to try to understand Joseph's actions. Deuteronomic law allowed death for intercourse with a betrothed woman (Deut 22:23–27). Joseph, not aware of the Spirit's role and assuming Mary to be pregnant by another man, decides not to put her to death but to exercise a less shameful action of divorcing her quietly.

But his point of view is inadequate because it is not God's perspective. The audience knows that Joseph has failed to incorporate a third factor, the Holy Spirit's role. Verses 20–21 correct Joseph's perspective by supplying him with this piece of knowledge. The "angel of the Lord" (a messenger sent from God) appears to Joseph in a dream and tells him that Mary's child originates "from the Holy Spirit." This angel repeats what the audience knew in verse 18. The scene functions to underline for the audience God's initiative through the Holy Spirit.

The angel, speaking on God's behalf, discloses that God has initiated this event for the particular purpose of saving his people from their sins (1:21). That is, the angel's visit manifests not only God's purpose but also what necessitates God's action. God regards the present as being sinful.

The authorial audience is assumed to know that the word for "sins" (ἁμαρτία, hamartia) generally means "missing the mark." In the Septuagint it has a more focused sense of an evil will and intention expressed in violating the divine will.[9] The genealogy has, of course, invoked numerous stories of human failure with respect to the divine will. The explicit reference to "the wife of Uriah" recalls David's failings with Bathsheba (1:6b; 2 Sam 11–12). The inclusion of Manasseh (1:10) and of the exile (1:11–12) invoke the former's idolatry and the Deuteronomist's view of exile as punishment for sin (2 Kings 21:1–18). God sees human existence as missing the mark, as not living according to the divine will. Humans need to be saved from this loss of direction and purpose. God's view of Jesus and the human condition is expressed through the angel's words.

But by mentioning Abraham and the exile, the genealogy is evidence of God's ability to save people from the impact of sin. The audience learns that, in God's point of view, sin is not the final or ultimate reality and that God's actions to rescue people from sin will now continue in Jesus. Further, by naming the child Jesus in 1:21 God sets up a fundamental perspective on all of Jesus' subsequent actions and words. By supplying this information at Jesus' conception, the author distinctively colors the rest of the gospel. The authorial audience must understand the significance of Jesus from God's point of view, as one whose mission is to provide salvation from sin.

The author reinforces this in verses 22–23. For the first time in the narrative a fulfillment formula interprets an event. Using the temporal plane the conception of Jesus is presented as carrying out ("fulfill")[10] what the Lord had previously revealed (lit., "what the Lord had spoken") through the prophet Isaiah. The conception is not a random event. It is consistent with and carries out the previously revealed will of God.[11]

This citation from Isaiah also provides further information about God's will for Jesus. It designates Jesus as Emmanuel (1:23). The author, assuming the audience is not familiar with Hebrew, interprets the term, "God with us."[12] God's point of view is that Jesus will manifest God's presence, God's saving presence.[13] As with 1:21, the function of this piece of information is to cause the audience to read the rest of the gospel in this perspective. The audience must understand Jesus' actions and words as fulfilling his God-given mission.

Verses 24–25 underline the basis for this mission by returning to the question of origin. The audience is again told that Jesus did not originate from human sexual intercourse. As verses 18 and 20 have already made clear, God through the Holy Spirit brought Jesus into being. Through his dream Joseph had his initial perspective corrected. Now, like a good disciple and as a model for the audience, he accepts the angel's (God's) point of view and he obeys the angel's command (compare 1:19 and 24–25). This helps the audience accept God's perspective on the rest of the story.

MATTHEW 2:1–12: RESPONSES TO GOD'S INITIATIVE

Chapter 2 reinforces God's perspective by evaluating human responses to God's action in the birth of Jesus. It also shows God's action to protect what God has initiated.

The visitors from the east (or Magi) manifest an ideal response. The author states that their purpose in traveling to Jerusalem is to worship Jesus "born king of the Jews" (2:2). They accomplish this with exceeding joy and the offering of gifts (2:10–11). The genealogy placed the coming of Jesus in the context of God's workings with Jews and Gentiles. So the actual coming of the Christ (2:2, 4) includes and affects Gentiles. These visitors rejoice in God's initiative and welcome it with worship. Their actions endorse and reinforce God's perspective.

The implied author discloses that "King Herod" (2:3) is "troubled" (lit.) by the news of the one "born king of the Jews" (2:2; Uspensky's psychological plane). He makes inquiries from the religious leaders about the birthplace of the Christ (2:4–6). He learns from the visitors from the East the time of the star's appearing (2:7–8). He declares at the end of verse 8 his purpose, "that I may come and worship him" (lit.).

The use of the verb "worship," the same one used for the visitors from the East (cf. 2:2), could ally Herod and the Magi (Uspensky's phraseological plane). But the audience already knows of Herod's fear from verse 3 and so doubts his sincerity. The subsequent warning of the Magi not to return to Herod (2:12) supplies the audience one more reason to be suspicious. It also distances Herod from the Magi. Because a dream was used by God in 1:20 to instruct Joseph, the audience understands the dream in 2:12 to be a warning from God. The warning denotes a negative evaluation of Herod (though no reason is provided as yet). By contrast, it signals God's protective favor on and approval for the Magi.

This section evaluates a third response to God's action. The religious leaders accurately instruct Herod from the scriptures about the birthplace of the Christ (cf. 2:1 and 2:5–6). However, in contrast to the visitors from the East, they do not travel from Jerusalem to Bethlehem to worship and offer gifts.

They do not act on their knowledge. The contrast negatively evaluates their failure to live in accord with God's truth. This failure reappears subsequently in other characters with the same evaluation.[14]

MATTHEW 2:13–23: GOD'S ACTIVE PRESENCE

In 2:13–23 Herod's response, already suspect because of the warning in the dream in verse 12, is developed to reinforce God's perspective. God plays an important and direct role in this section, similar to that of 1:18–25. In 2:13 God directly intervenes through "an angel of the Lord." In a dream (cf. 1:20; 2:12), the angel instructs Joseph to take Mary and Jesus and go to Egypt because Herod is about "to destroy him." God discloses Herod's real purpose. As in 2:12, God intervenes to alert characters to danger of which they were not aware. Whereas in 2:12 the intervention expresses God's favor for the visitors from the East, this appearance to Joseph protects God's saving work initiated in Jesus.

The implied author informs his audience in 2:15 that the family's stay in Egypt "fulfills" the words of Hos 11:1, "Out of Egypt I have called my son." Hosea's word viewed all Israel in the exodus as God's covenant people. The author gives Hosea's words new meaning in a different context. The text now finds its "right" interpretation in relation to Jesus (so also 2:5–6). It sees in Jesus' experience a reenactment of Israel's exodus experience and of God's saving actions.

In addition, (1) it underlines that Joseph, Mary, and Jesus' departure for Egypt is the divine will. The citation from Hosea allies the action involving Jesus with God's will previously revealed through the prophet and enacted in the exodus. (2) It confirms that Herod's attempt to destroy the child is contrary to God's will and cannot succeed. God outsmarts Herod. (3) It provides a further opportunity to assert God's perspective of Jesus. The words of introduction in 2:15 (lit., "what was spoken by the Lord," cf. 1:22) remind the audience that *God* calls Jesus "my son" and so indicates his special relationship with Jesus. (4) The citation offers the audience another opportunity to invoke the story of Moses who was also born in dangerous circumstances and who performed God's will in leading God's people Israel out of Egypt. The echoes of the story of Moses and the exodus ally Jesus with God's liberating will, placing him in continuity with God's previous actions of liberation on behalf of God's people and in association with such significant figures as Moses.

The accuracy of the divine warning in 2:13 about Herod's murderous intentions is demonstrated in 2:16. God's point of view is reliable. The angel of the Lord indicated Herod's intentions to "destroy the child" (lit., 2:13). So Herod kills the children under two years in and around Bethlehem (2:16).[15] This behavior exhibits sin (cf. 1:21). In killing the children Herod breaks God's will as indicated in the Ten Commandments (Exod 20:13). He refuses to welcome God's saving presence manifested in Jesus and to worship God. The reliability of God's point of view in warning of this event is underlined by connecting Herod's action with Jeremiah's word concerning the exile (2:17–18).

God's control and protective presence in this sinful world is evident in another dream appearance by the angel of the Lord (2:19–20). With the death of Herod the danger is past and the family is directed to return to Israel. But sin is not so easily overcome. Archelaus presents new danger. In a further dream Joseph receives new direction (2:22) to carry out the divine will (2:23).[16]

Throughout 2:13–23 God is actively present, faithfully protective of those carrying out the divine will in God's agent Jesus. The world is, as God has previously asserted in 1:21, a dangerous and sinful place. It needs salvation from sin. God's intervention is powerful enough to overcome the threats and advance the divine purpose.

MATTHEW 3:1–17: GOD'S POINT OF VIEW IS TRANSFERRED TO JESUS

John the Baptist is introduced in 3:1–12. His appearance in the "wilderness" recalls God's liberating action of the exodus and the exile. His call for people to repent and to undergo baptism, as well as his use of the scriptures (Isa 40:3) enables the audience to identify him as a spokesperson of God's will

(3:2–3). His clothing (camel hair and belt) recalls Elijah the prophet (3:4; 2 Kgs 1:8). The audience knows from the disclosure of God's will for Jesus in chapters 1–2 that John preaches a trustworthy message ("prepare the way of the Lord"). As a representative of God's perspective, his condemnation of the religious leaders in 3:7–10 is serious and consistent with their negative presentation in 2:4–6. On God's behalf he also indicates further aspects of Jesus' mission (3:11–12). In accord with Ezek 36:24–28 and Joel 2:28–29, he declares that Jesus will baptize with the spirit of the new age and will exercise judgment (the metaphor of harvest, Jer 15:7; Matt 13:24–30).

Jesus' baptism by John further establishes God's point of view (3:13–17). This scene allies Jesus and God by showing Jesus actively carrying out the divine will. This alliance establishes the basis for Jesus to be the reliable advocate of God's point of view through the rest of the gospel.

Without disclosing a reason, the author presents Jesus as seeking baptism from John (cf. 3:6). John refuses (3:13–14). Jesus, however, declares his baptism to be necessary to "fulfil all righteousness" (3:15). Using contextual clues the audience knows from the four previous uses of the key word "fulfill" (1:22; 2:15, 17, 23) that this verb means to enact or carry out God's saving will according to the scriptures. Its use with the noun "righteousness" suggests that righteousness should be understood as "what is right in God's eyes." This is the meaning of the adjective "righteous" used in 1:19 to describe Joseph. The audience's knowledge of the noun's use in the Hebrew Bible to denote God's will confirms this understanding.[17]

By choosing to use these two important words (Uspensky's phraseological plane), Matthew's Jesus persuades John (and the audience) that his baptism performs God's previously disclosed will.[18] This claim is consistent with the perspective of the narrative thus far. All of Jesus' actions have been presented as being in line with (fulfilling) God's will. Jesus' desire to do the divine will indicates his compliance with the role God has commissioned him to perform, to manifest God's saving presence (1:21, 23), to dispense the Spirit, and carry out judgment (3:11–12). Jesus' loyalty to God's will is emphasized in the temptation scene (4:1–11).

Verses 16–17 present God's legitimation for the obedient Jesus. The implied author narrates a revelation scene ("the heavens opened"). It discloses God's explicit blessing on Jesus after the baptism. The Spirit which enacted God's will in bringing Jesus into being (1:18, 20) descends from the opened heaven (from God) and "comes on/into" him empowering him for his God-given mission. A "voice from heaven" (God) speaks by quoting scripture, Gen 22:2, Ps 2:7, and Isa 42:1 ("This is my Son the Beloved, with whom I am well pleased").[19] The scriptural citations invoke obedience, suffering, and a kingly role. God designates Jesus "my son" (as in 2:15), a term that denotes someone in close covenant relationship with God who is an agent of the divine will. Jesus' significance in the gospel results from this divine perspective. His actions and teaching are the means by which he carries out his divinely given role of manifesting God's saving presence (1:21, 23).

From now on Jesus represents God's perspective through his actions and teaching. Not surprisingly, the narrative places Jesus on center stage. With only a few exceptions,[20] it will follow him, focusing on people's encounters with him. Jesus teaches and enacts the divine will.

CONCLUSION

We have thus far observed a number of conventions which the author employs to guide the audience in identifying God's point of view as the normative perspective for this gospel:

- The review of God's previous dealings with Israel in the opening genealogy (1:1–17).

- The use of an "angel of the Lord" to disclose God's will (1:20–21; 2:13, 19).

- The use of dreams to disclose God's will (1:20; 2:12, 13, 19, 22).

- The active presence of God through the Holy Spirit (1:18, 20; 3:11, 16).

- God's accurate and reliable disclosures of what will soon happen (1:20–21 and 2:1; 2:13 and 2:16–18).

- The use of the scriptures to show God's will being accomplished (1:22–23; 2:5–6, 15, 17–18, 23; 3:3, 17).

- God's voice (3:17).

- The advocacy of God's will by other characters (Joseph [1:24–25, 2:13–23]; the magi [2:1–12]; John the Baptist [3:1–15]).

- The contrast provided by the negative evaluation of those who reject the divine will (Herod [2:1–18]; the religious leaders [2:5–6; 3:7–10]).

- Jesus' words and actions (3:13–16).

The authorial audience identifies this perspective, agrees with it, and has its identity and lifestyle shaped accordingly. Whether an actual audience experiences these aspects is an important question. An actual audience may consent to this point of view only for the reading of this text; it may find it completely or partially compatible with its own outlook on life; it may deem it to be quite unacceptable as a basis for contemporary living.

NOTES

1. For discussion of point of view, B. Uspensky, *A Poetics of Composition* (Berkeley: University of California, 1973); J. M. Lotman, "Point of View in a Text," *New Literary History* 6 (1975) 339–52; S. Chatman, *Story and Discourse* (Ithaca: Cornell University, 1978) 151–58; N. Petersen, " 'Point of View' in Mark's Narrative," *Semeia* 12 (1978) 97–121; A. Culpepper, *Anatomy of the Fourth Gospel: A Study in Literary Design* (Philadelphia: Fortress, 1983) 20–34; Kingsbury, *Matthew as Story,* 33–37; idem, "The Figure of Jesus in Matthew's Story: A Literary-Critical Probe," *JSNT* 21 (1984) 3–36; D. Hill, "The Figure of Jesus in Matthew's Story: A Response to Professor Kingsbury's Literary-Critical Probe," *JSNT* 21 (1984) 37–52; M. A. Powell, *What Is Narrative Criticism?* (Guides to Biblical Scholarship; Minneapolis: Fortress, 1990) 23–25; J. C. Anderson, *Matthew's Narrative Web: Over, and Over, and Over Again* (JSNTSup 91: Sheffield: JSOT, 1994) 53–77.

2. Uspensky, *Poetics*, 1–100.

3. "Omniscient" (all-knowing) is not a helpful term. The implied author is not all-knowing with regard to all knowledge. Nor does the implied author tell everything that might be known about the characters and actions. The notion of "privilege" is more useful.

4. Uspensky (*Poetics*, 20–32) identifies naming as an important technique in the phraseological plane.

5. For discussion of the genealogy, see the commentaries; Brown, *Birth of the Messiah*, 57–95, 587–96; Johnson, *Purpose of the Biblical Genealogies*.

6. For discussion of the number "fourteen," see the commentaries and Brown, *Birth of the Messiah*, 74–84, 589–90.

7. The Deuteronomist historian holds Manasseh responsible for the fall of Jerusalem at the beginning of the exile because of the depth of his evil (2 Kings 21:1–18). Manasseh is presented in 2 Chron 33:12–13 as repenting.

8. 1:18 refers the audience directly to 1:1 by using the same word γένεσις (*genesis*). NRSV translates the first as "genealogy" and the second as "birth." Luz (*Matthew 1–7*, 103–4) prefers "origin" in both verses. For discussion, Brown, *Birth of the Messiah*, 58–59, 66–69; Davies and Allison, *Matthew*, 1.149–54.

9. W. Grundmann and G. Stählin, "ἁμαρτάνω, ἁμάρτημα, ἁμαρτία," *TDNT* 1.267–316, esp. 1.286–96.

10. The verb translated "fulfill" (πληρόω) appears sixteen times in Matthew, twelve times in introducing a Hebrew Bible citation (1:22; 2:15, 17, 23; 4:14; 8:17; 12:17; 13:35; 21:4; 26:54, 56; 27:9; the other four are 3:15; 5:17; 13:48; 23:32). Its meaning has caused much debate, especially in 5:17. Some scholars see it as primarily meaning "to do or obey" God's will. Others understand it to mean to bring into being what has been previously promised in the Hebrew scriptures. So J. P. Meier, *Law and History in Matthew's Gospel* (AnBib 71; Rome: Biblical Institute, 1976) 73–81; idem, *Vision of Matthew*, 224–26.

11. It should be noted that in the Hebrew text Isa 7:14 refers to the imminent birth of a Davidic prince (Hezekiah?) during the reign of Ahaz (approx. 735–715 BCE) as a sign of hope for Judah. His mother is a young woman (ʿ*almah*). When the verse was translated into Greek in the Septuagint, the translators used the Greek word, παρθένος (*parthenos*, "virgin") probably indicating that the mother is a virgin at the time of the oracle. In both versions the verse assumes conception through normal intercourse. In citing Septuagint material, the implied author typically ignores its historical and literary contexts, but uses verses which contain words or themes applicable to the gospel inci-

dent. The use of such material demonstrates the multiple meanings of texts created by their interaction with different contexts.

12. Matthew mostly omits Mark's explanations of Aramaic and Hebrew words and phrases:

Mark	Matthew
3:17	omitted from 10:2
5:41	omitted from 9:25
7:11	omitted from 15:5
7:34	omitted from 15:30
14:36	omitted from 26:39
15:22	retained in 27:33
15:34	retained in 27:46

13. Some commentators (J. C. Fenton, *Saint Matthew* [Philadelphia: Westminster, 1963, 1977] 80–82; D. Hagner, *Matthew 1–13* [WBC 33A; Dallas: Word, 1993] 21) understand this phrase to identify Jesus as God. However, since this claim has no other support in Matthew, it is preferable to understand Jesus as one who embodies, is an agent of, God's saving purposes and presence.

14. See the repeated references to hypocrisy (6:2, 5, 16; 7:5; 15:7; 22:18; 23:13, 15, 23, 25, 27, 29) and to plants that do or do not produce appropriate fruit (3:8–10; 7:16–20; 12:33–37; 13:3–9). See also D. O. Via, *Self-Deception and Wholeness in Paul and Matthew* (Minneapolis: Fortress, 1990).

15. A similar technique is used subsequently in the gospel. Jesus predicts his death and resurrection (16:21; 17:22; 20:17–19; 26:2, 32) after the audience has been told of the intentions of the religious leaders to kill him (12:14). Jesus' prediction is shown to be reliable by both the prior knowledge and its subsequent fulfillment. As another example, note the sequence for Judas's betrayal: Judas's offer (26:14–16), Jesus' prediction (26:21–25, 46), Judas's action (26:47–50).

16. Commentators do not agree on what text is being invoked. See Davies and Allison, *Matthew*, 1.275–80; Brown, *Birth of the Messiah*, 209–13, 223–25.

17. Debate over the meaning of "righteousness" has often posited a false antithesis between human ethical conduct and divine activity. So B. Przybylski (*Righteousness in Matthew and His World of Thought* [SNTSMS 41; Cambridge: Cambridge University, 1980] 1–12, 78–99) concludes that in Matthew the term always indicates God's demand on human beings for proper conduct (99). But the use of the word in the Psalms and prophets indicates a "both-and" approach. God's will is carried out by God (acting faithfully to the covenant commitments) and by humans. Different usages may emphasize one dimension rather

than another. See Ps 22:31 ("deliverance"); 99:4; Isa 51:5–8; 60:21; 61:1–3. Meier, *Law and History*, 76–79.

18. Davies and Allison, *Matthew*, 1.325–27; Meier, *Law and History*, 76–80.

19. For uses of direct and indirect speech in the phraseological plane, Uspensky, *Poetics*, 32–50.

20. For example, John the Baptist (3:1–12), Herod and John (14:1–12), the religious leaders (26:3–5; 27:1–2), Judas and the chief priests (26:14–16), Peter (26:69–75), Judas (27:3–10), religious leaders and Pilate (27:62–66), chief priests and guards (28:11–15).

Chapter 9

Maintaining God's Point of View

We have identified a number of conventions which are employed in the opening three chapters of the Gospel of Matthew. These enable the audience to identify God's perspective as normative for the world of the gospel. We have also observed that in his baptism Jesus "fulfill[s] all righteousness" (3:15). He accepts the tasks God calls him to do and so becomes the representative of God's point of view.

In this chapter we move beyond the opening chapters to identify twelve conventions which enable the authorial audience to maintain this point of view. Some of these conventions are familiar from the opening chapters.[1] Others are added, particularly Jesus' increased role as representative of God's point of view. We will also observe the presence of opposing points of view.

God Speaks Directly

In the transfiguration scene (17:1–13), God repeats the statement from the baptism which expresses approval of Jesus (17:5; cf. 3:17) though the statement functions somewhat differently. It confirms Peter's confession of Jesus as God's son (16:16) and is strengthened by the addition of God's command, "Listen to him." It also follows Jesus' statement in 16:21 that he must go to Jerusalem to die. The audience understands that this disclosure comes with God's stamp of approval. In a subsequent parable Jesus refers to a vineyard owner's son who is killed by resisting tenants (21:37–39). In using this image in a self-reference Jesus agrees with God's designation of him as God's Son or commissioned agent (cf. 2:15; 3:17). He expresses the same agreement before the high priest in his trial (26:63–64).

Fulfillment Citations

These present Jesus' words and actions as complying with and embodying the previously disclosed divine will (4:14–16; 8:17; 12:17–21; 13:14–15, 35; 21:4–5; 27:9).

Citation of Scripture

This offers a variation on number 2. Jesus cites Scripture for several purposes. Scripture justifies and interprets his actions as consistent with God's will.[2] He interprets Scripture for the guidance of his followers (5:21–48; 8:4). He uses Scripture to discredit his opponents by showing their lives to be inconsistent with God's will (9:13; 15:7–9; 21:13, 16; 22:37–39, 44). Both the devil (4:6) and Pharisees (19:7) also cite Scripture but in these scenes Jesus demonstrates that they do not interpret it correctly.

The Association of Old Testament Characters with Jesus[3]

These include Elijah (11:12–15; 17:10–13), David (12:3–7), Jonah and the Queen of the South (12:40–42; 16:4), Moses (2:13–23; 5:1; 8:1), Moses and Elijah (17:3), Daniel (24:15), Noah (24:36–39).

The Prominence of Angels

Angels are alluded to or appear subsequently as agents of God's will (4:6; 18:10; 26:53; 28:2–7).

Parables Disclose God's Point of View on Human Actions and Destiny[4]

For example, human responses to God's word and actions vary (13:3–9, 18–23), but humans remain accountable in the judgment (13:24–30, 36–43; 22:1–14); disciples are to forgive because God has forgiven them (18:23–35); God's way challenges human values and practices (20:1–16); humans are to do God's will (21:28–32); God's efforts throughout Israel's history lead to the rejection of Israel's leaders and the inclusion of Gentiles (21:33–46); faithful disciples have nothing to fear when Jesus returns, but unfaithful disciples will be condemned (24:45–25:30). Frequently, the main character (the sower [13:3, 24], the king [18:23; 22:1], the householder [20:1; 21:33], the vineyard owner [21:28], the master [24:45], the bridegroom [25:1, 10], the property owner [25:14]) represents God's point of view. The actions and judgments of this character, however unusual, cannot be faulted. Often they bring divided responses, but this central character's perspective evaluates those responses.

Jesus' Teaching and Actions Disclose God's Will[5]

(1) One key scene is 11:25–27. In overhearing Jesus pray, the audience is reminded of God's revelatory work in Jesus (11:25–26), grounded in the exclusive relationship of Father and Son (11:27a–c) into which others can be incorporated through Jesus' revelation (11:27d). (2) This revelation concerning the presence and future purposes of the reign of God results from God's gracious action in Jesus' teaching and deeds (cf. 11:4–6, 25–27). In two other verses the verb "it has been given"[6] signifies God's action. Jesus declares that God gives understanding to the disciples in 13:11 (in contrast to the crowds to whom "it has not been given").[7] Only "those to whom it is given" can "accept" Jesus' difficult teaching on marriage (19:11). (3) Jesus discloses God's will "hidden from the foundation of the world" (13:35b; 19:4). (4) God's revelatory activity in Jesus is again affirmed in 16:17. "My Father who is in heaven" causes Peter's confession about Jesus' identity ("the Christ the Son of the living God"). His insight does not derive from ordinary human agency ("flesh and blood"). (5) The citation from Isaiah in 12:17–21 repeats the words of God from the baptism. They underline Jesus' special relationship with God and the nature of Jesus' actions in accord with 1:21, 23. (6) Jesus' references to God as "My Father (in Heaven)" remind the audience of their close relationship.[8] This relationship provides the basis for the authoritative teaching in the five discourses (chs. 5–7, 10, 13, 18, 23–25).

(7) Statements which begin "I have come (not) to" or "the Son of Man has come (not) to" also indicate that Jesus' teaching and actions disclose God's point of view. For example:

- 5:17—I have come not to abolish [the law and the prophets] but to fulfill [them].

- 9:13—For I have come not to call the righteous but sinners.

- 20:28—The Son of Man came not to be served but to serve, and to give his life a ransom for many.[9]

In these statements Jesus declares his purposes in ways that are consistent with God's point of view established in the opening chapters. The claim of 5:17 coheres with the use of fulfillment citations in the opening four chapters to indicate the enactment of God's previously revealed will in the life of Jesus (1:22–23; 2:15, 17, 23; 4:12–16). In 9:13 Jesus, having forgiven the paralyzed man his sins and healed him (9:1–7), describes his purpose as calling sinners from sin. This statement expresses a purpose consonant with that announced by God's angel, to save from sins (1:21). In 20:28 Jesus indicates how he intends to carry out the purpose of saving from sin. His death is the means of delivering those who are captive to sin.

The use in 8:29 is slightly different in that it is a question (not a statement) from demons not from Jesus: "Have you come here to torment us before the time?" Nevertheless, this verse functions to provide a display of Jesus' purpose consistent with the point of view of the opening chapters. Jesus casts out the demons showing his power over Satan (4:1–11). His action is an inbreaking of the saving presence of God, the reign of heaven (4:17; 12:28).[10]

(8) In addition to the "came . . . to" statement of 20:28, Jesus' death and resurrection are identified as being God's will in other ways. Jesus discloses that he "must" (16:21) go to Jerusalem to die. His compulsion derives from his compliance with God's will demonstrated throughout the rest of the narrative. The Gethsemane scene reinforces this sense of obligation. Here the audience experiences Jesus praying (alone and in echoes of the Lord's prayer [6:10]) "My Father, if this cannot pass unless I drink it, your will be done" (26:42). The crucifix-

ion events are also asserted to be in accord with the scriptures (26:54, 56; see ch. 14).[11]

(9) Jesus' ability to reveal God's will and knowledge about the heavenly sphere, the sphere of God not humans, also reminds the audience that God's point of view controls the narrative. Jesus reveals what happens in the heavens concerning angels (18:10; 26:53). He discloses the future events of resurrection (22:30) and the return of the Son of Man (26:64; also chs. 24–25) about which only God knows the time (24:36).

(10) Jesus also discloses God's ways of acting towards human beings and disciples:

- 5:45—For he makes his sun rise on the evil and the good, and sends rain on the righteous and unrighteous.

- 6:14—For if you forgive others their trespasses, your heavenly Father will also forgive you.

- 6:15—But if you do not forgive others, neither will your Father forgive your trespasses.

- 6:26—And yet your heavenly Father feeds them. Are you not of more value than they?

- 6:30—But if God so clothes the grass of the field, which is alive today and tomorrow is thrown into the oven, will he not clothe you—you of little faith?

- 6:32—And indeed your heavenly Father knows that you need all these things.

- 6:33—And all these things will be given to you.

- 7:11—How much more will your Father in heaven give good things to those who ask him.

- 9:38—Therefore ask the Lord of the harvest to send out laborers into his harvest; (see also 10:29–31).

- 18:19—If two of you agree on earth about anything you ask, it will be done for you by my Father in heaven.

Implicit in such statements are instructions about God's will for the identity and lifestyle of disciples in the present.

(11) Jesus also explicitly instructs disciples that as children of God (5:43–48) they must imitate "the Father"[12] and do God's will (6:10b; 7:24–27; 12:46–50).

(12) At times Jesus' responses to people provide commentary for the audience. They show what is commended (and therefore to be emulated) and what is rejected. In several scenes he indicates that the simple act of approaching him manifests faith. Though the characters do not use the word "faith," Jesus names this desirable quality and so makes it explicit for the audience (8:10; 9:2, 22, 29). At other times he names and makes explicit an undesirable quality, the fear and little faith of the disciples (8:26; 14:31).

(13) Revelations about God's ways of acting in the future judgment are used frequently to express God's view of present behavior. In the Sermon on the Mount (chs. 5–7) a general instruction about living righteously also warns against living for human approval. To do so means losing God's future reward in the judgment (6:1). The same approach is taken with respect to doing deeds of mercy (6:4), praying (6:6), and fasting (6:18).

(14) A warning against destructive relationships within the community of believers (18:9–14) is reinforced in three ways. Jesus discloses the behavior of "their angels" in heaven (18:10). He tells a parable about a man who leaves his ninety-nine sheep to seek out the one which "goes astray" (18:11–13). He also makes an explicit statement of God's will:

> It is not the will of your Father in heaven that one of these little ones should be lost (18:14).[13]

(15) The requirement to forgive community members (18:21–35) is reinforced by the disclosure of God's punishment for an unwillingness to forgive:

> So my heavenly Father will also do to everyone of you, if you do not forgive your brother or sister from your heart (18:35).

(16) Each of the major sections of teaching ends with scenes of the future judgment:

- Chapters 5–7—Sermon on the Mount (7:13–27)

- Chapter 10—Missionary Discourse (10:32–42)

- Chapter 13—Parables (13:36–50)

- Chapter 18—Community Discourse (18:21–35)

- Chapters 24–25—Eschatological Discourse (25:31–46)

These scenes graphically present condemnation and vindication in the judgment.[14] They show that what Jesus reveals as God's will for the present is the standard by which God will judge people in the future (7:24–27). They warn about the terrible consequences awaiting those who do not live in the ways indicated by Jesus as God's will. They also encourage faithful discipleship by reassuring the audience that God welcomes and rewards faithful obedience (for example, 10:32–33, 40).[15]

The Pervasiveness of Sin

Jesus reiterates God's view of the human situation. It is marred by sin from which humans need rescuing (1:21). In 7:11 Jesus asserts the evil nature of human beings in contrast to God's graciousness. In 9:36 Jesus compassionately describes the crowds as "harassed and helpless." His way of helping is to send the disciples to "the lost sheep of . . . Israel" (10:6) to proclaim the good news of God's saving presence (the reign of heaven, 10:7). This response recalls the beginning of Jesus' own public ministry. To be "harassed and helpless" is to know death and darkness. This describes the world of sin into which comes the light of God's saving presence (4:16–17).

In 11:28 Jesus summons "all you that are weary and are carrying heavy burdens" to find "rest." In terms of Jesus' mission, "rest" is to know God's saving presence, the reign of heaven which Jesus manifests. Those who need such rest are those who lack it, either because of the religious leaders (cf. 23:4) or, more likely, because of the burden of sin.[16] In 15:12–20, Jesus explains to the disciples that the human heart produces all sorts of "evil intentions" and destructive actions.

Jesus Evaluates Other Voices and Actions

Jesus constantly evaluates other points of view in relation to God's, exposing their inadequacies. In the Sermon on the Mount (chs. 5–7), Jesus negatively evaluates:

- The opposition to God's actions expressed in persecuting disciples. He blesses the disciples (5:10–12).

- Claims of the religious tradition. He offers contrasting interpretations and requirements (5:21, 27, 31, 33, 38, 42).

- The behavior of "hypocrites" and "Gentiles." He instructs disciples not to imitate their behavior and teaches a different piety (6:2, 5, 7, 16).

- Prevailing cultural attitudes to material possessions and to life (6:31). He exhorts trust in God (6:25–34).

- Inappropriate relationships among believers. He advocates nonjudgmental behavior and actions (7:1–5).

- The popular, easy way of life which leads to destruction. He offers an alternative, difficult, unpopular way of life, committed to God's will, leading to life (7:13–14).

- The actions of the "false prophets." Their deeds indicate wrong motives and failure to do the will of God (7:15–23).

Through the gospel he corrects the points of view of the disciples (14:15–21, 26–27; 15:15–20; 19:10, 13b–15), other characters (the mother, 20:21; the Sadducees, 22:23), and the crowds (20:31; 21:11). More often, Jesus' opponents fill this role (see below).

Testimony of Other Characters

Other characters reinforce God's point of view by bearing positive witness to Jesus: John the Baptist (3:1–12; 11:2–6); the trusting centurion recognizes Jesus' authority (8:5–13); the confessing disciples (14:33); and at times the crowds (7:28–29; 9:8). Other characters supply contrasting perspectives. The disciples of the Pharisees and the Herodians ironically recognize that Jesus teaches "the way of God in accordance with truth" but Jesus' comments expose their malice and hypocrisy (22:15–18). The religious leaders witness Jesus forgiving sins and accuse him of blasphemy (9:3). The audience knows that this point of view is wrong because: (1) Jesus labels it "evil" (v. 4), (2) Jesus argues that his healing miracle demonstrates his authority to forgive (vv. 5–8), and (3) the audience knows from 1:21 that Jesus' God-given mission is to save the people from their sins. Jesus' life-giving powers are similarly demonstrated in the midst of death and scoffing crowds (9:24; 9:18–26).

Titles of Address[17]

God's point of view is that Jesus manifests God's saving presence (1:21, 23) as God's Son (2:15; 3:17; 17:5). This provides the basis for evaluating other interpretations of Jesus' identity. To call Jesus the "carpenter's son" (13:55), John the Baptist (14:2; 16:14), Elijah, or Jeremiah (16:14) does not agree with God's point of view, reveals human misunderstanding, and exposes the rejection of God's perspective.

Characters who address Jesus as "Son of God" agree with God's evaluation (14:33; 16:16; 27:54). The same applies to the use of the titles "Christ" (16:16, 20; 26:63), "king of the Jews" (2:2, 4; 27:11, 17, 22), "the one who is to come" (11:2–3), and "Son of David" (15:22). The latter title is generally used for Jesus by outsiders in need of healing and mercy.[18] Only disciples and those with faith reverently address Jesus as "Lord" (8:2, 5, 25; 14:28) while those lacking these qualities call him "teacher" (8:19; 12:38; 19:16; 22:16), "prophet" (21:11), or "rabbi" (compare 26:22 [disciples] and 26:25 [Judas]).

Blessings and Curses

God's favor is expressed through blessings on disciples (5:3–12, 13:16–17; 16:17) and God's displeasure through curses on the religious leaders (ch. 23).

GOD'S POINT OF VIEW AND SATAN

This discussion of the ways in which the audience sees God's point of view through the action and words of Jesus has included reference to opposition to that point of view. The audience identifies this opposition with two sources, Satan and human beings.

The temptation scene in 4:1–11 establishes "the devil," "the tempter," or "Satan" (4:1, 3, 5, 8, 10, 11) as the cosmic source of opposition to God's purposes in Jesus. In the baptism scene, the audience saw Jesus' allegiance to God's will and heard God express pleasure in "my beloved Son" (3:16–17). But in the temptation which immediately follows, the devil tries to turn Jesus from that allegiance. Twice the devil questions God's point of view by saying "*If* you are the Son of God . . . " (4:3, 6). The use of "if" questions whether God's declaration about Jesus as God's Son (3:17) is either adequate or truthful. The devil suggests its veracity requires proof. One significance of the three commands the devil gives to Jesus (4:3, 5, 9) lies in the requirement that Jesus do what Satan orders, rather than trust God's declaration and follow God's plan. The third command especially illustrates this contrast. The devil offers Jesus "all the kingdoms of the world" (4:8) whereas Jesus' task is to announce "the kingdom of heaven" (4:17). The devil commands Jesus to worship him whereas Jesus' commitment is to God (4:9–10).

Jesus wins the struggle as the devil leaves him (4:11). But the devil does not leave the world of the story. The opposition between God and Satan continues. Satan takes up residence in people's lives through demons (12:43–45). In casting out demons (4:24; 8:16, 28–34; 9:32–34; 12:22–32; 17:14–21), Jesus and his disciples (10:1, 8) show the presence of the reign of God overcoming Satan's realm (12:28; 10:7–8). The parables in chapter 13 disclose that Satan actively works in the world to oppose God (13:4, 19, 25, 38–39). The devil even produces children (13:38). Saving from sin means in part setting free from the power of Satan in demons. In explaining his parables, Jesus indicates that Satan will go on opposing God's work until the judgment which ends the present age (13:30, 39–43).

Satan's opposition is expressed through various characters including disciples (Peter, 16:23). The leading representatives, however, are the religious leaders.[19] Throughout the gospel, conflict between Jesus and the religious leaders occurs continually and openly (see chs. 9, 12, 15, 16, 21–23). The religious leaders plot and carry out Jesus' death.[20] Ironically, they think they are destroying Jesus. Instead, they enable God's saving will to be carried out.

The audience uses two particular words to identify the religious leaders as the devil's agents: (1) In 4:3 the devil is called "the tempter" (ὁ πειράζων, *ho peiradzōn*), the one who tempts or tests Jesus (4:1). The same verb, "to tempt" or "to test," indicates the purpose of the religious leaders toward Jesus (16:1; 19:3; 22:18, 34–35). Like Satan, they oppose God's purposes by trying to divert Jesus from doing and teaching the will of God. (2) The devil is also described as "the evil one" (13:19, 38; ὁ πονηρός, *ho ponēros*). The same adjective describes the religious leaders and their actions as "evil" (9:4; 12:34, 39, 45b; 16:4; 22:18). Disciples pray to be delivered from "evil/the evil one" (6:13b).

Satan's temptation of Jesus (4:1–11) is paradigmatic for the behavior of the religious leaders in other ways. Like Satan, the religious leaders challenge God's evaluation of Jesus. They deny that God acts in Jesus (9:3), ironically ascribing God's actions to Satan (9:34; 12:22–32). They join passers-by to reject God's evaluation of Jesus as God's Son (27:39–44; 26:62–64). In calling for Jesus to come down from the cross they resist God's will (27:40; cf. 16:21). Furthermore, as in the temptation (4:1–11), Jesus shows their opposition to be based on misunderstandings of the scriptures (9:10–13; 12:1–8; 15:1–9; 19:3–9; 22:23–33). Jesus says to them, "You are wrong because you know neither the scriptures nor the power of God" (22:29).

THE DEVIL MADE ME DO IT? "THE THINGS OF HUMAN BEINGS"

Satan's opposition to God's point of view and will is also identified by another set of terms. In 16:22–23 Peter rebukes Jesus for speaking of his forthcoming death. In turn Jesus rebukes Peter, calling him Satan. Jesus identifies Peter's problem as "setting your mind not on the things of God but on the things of human beings" (16:23, author's translation).

This opposition between divine and human perception appears elsewhere. (1) The parables disclose that while Satan prevents one quarter of those who hear "the word of the kingdom"[21] from accepting it (13:19), social factors such as hardship and the "cares of the world and the lure of wealth" hinder half of the recipients (13:21–22). (2) In 19:26 Jesus contrasts the limits of human achievement with God's unlimited possibilities. To enter the reign of God by one's own accomplishments is impossible. But it becomes possible with the gift of God's saving presence. (3) In 21:23 the religious leaders question Jesus about the source of his authority. Jesus responds by asking them whether John's authority and baptism derive "from heaven or was it of human origin?" (21:25). The audience knows the right answer from earlier chapters. The religious leaders, however, are not willing to make the right answer because of its implications (21:25b).[22]

(4) In a major conflict scene (15:1–20), Jesus rebukes the religious leaders for preferring "the things of human beings" rather than of God. They break the commandment of God because they favor their traditions (15:3). In supporting their human traditions rather than God's will, they "make void the word of God" (15:6). By citing the direct speech of God in Isaiah 29, Jesus discloses that their fundamental problem is the allegiance of their hearts (15:8). The heart signifies the center of human commitment, thinking, willing, and acting. Hearts that "are far from me" do not worship God (cf. the religious leaders in 2:4–6; the devil's temptation in 4:9–10) and so do not perceive accurately. They confuse their own perceptions with God's by "teaching human precepts as doctrines" (15:9). In following their own perceptions rather than God's, they cannot live according to God's will. Accordingly their lives manifest evil in all sorts of socially destructive forms (15:10–11, 17–20; cf. 7:11). Humans need salvation from such sins by transferring their allegiance to God through the act of "following" Jesus. In this realignment of perspective, humans accept God's point of view and commit themselves to God's will as manifested in Jesus. This is the role, identity, and lifestyle assumed of the authorial audience.

SUMMARY

The implied author of the Gospel of Matthew spends much energy establishing the point of view which the authorial audience must identify and adopt. The story of Jesus is told from

God's perspective. In the actions and teachings of Jesus, God's Son or commissioned agent, God acts to manifest God's saving presence in a sinful world.

We have also identified points of view that oppose and conflict with God's point of view. These center in Satan but also belong to the sphere of human beings. An actual audience can (like the authorial audience) understand and accept God's point of view and live accordingly, or, like Satan and the religious leaders, resist it.

In the following chapters we will look at how God's point of view and the points of view opposed to it affect the audience's interaction with the plot, characters, and setting of the story.

NOTES

1. For the notion and function of redundancy, or repetition, in the gospel, see Anderson, *Matthew's Narrative Web*.

2. For example 4:4, 7, 10; 8:4; 9:13; 11:4–6, 10; 12:3–7; 15:4; 19:4–7, 18–19; 21:9, 13, 16, 42; 22:32; 23:39; 27:46.

3. It is impossible here to indicate the numerous implicit references and allusions to various other biblical figures and traditions, notably Moses and wisdom traditions.

4. See W. Carter and J. P. Heil, *Reading Matthew's Parables* (forthcoming).

5. I am drawing attention to the explicit ways in which the point of view established in the opening chapters continues to be asserted.

6. Most commentators note the use of a "divine passive" which assumes, but does not state, God as the subject.

7. The disciples' knowing in 13:11 is a synonym for their understanding (cf. 13:51).

8. See 7:21; 10:32–33; 11:27; 12:50; 15:13; 16:17; 18:10, 14, 19, 35; 20:23; 25:34; 26:29, 39, 42, 53.

9. 10:34–35 should also be noted as a recognition of the divisive impact of Jesus' mission. Not all accept or welcome God's saving presence. See below.

10. Space prevents a consideration of the related passages 11:16–19 and 17:10–13.

11. Some (Hill, *Gospel of Matthew*, 343; Harrington, *Matthew*, 375) argue that 26:54, 56 refer to the flight of the disciples (26:31; cf. Zechariah 13:7). 26:56b might support this. However, the reference in 26:56a to "all this" points to a much wider reference.

12. Cf. 5:16, 45, 48; 6:1, 4, 6, 8, 14, 15, 18, 26, 32; 7:11; 10:20, 29; 18:14 [?]; 23:9.

13. The verb "lost" or "perish" indicates eschatological destruction (7:13).

14. See Bornkamm, "End-Expectation and Church," in *Tradition and Interpretation*, 15–51; L. E. Keck, "Ethics in the Gospel According to Matthew," *Iliff Review* 40 (1984) 39–56, esp. 48–49, 52–55.

15. Davies and Allison, *Matthew*, 2.213; Hagner, *Matthew 1–13*, 288.

16. Davies and Allison, *Matthew*, 2.288–89.

17. For the limitations of focusing on titles, L. E. Keck, "Toward the Renewal of New Testament Christology," *NTS* 32 (1986) 362–77.

18. So 9:27; 12:23; 15:22; 20:30, 31; 21:15. "Son of David" also means "Lord" as 22:41–46 makes clear. Jesus is Son of David in descending from David (through Joseph's naming of Jesus, 1:25) but is Lord because of the tasks to which God calls him. For discussion of "Son of David," J. D. Kingsbury, "The Title 'Son of David' in Matthew's Gospel," *JBL* 95 (1976) 591–602; D. Duling, "The Therapeutic Son of David: An Element in Matthew's Christological Apologetic," *NTS* 24 (1977–78) 392–410; W. Loader, "Son of David, Blindness, Possession, and Duality in Matthew," *CBQ* 44 (1982) 570–85.

19. The various groups—Pharisees, Sadducees, scribes, high priests, elders—form one entity, the religious leaders. See further in ch. 15 below.

20. See 12:14; 16:21; 20:18–19; 21:45–46; 22:15; 26:3–5, 14–16, 47, 57; also chs. 14–15 below.

21. See the discussion of the related term "gospel of the kingdom" (4:23; 9:35; 24:14) in J. D. Kingsbury, *Matthew: Structure, Christology, Kingdom* (Philadelphia: Fortress, 1975) 128–37.

22. 22:15–22 is a little different in that it does not offer a strict antithesis between "the things of God" and "the things of Caesar." Clearly "the things of God" are superior, but they are not exclusive. There remains a place for performing appropriate obligations to Caesar, such as paying taxes.

Chapter 10

Shaping Matthew's Plot

In addition to identifying the gospel's point of view, the audience utilizes the author's clues or conventions to fit the various events and characters together into a coherent plot. Focusing on the plot is a fresh way of thinking about the gospel's structure.[1] In this chapter we briefly review two ways of looking at the gospel's structure. We outline some of the tasks an audience performs in shaping a plot. In the next chapter we discuss Matthew's plot.

B. W. BACON'S PENTATEUCHAL THEORY

B. W. Bacon's Pentateuchal theory offered an influential analysis of the gospel's structure early in this century.[2] Bacon noticed a fivefold alternation between the gospel narratives and Jesus' discourses or speeches. A repeated formula closed each speech:

Narrative	3:1–4:25	
Discourse	5:1–7:27	Sermon on the Mount
Formula	7:28–29	"Now when Jesus had finished saying these things . . . "
Narrative	8:1–10:4	
Discourse	10:5–42	Mission Instruction
Formula	11:1	"Now when Jesus had finished instructing his twelve disciples . . . "

Narrative	11:2–12:50	
Discourse	13:1–52	Parables about the reign of heaven
Formula	13:53	"When Jesus had finished these parables . . . "

Narrative	13:54–17:27	
Discourse	18:1–35	Instructions about community relationships and practices
Formula	19:1	"When Jesus had finished saying these things . . . "

Narrative	19:2–22:46	
Discourse	23:1–25:46	Instruction on living until the end (eschatological discourse)
Formula	26:1	"When Jesus had finished saying all these things . . . "

Bacon argued that this fivefold pattern resembled the five books of the Pentateuch and its alternation of narrative and discourses or speeches. Bacon proposed that Matthew, a converted rabbi, structured the gospel this way to depict Jesus as a new Moses and his teaching as new Pentateuch or new law to guide the church against lawlessness.

Although many have followed Bacon's view, it is no longer widely supported.[3] Its most serious problem is its failure to give adequate attention to the birth narrative (chs. 1–2) and the passion and resurrection stories (chs. 26–28). Bacon's description of these sections as "preamble" and "epilogue" indicates his failure to integrate these sections into his scheme. Moreover, Bacon's emphasis on the number five has raised questions. The content and setting of chapters 23 and 24–25 are significantly different, suggesting six discourses. Bacon's claim that the pattern of alternating narrative and discourse derives from the Pentateuch is also dubious. It is difficult, for instance, to see such a pattern in Leviticus or Numbers. The most serious concern is that Bacon's emphasis on the five sections pays little attention to the gospel's story.

J. D. KINGSBURY: REPEATED FORMULA

J. D. Kingsbury has offered a second analysis of the gospel's structure. Kingsbury has drawn attention to a phrase or formula which he considers "pivotal to the broad outline" of the gospel.[4] In 4:17 and 16:21 the phrase "From that time Jesus began to . . . " appears.[5] Kingsbury suggests that this formula indicates important new phases in Jesus' ministry. His public ministry begins in 4:17 while 16:21 begins instruction about his death and resurrection. Kingsbury proposes an outline for the gospel:

- 1:1–4:16—The Person of Jesus Messiah

- 4:17–16:20—The Proclamation of Jesus Messiah

- 16:21–28:20—The Suffering, Death, and Resurrection of Jesus Messiah[6]

Kingsbury's proposal helpfully identifies the broad outline of the gospel in thematic form as well as highlights several important turning points in the story. His outline, though, is not detailed enough to recognize other significant developments. This failure raises questions about the adequacy of this one formula to express the structure of the whole gospel. Moreover, this analysis does not account for the use of part of the formula in 26:16 ("And from that moment . . . "). If 4:17 and 16:21 merit the emphasis placed on them, the use of part of this key formula in 26:16 without signalling an important division seems strange. There is also the issue of other repeated formulas through the gospel. Attention to this one and the neglect of others seems somewhat arbitrary.

ATTENTION TO THE PLOT

Recent literary approaches have considered the issue of structure in terms of the gospel's plot. Kingsbury has sought to confirm and extend his analysis by this approach.[7] Other helpful discussions of the plot have appeared.[8]

What Is a Plot?

Discussions of plot by literary theorists have highlighted several important dimensions. Aristotle, for instance, emphasizes *unity* as a key characteristic of a plot.[9] The action must have a beginning, middle, and end. Neither the beginning nor the end will be "at some chance point." The end is the "necessary" or "usual" sequel of what comes before it. The middle "both comes after something else and has another thing following it."

Though Aristotle is not explicitly discussing ancient biography, his emphasis on unity remains important. Ancient biographies consist of numerous anecdotes of incidents or events.[10] They are not randomly selected. Authors commonly arrange this material in chronological order. The audience expects initial attention to ancestry and birth, followed by scenes depicting great deeds and virtues, leading to death and its consequences.[11] The audience looks to establish a connected *sequence* through this material.

Several conventions assist the audience in formulating this connectedness. Aristotle warns that a unity is not created simply because a work "revolves about one man." Rather, events must contribute to a larger unified action. Aristotle highlights *causality* as an integral part of this unity and sequence. Events are the consequences of previous events and the cause of subsequent events.[12]

In Matthew, the author uses connectives as one convention to assist the audience. Connectives such as "for" (γάρ, *gar*), "therefore/so/then"[13] (οὖν, *oun*, less commonly "now/thus"),[14] and "for/because" (ὅτι, *hoti*)[15] connect events in various ways. These connectives indicate sequence, consequences, implications, explanations, and reasons. The audience must formulate connections among events to create a unified, enchained sequence.

A further aspect of the "logic of connection"[16] concerns *time relationships* in the plot.[17] The author *orders* events in a variety of possible relationships. The most common is a sequence in which one event follows another. Often in Matthew these sequential relationships are vague, indicated by "then,"[18] "and/but,"[19] "and/also,"[20] "again,"[21] or genitive absolute constructions translated as "while," "as," "when," or "after" (8:5, 16, 28; 9:18, 32; 11:7; 12:46). Infrequently, the implied author expresses more specific time relationships.[22] Most noteworthy is the author's insistence that the resurrection happened on the third day after Jesus' death.[23]

Other time relationships are indicated by a departure from normal sequencing. The audience is assumed to be able to recognize the disruption to the chronological sequence. *Flashbacks* are one such departure: In 14:1–12 Herod considers Jesus (14:2) as John the Baptist "raised from the dead." This view requires John's earlier death to be narrated (so 14:3–12).[24] The genealogy (1:2–17), the line from which Jesus is descended, reaches back over many centuries to Abraham.[25] The fulfillment citations stop the forward movement of the plot to interpret the action by invoking an earlier event or saying. Jesus reveals the will of the creator "at the beginning" (13:35; 19:4).

The author also uses *flashforwards,* references to future events mentioned before their time in the story.[26] The audience recognizes, for example, scenes of future judgment (7:21–23; 25:31–46), future difficulties that disciples will face in mission (5:10–12; 10:17–23), and instructions about how the church is to order its life (18:15–20).

With hindsight it also recognizes *foreshadowing.*[27] An event anticipates an event or emphasis later in the story by sharing similar features. Features of the birth story foreshadow the passion narrative (the threatened and scheming religious and political authorities, the title "King of the Jews"; 2:2; 27:11, 29, 37). References to the inclusion of Gentiles in God's purposes (1:1, 5–6; 2:1–12; 4:12–16; 8:5–13) foreshadow the final command of the risen Jesus to engage in Gentile mission (28:16–20). Jesus' statements about his approaching death anticipate and provide advance notice of that event.

The audience also must interpret the passing or *duration* of time. The author varies the speed or pace of the narrative.[28] Large periods of time are passed over quickly. One verse covers the forty days and nights of Jesus' fasting (4:2) while three chapters cover the time from Jesus' conception to the start of his public ministry (1:18–4:16). Short periods can be covered more slowly. Seven chapters, one quarter of the gospel, narrate the last week of Jesus' life (chs. 21–28). Scenes that employ dialogue seem to narrate events as they happen (cf. 17:14–20).[29]

Summaries move the story more quickly than narrating each of the events. This technique appears several times in the stories of Jesus' early life (the journeys, 2:1, 9, 12, 14, 21 and unspecified periods of residence, 2:15, 23; 4:12–13). It also features in the subsequent narrative (14:13, 34; 15:39; 19:1) including summaries of Jesus' teaching, preaching, and healing (4:17, 23; 9:35; 11:1, 20).[30] The impact for the audience is diverse. Summaries pass over time and events quickly, highlighting what is narrated in more detail. They also provide an economical way of showing the audience the magnitude and extent of Jesus' activity. The alternation of summaries with detailed narration of healing and teaching provides the audience with specific examples.

The narrative also moves over time periods without supplying any information. 1:18–2:25 takes the audience from the conception to Jesus' birth with minimal information about the time of Mary's pregnancy. A similar large stride is taken from Jesus' childhood (2:23) to his baptism (3:13). Periods of time also seem to be omitted between the temptation (4:11) and the beginning of Jesus' ministry in 4:17.

The *frequency* with which events are narrated comprises another aspect of time relationships.[31] The author employs much repetition to highlight important material and to help the audience unify the presentation. We have observed repeated phrases such as the transition formula at the end of the speeches or the introduction to the fulfillment citations. Several scenes are repeated: Jesus and the sea (8:23–27; 14:22–33); the healing of two blind men (9:27–31; 20:29–34) and of a mute demoniac (9:32–34; 12:22–32); and the miraculous feeding of the five and four thousand (14:13–21; 15:32–39). These repetitions emphasize the events' importance and enable the audience to connect them as a common unifying feature.[32]

Frequency is used in another way. A single instance in the story may indicate a frequently repeated behavior. For instance, Jesus instructs disciples that they are to forgive "seventy times seven" (18:21–35, 22). The use of the Greek imperfect tense can indicate events that happened several times. The imperfect in 14:4, for instance, can suggest that John spoke of the inappropriateness of Herod's marriage several times. Summary passages also include imperfects to indicate repeated actions.[33]

Repetition forms an inclusio or framework enabling the audience to draw material together. The theme "God with us" begins and ends the gospel (1:23; 28:20) underlining for the audience this key dimension of its identity. Summary passages of Jesus' healing and teaching actions frame the first part of his public ministry (4:23–25 and 9:35). Common features mark the beginning and end of the Sermon on the Mount (the mountain, Jesus teaching, the crowds, 5:1–2; 7:28–29). Repeated phrases indicate the beginning and end of sections within the Sermon

("the law or the prophets," 5:17 and 7:12; "you will know them
by their fruits," 7:16 and 7:20). Such redundancy underlines
key emphases, draws the audience's attention to them, and
ensures clear communication thereby facilitating acceptance of
the author's point of view.[34]

From Connections to Hierarchy: Kernels and Satellites

We have observed some of the conventions the author
employs to enable the audience to establish unity, sequence,
causality, and time relationships (order, duration, frequency)
among the events. The audience must also determine what
Seymour Chatman calls "the logic of hierarchy."

"Some [events] are more important than others," says
Chatman.[35] Among all the events which comprise the plot, the
audience identifies the most important ones to comprehend the
plot's unity and causality. An author can use a variety of
conventions to highlight these events, such as repeated phrases,
new actions, or an emphasis on an important issue.

Chatman distinguishes between "kernels" and "satellites."[36] The audience recognizes *kernels* (1) because they are
significant and major "branching points" or "hinges." They
are events that advance the plot. (2) Moreover, as "branching
points" they raise questions to be addressed by subsequent
kernels. (3) Kernels are "consequences of earlier [kernels]"
since they "satisfy questions" arising from the narrative logic
of the text. (4) Kernels function as the central event in a
narrative block, to which the other events in the block are
connected and from which they derive. They are the most
crucial parts of the narrative structure, which if deleted,
would "destroy the narrative logic."

Satellites are minor events that derive from kernels and
which work out and elaborate kernels. "Their function is that
of filling in, elaborating, completing the kernel; they form the
flesh on the skeleton." In turn, events are organized into *narrative blocks*. Each block is composed of a major event or kernel
and a series of minor events or satellites. Retroactively through
the narrative, but ultimately from the perspective of the end,
the audience identifies the kernels and satellites of the plot.

This chapter has identified some of the conventions an author employs and some of the tasks the audience performs as they order the plot. Chapter 11 will outline the plot of Matthew's gospel, with attention to the hierarchy of events (kernels and satellites), unity, sequence, causality, and time relationships.

NOTES

1. Senior, *What Are They Saying about Matthew?* 20–27; Davies and Allison, *Matthew,* 1.58–72; Luz, *Matthew 1–7,* 33–44; W. Carter, "Kernels and Narrative Blocks: The Structure of Matthew's Gospel," *CBQ* 54 (1992) 463–81, esp. 463–65 and the literature cited.

2. Bacon, *Matthew.*

3. For critique, Kingsbury, *Matthew: Structure, Christology, Kingdom,* 1–7.

4. Kingsbury, *Matthew: Structure, Christology, Kingdom,* 8.

5. Using his then redaction approach, Kingsbury (*Matthew: Structure, Christology, Kingdom,* 7) noted it was a formula "peculiar to Matthew." That is, since Matthew had added it to Mark, the phrase was understood to indicate something important about the author's intention.

6. Kingsbury, *Matthew: Structure, Christology, Kingdom,* 9.

7. For example, Kingsbury, "Figure of Jesus," 3–36; idem, *Matthew as Story,* 40–93.

8. F. Matera, "The Plot of Matthew's Gospel," *CBQ* 49 (1987) 233–53; M. A. Powell, "The Plot and Subplots of Matthew's Gospel," *NTS* 38 (1992) 187–204; J. D. Kingsbury, "The Plot of Matthew's Story," *Int* 46 (1992) 347–56; Carter, "Kernels and Narrative Blocks"; Anderson, *Matthew's Narrative Web,* 133–91.

9. Aristotle, *The Poetics* (LCL; Cambridge: Harvard University, 1939) Sections 7–10.

10. Cox, *Biography in Late Antiquity,* 58; Burridge, *What Are the Gospels?* 141–42, 202–4; Aune, *New Testament in its Literary Environment,* 29, 34–35, 50.

11. Burridge, *What Are the Gospels?* 207–9, also 119–20, 139–41, 145–47.

12. K. Egan, "What Is a Plot?" *New Literary History* 9 (1978) 455–73. Aristotle, *The Poetics.*

13. For example, γάρ (*gar,* "for") introduces scriptural reasons (2:5b; 4:6b, 10; 13:15; 26:31), frequently provides reasons or explanations in Jesus' teaching (5:12b, 18, 20, 29b, 30b, 46; 6:7b, 8b, 14, 16,

21, 24, 32, 34b; 7:2, 8, 12b, 25b, 29; 9:13, 24; 10:10, 17, 19, 20, 23, 26, 35; 11:30; 12:33, 34, 37; 13:12, 17; 16:25, 26, 27; 19:14; 20:1; 23:3b, 5b, 8, 9b, 13b, 17, 19, 39; 24:5, 6b, 7, 21, 24, 27, 37, 38; 25:3, 14, 29, 35, 42; 26:52b), and provides explanations for actions (4:18b; 7:29; 8:9; 9:20–21; 14:3–4, 24; 19:22; 21:26b; 26:73; 27:18, 19; 28:2). See R. A. Edwards, "Narrative Implications of *Gar* in Matthew," *CBQ* 52 (1990) 636–55.

14. Cf. 1:17; 3:8, 10; 5:19, 23, 48; 6:2, 8, 9, 22, 23, 31, 34; 7:11, 12, 24; 9:38; 10:16, 26, 31, 32; 12:12, 26b; 13:18, 27b, 28b, 40, 56b; 17:10; 18:4, 26, 29, 31; 19:6b, 7; 21:25b, 40; 22:9, 17, 21, 28, 43, 45; 23:3, 20; 24:15, 26, 42; 25:13, 27, 28; 26:54; 27:17, 22, 64; 28:19. In several verses the NRSV appears not to translate the word (3:8; 6:8; 7:12; 12:12; 13:40; 18:4, 31).

15. Cf. 2:18e; 5:3, 4, 5, 6, 7, 8, 9, 10, 12, 34, 35 (2x), 36, 45; 6:5, 26; 7:13; 9:36; 11:20b, 21, 23, 29b; 12:41b, 42b; 13:13; 14:5; 15:23d, 32; 16:17, 23d; 17:15; 20:7, 15; 23:10, 13, 15, 23, 25, 27, 29; 25:8, 13.

16. Chatman, *Story and Discourse,* 53.

17. G. Genette, *Narrative Discourse: An Essay in Method* (Ithaca: Cornell University, 1980) 33–160; G. Genette, "Time and Narrative in *A la recherche du temps perdu,*" in *Aspects of Narrative* (ed. J. H. Miller; New York: Columbia University, 1971) 93–118.

18. τότε *(tote),* 2:7, 16, 17; 3:5, 13, 15b; 4:1, 5, 10, 11, 17; 5:24b; 7:5, 23; 8:26; 9:6, 14, 15b, 29, 37; 11:20; 12:13, 22, 29b, 38, 44, 45; 13:26b, 36, 43; 15:1, 12, 28; 16:12, 20, 21, 24, 27b; 17:13, 19; 18:21, 32; 19:13, 27; 20:20; 21:1b; 22:8, 13, 15, 21; 23:1; 24:9, 10, 14b, 16, 21, 23, 30, 40; 25:7, 31b, 34, 37, 41, 44, 45; 26:3, 14, 16, 31, 36, 38, 45, 50, 52, 56b, 65, 67, 74; 27:3, 9, 13, 16, 26, 27, 38, 58b; 28:10.

19. δέ *(de)* appears about 495 times, forty-four in ch. 1 alone. As examples, see 8:16, 18; 9:36; 12:15, 43.

20. καί *(kai)* appears about 1189 times, seven times in 4:24; 8:9; six times in 7:27; 13:15; five times in 2:11; 4:25; 7:25; 9:35; 21:12, 33. In 4:23–25 it appears fifteen times, in 20:17–20 ten times.

21. πάλιν *(palin)* appears either as first word or within clauses in 4:7, 8; 5:33; 13:45, 47; 18:19; 19:24; 20:5; 21:36; 22:1, 4; 26:42, 43, 44, 72; 27:50.

22. See 13:1; 15:32; 17:1; 18:1; 26:2.

23. See 16:21; 17:23; 20:19; 26:61 (temple); 27:40 (temple); 27:63; 27:64.

24. Genette (*Narrative Discourse,* 48–67) identifies this technique as analepsis.

25. Genette (*Narrative Discourse,* 48) identifies the temporal distance between the "present" moment in the story and the moment

or events being referred back or forward to as *reach*, while their duration is identified as *extent*.

26. Genette (*Narrative Discourse*, 67–79) identifies this technique as prolepsis.

27. C. Lohr, "Oral Techniques in the Gospel of Matthew," *CBQ* 23 (1961) 403–35, esp. 411–13.

28. Genette, *Narrative Discourse*, 86–112, esp. 94.

29. Genette (*Narrative Discourse*, 87) warns that "a scene with dialogue has only a kind of *conventional* equality between narrative time and story time" because of factors such as the speed of the exchange, silences, other pleasantries, or omitted aspects of the conversation.

30. For healings, 4:24; 8:16–17; 9:35; 11:4–5; 12:15; 14:14, 36; 15:30.

31. Genette, *Narrative Discourse*, 113–160.

32. Anderson, *Matthew's Narrative Web*, 44.

33. Note the continual "baptizing" by John (3:6), the "following" of the crowds (4:25), the "begging" of those wanting to touch the fringe of Jesus' cloak (14:36), the repeated "sitting" and teaching in the temple (26:55).

34. S. Wittig, "Formulaic Style and the Problem of Redundancy," *Centrum* 1 (1973) 123–36; S. Suleiman, "Redundancy and the 'Readable' Text," *Poetics Today* 1 (1980) 119–42; Anderson, *Matthew's Narrative Web*, 44.

35. Chatman, *Story and Discourse*, 53.

36. Chatman, *Story and Discourse*, 53–56.

Chapter 11

Matthew's Plot: Kernels and Satellites

I propose that the audience orders the gospel's plot by identifying six kernels (major branching points) and narrative blocks.[1] I am suggesting that the audience identifies six scenes (kernels) which are central to the gospel's plot. Other scenes (satellites) fill out and expand these key scenes in six narrative blocks:

1. 1:18–25 (1:1–4:16). God initiates the story of Jesus in the conception and commissioning of Jesus to manifest God's saving presence.

2. 4:17–25 (4:17–11:1). Jesus manifests God's saving presence in his public ministry of preaching and healing.

3. 11:2–6 (11:2–16:20). Jesus' actions and preaching reveal his identity as God's commissioned agent, necessitating a response of acceptance or rejection from human beings.

4. 16:21–28 (16:21–20:34). Jesus teaches his disciples that God's purposes for him involve his death and resurrection. This event also shapes discipleship.

5. 21:1–27 (21:1–27:66). In Jerusalem Jesus conflicts with and is rejected by the religious leaders. He dies at their hands, giving his life for the forgiveness of sin.

6. 28:1–10 (28:1–20). God's saving purposes are not thwarted. God overcomes opposition, sin, and death by raising Jesus. Jesus commissions his disciples to worldwide mission promising to be with them.

THE FIRST NARRATIVE BLOCK (1:1–4:16)

The audience recognizes the first kernel, 1:18–25, because it narrates new action in the plot. God initiates this action when Mary conceives Jesus by the Holy Spirit. The opening seventeen verses place Jesus' coming in relation to God's previous dealings with human beings. As noted in chapter 8, this genealogy expresses God's point of view. History is under divine control and subject to God's sovereign will and guiding promises.[2] The coming of Jesus the Christ (1:16–17) is embedded in the larger story of God's dealings with Israel, in the stories of Abraham, of David, of exile, etc. By evoking this context and point of view, the author ensures that the audience sees Jesus' birth in terms of the sacred story. The genealogy functions as an interpretive framework which shapes the understanding of the story.[3]

This first kernel provides the "foundation for what follows,"[4] the event which cannot be deleted without damaging the narrative logic. With the action of Mary's conception of Jesus through the Holy Spirit (1:18–25), *God* (not Joseph and Mary, 1:18c, 20d, 25a) begins the story. From the outset the author presents God as the initiator of the plot. God acts to overrule human processes ("before they lived together," 1:18) and wishes (1:19–20) in the conception of Jesus. In so doing, God acts to save humans from sin and to be revealed (1:21–23) through Jesus.

From this kernel (1:18–25), the action is "filled in and elaborated" by a series of satellites through the narrative block (1:1–4:16). The birth of Jesus in 2:1a results from God's act through the Holy Spirit. The visitors from the East welcome God's action in Jesus and come to worship him (2:11). Herod the King, threatened by God's act in the birth of the "King of the Jews" (2:2), reacts violently. Jesus' family flees to Egypt guided and protected by the presence of God (2:13–23). John the Baptist prepares people for Jesus' coming (3:1–12) and announces two further aspects of Jesus' mission, to baptize with the Holy Spirit (3:11) and to judge (3:12). Jesus' baptism (3:13–17) indicates both his acceptance of the divinely commissioned role (cf. 1:21, 23) and God's confirmation of Jesus' mission and identity as God's "Son" or commissioned agent

(3:17). The temptation (4:1–11) tests Jesus' identity (4:6) and fundamental allegiance to do God's will (4:9–10). It exposes the opposing cosmic forces with a stark alternative of obedience to the devil or to God. Matthew 4:12–16 closes this first narrative block with Jesus' move to Capernaum in readiness for his public ministry.

This closing satellite (4:12–16) emphasizes the kernel's content that God commissioned Jesus to save the people from their sins (1:21) and to manifest God's presence (1:23). Jesus' presence in Capernaum fulfills Isaiah's prophecy. The use of Isa 9:1–2 in 4:15–16 invokes the notion of God acting with salvific intent to bring light into darkness. The use of the verb "has dawned" (4:16) from Isa 58:8–10 emphasizes divine presence (Isa 58:9) as a key aspect of this divine salvation. The identification of Galilee as "Galilee of the Gentiles" (4:15) underlines the universal scope of God's purposes. Matthew 1:1–4:11 presents this aspect of Jesus' mission in the title "son of Abraham" (1:1), the presence of the women in the genealogy (1:3, 5, 6), the worship of the visitors from the East (2:1–12), the journey to and revelation in Egypt (2:13–15, 19), the attack by John the Baptist on the Pharisees for claiming privileged kinship with Abraham (3:9), and the temptation of the devil (4:8–9) regarding "all the kingdoms of the world." Matthew 4:12–16 closes the first narrative block by drawing together for the audience key themes or emphases from that section.

THE SECOND NARRATIVE BLOCK (4:17–11:1)

Chatman argues that audiences recognize kernels because they advance the plot as "hinges" or "branching points." In 4:17–25 a significant development takes place, causing the audience to identify 4:17–25 as the second kernel. Jesus begins to preach and heal, calling people to encounter God's rule and presence.

The audience also identifies a scene as a kernel because it functions to "satisfy questions" arising from the narrative logic of the text (causality). Kernels are "consequences of earlier [kernels]." The beginning of Jesus' ministry in 4:17–25 answers a question raised by the first narrative block (1:1–4:16) and kernel (1:18–25). Their emphasis on Jesus' origin and identity in the initiative of God who commissions Jesus to manifest God's saving presence among human beings (1:21, 23) raises a question. How is Jesus to carry out the commission given to him? How are other human beings to encounter what Jesus manifests: God's salvation (1:21), divine presence (1:23), the gift of the Spirit (3:11), eschatological vindication (3:12), knowledge of the divine will (3:13–17), and triumph over the devil (4:1–11)?

The second kernel (4:17–25) begins to answer these questions. Jesus' teaching, preaching, and healing carry out his commission. A positive human response means access to its benefits. Jesus' call to the four fishermen to follow him presents the demand of God to repent (4:17). In those words God's forgiveness, presence, and rule are manifested and encountered. In Jesus' actions of healing and exorcism (4:24), God's triumphant presence and victory over the devil is made known (cf. 12:28). Matthew 4:17–25 thus addresses the "how?" question raised by 1:1–4:16. As a kernel it satisfies this question which arises from the previous kernel and narrative block.

The connection between 4:17 and 4:18–25 is an important aspect of this kernel. Jesus' one-line sermon in 4:17, "Repent, the reign of God is at hand," provides a programmatic statement. The audience understands this proclamation in relation to 1:1–4:16. The arrival of the "kingdom of heaven" means God's saving presence, triumph, and will.[5] But 4:18–25 provides further definition. These verses offer examples and summaries of how God's salvific will takes effect among human beings through Jesus' proclamation and healing. In 4:18–22 the call to repentance means leaving the claims and priorities of the economic and social worlds to follow Jesus (4:19), thereby acknowledging God's rule as the basis of one's identity and lifestyle.[6]

Further, the audience identifies a kernel by its function as the central event of a narrative block to which it connects other events (satellites). The emphasis on Jesus' preaching and healing activity in 4:17–25 provides the central focus for the second narrative block (to 11:1). The subsequent events work out the "choices made at the kernel."[7] Having begun his proclamation and called disciples (4:17–22), Jesus must teach them (5:1) and the crowds (7:28) about the reign of heaven (5:3, 10; 6:10, 33; 7:21) in the Sermon on the Mount (chs. 5–7). In chapters 8–9 the audience encounters healing miracles. These fill out, elaborate, complete the kernel's references (4:23–4) to Jesus' healings. As H. Held has argued,[8] these accounts are presented with an emphasis on discipleship, maintaining the focus on teaching and proclamation. The audience also finds explicit proclamation concerning the reign of heaven (8:11–12), along with demonstrations of God's presence and power to save from the created order (8:23–27), human decisions (8:18–22; 9:9), death (9:18–26), the devil (8:31–32; 9:33), and sin (9:1–7). In chapter 10 Jesus commissions the disciples, called "fishers of human beings" (lit.) in 4:19, to perform the same tasks as he does: to heal and cast out spirits (4:23–24; 10:1, 8) and proclaim the reign of heaven (4:17; 10:7). The promised Spirit helps in this task (10:20; cf. 3:11). An inclusio in 11:1 of Jesus' preaching and teaching activity ends the block. These satellites derive from the kernel, filling it in, "elaborating, completing the kernel, forming flesh on the skeleton."[9]

Finally, this second kernel raises a crucial question for the audience. It introduces the issue of response to, and recognition of, Jesus as God's commissioned agent manifesting God's saving presence. This factor of response has not been absent in the first narrative block in relation to Jesus' birth (1:1–4:16). However, 4:17–25 refocuses it in terms of Jesus' public activity and ministry. God's saving action does not take effect automatically in the human sphere but requires a response from human beings. Receiving Jesus' preaching of the presence and reign of heaven is a positive response to God's saving purposes based on a recognition of Jesus as the commissioned one. In 4:17–22 positive responses to Jesus dominate (also 7:28–29), but responses of rejection increasingly occur in the satellites (so 8:18–20, 34; 9:3, 11, 14–17, 34). The presentation in 4:17–25 of diverse responses to the divine initiative manifested in Jesus thus poses a fundamental question: will people recognize Jesus as God's commissioned agent (Christ and Son) and encounter in Jesus' preaching God's presence, forgiveness, Spirit, and victory over the devil?

In summary, the audience recognizes that 4:17–25 functions as the second kernel in the structure of the gospel. It advances the plot by indicating the beginning of Jesus' ministry. It satisfies the question that has arisen in the earlier narrative as to how Jesus will carry out his task. It stands at the center of the narrative block (4:17–11:1) where its implications are filled in and elaborated by the satellites. It raises a question that will be brought into focus by the next kernel.

THE THIRD NARRATIVE BLOCK (11:2–16:20)

The audience recognizes 11:2–6 as the third kernel because it articulates the central question confronting those who encounter Jesus' ministry as presented in 4:17–11:1: Is Jesus the one commissioned by God to carry out God's saving purposes? It also provides means whereby that question can be answered. In the works and words of Jesus' ministry his true identity can be discerned so the appropriate response can be made. The logic of the narrative flow to this point thus emerges: While 1:1–4:16 emphasizes *God's* initiative in commissioning Jesus to fulfill the divine plan, and 4:17–11:1 focuses on *how* Jesus fulfills that plan, 11:2–6 (to 16:20) elaborates the *significance* of Jesus' actions and words for revealing his identity and necessitating a response.

The beginning of the third kernel (11:2) names "the works of the Christ" (lit.; NRSV has "what the Messiah was doing") as the focus of John's inquiry. The use of this title reminds the audience of the correct answer (cf. 1:1, 17) to John's question before he asks it, "Are you the one who is to come?" (11:3). The citations from Isaiah (11:4–5) indicate how the question can be answered positively, namely by interpreting Jesus' actions. People can discern in Jesus' preaching and healing his identity as the one commissioned by God to manifest God's saving presence.[10]

Jesus' final comment in the kernel (11:6) points to the outcome of the respective responses. There is the blessing of God's favor for those who are not offended. The use of the negative verb ("who takes no offense") implies, though, the possibility of a negative response, that of taking offense. The giving of a blessing suggests a curse on those who are offended. Matthew 11:2–6 is another "branching point" for the subsequent narrative: recognizing Jesus' identity and its role in his actions.

Several satellites underline Jesus' identity and role as revealed in his "works" (11:25–30; 12:15–21; 14:22–33). In 11:25–30 Jesus addresses God with the intimate title "Father" and a title of majesty, "Lord of heaven and earth." Both titles remind the audience of Jesus' special relationship with God, the basis for God's gracious revealing work (11:26). The mixed reception of this revelation, though, comes immediately into focus. The audience knows from the context that the "wise and intelligent" from whom "these things" are hidden, are those who reject Jesus (9:1–13; 11:19–24). The "infants" to whom "these things" are revealed indicate disciples who have accepted Jesus' revelation. Jesus' revelation divides people into those who do or do not take offense.

Matthew 11:27 recalls the source of this revelation, the special relationship existing between Father and Son. God has handed over to Jesus "all things" (11:27). In the gospel's context the audience understands that these "things" refer to God's saving presence, the reign of God, revealed in Jesus' actions and teaching (1:21, 23; 4:17). As the Son, Jesus experiences ("knows") and discloses God's saving will and presence. Jesus performs the function of Lady Wisdom (Sophia, cf. 11:19) who in biblical and noncanonical writings shares close relationship with God, reveals divine mysteries, and invites people to experience God's presence.[11]

In verses 28–30 Jesus invites those who are not disciples, those burdened by sinful human existence, to experience what he is commissioned to manifest, the presence of God's saving power, reign, and will. In inviting people to take his "yoke" Jesus employs an image which the audience knows refers to the Torah (Moses' teaching). Jesus' yoke is understood to be the revelation of God's purposes and will. In making this invitation Jesus identifies himself as Torah.[12] The move from using wisdom traditions in 11:25–27 to Torah in 11:28–30 is not surprising for the audience. Torah was regarded as the abiding place of wisdom.[13] The use of both traditions emphasizes Jesus' revelatory role.

Another satellite, the walking on the water scene (14:22–33), also discloses Jesus' identity. The disciples recognize that Jesus manifests God's saving presence by doing what God does. Like God Jesus walks on the water (Job 9:8; Ps 77:16–20;

107:23–32). Like the creator Jesus sets the water in its right place, overcoming its chaos by calming the storm (Gen 1:6–10). Like God Jesus saves people from drowning (Jonah 1–2; Ps 69:1–2, 15, 16–18). To do this Jesus stretches out his hand (Matt 14:31), just as God does (Isa 41:10, 13; Ps 144:7). Jesus talks like God (Matt 14:27) saying "It is I," (lit. "I am"; Exod 3:14; Isa 43:10–13) and urging them not to fear (Isa 41:10–11, 13; Gen 15:1; Matt 1:20).

Initially the disciples respond by showing fear (14:26–27). Peter displays momentary courage in leaving the boat to walk to Jesus on the water (14:28–29). As he sees the waves, however, fear overtakes him and he cries out "Lord save me!" Jesus rebukes his doubt and "little faith" and calms the storm (14:31–32). This act brings a response of worship[14] and the confession, "Truly you are the Son of God." This confession indicates they have discerned God's saving presence in Jesus' actions and share God's point of view (2:15; 3:17).

Jesus' "works," though, bring other responses. People resist the ministries of John (11:7–18; 14:1–12) and Jesus (11:19). Though they witness Jesus' "deeds of power" (11:20, 21, 23) some cities refuse to repent (11:20–24; cf. 12:38–42). Eschatological condemnation awaits them. The religious leaders resist his healing on a Sabbath (12:9–14). After seeing a blind and mute demoniac healed, with amazement the crowds question whether Jesus might be the Son of David (Messiah/Christ). Their question begins with μήτι (mēti) signifying their expectation of a negative answer (12:22–23). The religious leaders attribute his powers to Satan (12:24). They do not recognize that Jesus' works evidence the presence of God's Spirit and the reign of God (12:28; cf. 3:11; 4:17). His hometown responds with amazement and questions the origin of his "wisdom and these deeds of power" (13:54). They speculate on his family origins (13:55–56), but they also cannot recognize the commission or reign of God. They take "offense at him" (13:57; cf. 11:6a). "Because of their unbelief" he did not "do many deeds of power there" (13:58). In other locations he continues to heal and display gracious power, but no responses are indicated (14:13–21, 34–36; 15:32–39) with the exception of those who "praise God" (15:29–31).

Other satellites indicate the division caused by Jesus' preaching. The parables, for instance, show negative and positive responses (13:1–9, 18–23), as well as their eschatological consequences (13:24–30, 36–43, 47–50). They reflect the division between the disciples who understand and those who do not understand and accept (13:10–17, 34–35, 51–52). Particularly pronounced is the conflict with the religious leaders who refuse to recognize Jesus' teaching as a revelation of God (12:1–8, 24–45; 15:1–20; 16:1–12). In 12:14 they decide "to destroy him." They "take offense" at him (15:12; cf. the kernel, 11:6).

By contrast are the "infants" (11:25). They make up the new family of Jesus which displaces birth relationships with a common commitment to do the will of God (12:46–50). They receive his teaching (13:10–17). They recognize in his acts the presence of God (14:33). The Canaanite woman (15:21–28) displays such great faith and persistence that she overcomes Jesus' reluctance to display healing mercy to a foreigner, her demon-possessed daughter. Her response foreshadows the later command to worldwide mission.

The audience recognizes that the final satellite, Jesus' conversation at Caesarea Philippi (16:13–20), concludes the narrative block by summarizing its central issue. Jesus' question in 16:13, "Who do people say that I am?" restates the issue of identity and response (cf. 11:3). Verse 14 expresses the misunderstanding and rejection of Jesus by the religious leaders (12:14), the crowds (13:13), the people of Nazareth (13:57), and Herod (14:2). Verses 15–17 show Peter repeating the correct understanding which all the disciples expressed in 14:33. Jesus affirms that the basis of this confession is the revelation of God (16:17) and gives instructions about the future community of disciples, the church (16:18–19). But he forbids the disciples from proclaiming that he is the Christ (16:20). The audience is left wondering why this is.

THE FOURTH NARRATIVE BLOCK (16:21–20:34)

The fourth kernel (16:21–28) reveals to the audience a further dimension to Jesus' identity and task. In this kernel Jesus teaches for the first time that as God's agent commissioned to manifest God's saving presence, he must be crucified in Jerusalem and be raised by God. The confession of the disciples that Jesus is the Christ, God's Son (16:16; 14:33), is not adequately understood apart from this notion of suffering and vindication. Jesus is to fulfill his divinely given role (1:21, 23) not only in preaching, teaching, and healing (4:17–11:1; 11:2–16:20), but also in death and resurrection. Peter opposes God's will, an action attributed to Satan's influence (16:23).

Further, the audience learns that Jesus' death and resurrection are linked to discipleship. His death provides the paradigm for their existence in the time until the Son of Man returns (16:24–28). As the fourth kernel, 16:21–28 introduces two significant developments in the plot, one concerning Jesus' task, the other concerning the nature of the community of disciples.

The satellites of the fourth narrative block (16:21–20:34) develop both dimensions. In the transfiguration (17:1–9) the audience sees Jesus glorified as a demonstration of his future destiny. It hears God confirm Jesus' identity and command to listen to his new instruction (17:5). Jesus restates his destiny of death and resurrection (17:12; 17:22–23; 20:17–19; 20:28), but the disciples struggle to understand (16:22–23; 17:23). They cannot heal the epileptic boy and are rebuked for their "little faith" (17:20). They cannot understand Jesus' teaching about marriage which severely curtails male power over a woman (19:3–12). They drive back the children only to be told that the reign of heaven belongs to such marginal outsiders (19:13–14; cf. 11:26). The mother of James and John seeks places of eminence for her sons only to be reminded that service not power embodies God's reign (20:24–28).

The remaining satellites instruct the disciples on the way of life that their soon-to-be crucified but risen Lord requires in the reign of heaven (18:1, 23; 19:12, 23; 20:1). Community relationships marked by humility, mutual consideration (18:1–14), and forgiveness (18:21–35) are foremost in chapter 18. Chapters 19–20 utilize the audience's knowledge of the four standard elements of the ancient world's hierarchical household structure to propose a different order for households of the reign of God. Jesus resists the unlimited power of the husband over the wife (19:3–12), calls all disciples to live the marginal existence of children (19:13–15), opposes the use of wealth as the means of defining human identity and social relationships ("the rich man" 19:23; 19:16–30), and urges all disciples to imitate Jesus' act of service (his death, 20:17–19, 28) as servants and slaves for each other (20:17–28). Only disciples who share God's perspective (20:15, 20:1–16) and have their eyes opened (20:33) can see or understand these things.[15] The satellites maintain the focus on Jesus' death and resurrection, and draw out the implications of being a disciple of the crucified Jesus.

THE FIFTH NARRATIVE BLOCK (21:1–27:66)

The audience recognizes the fifth kernel (21:1–27) from two functions. First, it moves the plot forward towards Jesus' final rejection and crucifixion. After being in Judea Jesus enters Jerusalem (21:1–12), the place where the conflict with the religious leaders will be intensified and will result in his death. This confrontation is emphasized in 21:15–16 as the "chief priests and scribes" become indignant with Jesus. In 21:18–22 Jesus curses the fruitless fig tree, a metaphor for the condemnation of the "fruitless" unrepentant leaders and of the temple. In 21:23–27 the "chief priests and elders" question Jesus' authority.

The conflict builds through the satellites. Jesus tells a series of parables against "the chief priests and Pharisees" (21:45; 21:28–22:14) who argue with him over his authority (22:15–46). He condemns them in the woes of chapter 23. Under attack, the religious leaders do not merely take counsel (12:14) to destroy Jesus. They actively seek to arrest (21:46) and entangle (22:15) him, successfully plotting and carrying out his arrest (26:4, 47) and death (27:2, 20, 41).

The opposition of the religious leaders contrasts with God's point of view. Jesus' entry is presented in 21:4–5 as fulfilling Zechariah's vision (Zech 9:9; 14:4) that at the end of the age God would stand on Mount Zion. The crowds greet him using the words of Ps 118:26. The audience knows, though, that the crowd's identification of Jesus as a prophet is inadequate in contrast to the disciples' earlier confession (21:9–11; cf. 16:14–16; 3:11). Jesus' actions in the temple—cleansing it

(21:12–13), healing (21:14), receiving and defending the praises of the lowly children (21:16)—are in accord with the scriptures (Isa 56:7; Jer 7:11; Pss Sol 17:30; Ps 8:3).[16] The religious leaders are indignant (21:15). They are caught opposing God's saving presence manifested in Jesus.

The audience also recognizes 21:1–27 as a kernel from its second function. It addresses the question raised in the previous kernel, 16:21–28. There Jesus indicated that his death and resurrection are parts of his divine commission. The audience knows that the religious leaders are the ones who would effect his death (16:21; also 17:10–12; 20:18) but does not know *how* his death would come about. This fifth kernel, 21:1–27, supplies key aspects of the answer to this question.

One part of the answer emerges from Jesus' activities in the temple and the indignant response of the religious leaders (21:15–16). Jesus' action against the moneychangers and the animal keepers (21:12–13) is an attack on sacrificial practices. The question of how Jesus is to carry out his commission to save from sin (1:21) by giving his life as a ransom (20:28) is given clearer definition in contrast to the temple sacrificial system.[17] The cursing of the fruitless fig tree in 21:18–22 demonstrates judgment on the temple and its leaders. They no longer enjoin faithful prayer. They disbar people from worship (21:12–16). The temple will figure prominently in the satellites as Jesus' prediction of its downfall (23:38; 24:1–2) becomes a charge in his trial (26:61) and a taunt in his crucifixion (27:40).

This kernel offers a further answer to the questions about how Jesus' death comes about by articulating the issue in dispute between Jesus and the religious leaders. Jesus' actions (21:1–27) confront the leaders with the question of his authority and its source ("By what authority are you doing these things, and who gave you this authority?" 21:23). The question of the source of Jesus' authority is ultimately a question of his identity, but the leaders will not recognize Jesus' identity and role as being "from heaven" (21:25). As the satellites indicate, by not believing they do not do the will of God (21:28–32). Such a refusal, later shared by the people (27:20, 25), means exclusion from the reign of God (21:33–22:14; ch. 23), a verdict that so angers the leaders that they effect Jesus' death (21:45; 26:3–4). In contrast, the disciples who do recognize Jesus' authority and identity (so too the Gentile centurion, 27:54), are exhorted to endure the future hardship (24:13, 42, 50; 25:13) with righteous acts (chs. 24–25).

The kernel has moved the plot forward toward Jesus' death by bringing Jesus to Jerusalem and into conflict with the Jewish leaders. Matthew 21:1–27 has thus set about answering the question raised by the previous kernel (16:21–28). In turn 21:1–27 raises further questions for the audience and so guides it to the final kernel (28:1–10). Is the death of Jesus the end and defeat of God's plan and action? Is it the triumph of the religious leaders? Will Jesus' prediction of being raised (16:21) come true? The final satellite of this fifth narrative block (27:62–66) begins to raise these questions with its description of the leaders' efforts (27:62) to seal the tomb against any prospect of resurrection.

THE SIXTH NARRATIVE BLOCK (28:1–20)

The audience identifies a sixth kernel in 28:1–10. Jesus' resurrection supplies the hinge, the branching point which moves the plot forward into a new future when it seems there can be no future. The death of Jesus seemed to be the end of the story. This kernel, though, indicates that his death is not the victory of the religious leaders over God's plans. It did not bring Jesus' commission to nought. Jesus' prediction of his resurrection, like that of his death (the fourth kernel, 16:21–28), is accurate.

The women come to the tomb to await Jesus' resurrection.[18] The audience observes from the earthquake (28:2), the appearance of "an angel of the Lord descending from heaven" (28:2–3), and the announcement that Jesus is risen (28:5–7) that a new divine act has occurred to secure the divine purposes and will (the first kernel 1:18–25). Satan's ultimate opposition, death, carried out through the religious leaders, cannot remove or thwart God's saving presence manifested in Jesus. Thus 28:1–10 satisfies the questions of the previous kernel and narrative block concerning the ultimacy of Jesus' death. It forms a major event which cannot be "deleted without destroying the narrative logic."[19]

This event also moves the plot forward so that the satellites of 28:11–15 and 16–20 can elaborate this kernel. The religious leaders confirm their earlier rejection of Jesus by refusing to recognize any divine presence in, or vindication of, Jesus, and so spread a story (28:13–15) different from that proclaimed by the angel (28:5–7). But the disciples who have believed (and doubted) the proclamation of resurrection (cf. 28:7, 10) obediently gather at the mountain in Galilee (28:16). They are commanded to teach and disciple all nations (28:19), being assured of the divine presence through the risen Jesus (cf 1:23; 18:20). The gospel is open-ended since the worldwide missionary activity of the disciples (and audience) will provide further satellites.

AFFECTIVE IMPACT

Since Aristotle, literary critics have addressed the emotional or affective impact of plots on readers and audiences. Chatman identifies six types of plots which cause audiences to feel variously shock, pity and fear, disgust, satisfaction.[20] The final chapter of Matthew moves through a range of emotions, with a diverse impact on the audience.

After the sadness of Jesus' death, the women's journey "to see the tomb" establishes expectation (28:1). Jesus had taught about his death and resurrection so they come to the place of his death awaiting that resurrection. The earthquake and marvelous appearance of the angel intimidate the guards (28:4). Ironically, in this place of new life they become "like dead men." The angel reassures the women (28:5), proclaims that Jesus has risen, and commissions the women to proclaim the message to the disciples (28:5–7).

The women respond obediently "with fear and great joy" (28:8). When they meet Jesus, they worship him (28:9). Like the angel, Jesus reassures them and commissions them to proclamation (28:5, 7, 10). By contrast, futile scheming and self-protecting intrigue lead the religious leaders to offer an alternative interpretation of the events (28:11–15). In the final scene (28:16–20) the disciples worship and doubt (28:17) as well as hear the commission to worldwide mission. A reassuring promise accompanies this challenge (28:20).

The prominence of these emotions offers the authorial audience several responses. Like the women and the disciples, the audience is set in the presence of the marvelous and heavenly triumph of God's saving presence and purposes. It is invited to share in these things in a life of obedience, fear, joy, and worship (28:8–9, 17–20). Through its activity of making sense of the gospel's plot, the audience learns cognitively and affectively about who Jesus is and what he requires. It gains examples of how it is to live as his followers. By accepting God's point of view, the authorial audience joins in joyful worship (even with its fears and doubts). It is reminded that other interpretations and perspectives about Jesus exist (28:4, 11–15) but is strengthened by the plot's content (examples and instruction) to resist. The authorial audience is left with a final commission to active mission and the empowering reassurance that the risen Jesus accompanies it in that task.[21] An actual audience decides whether it will take on this identity, fulfill these roles, and perform these tasks in its daily life.

NOTES

1. The substance of this chapter is drawn from my article "Kernels and Narrative Blocks: The Structure of Matthew's Gospel," *CBQ* 54 (1992) 463–81. Used by permission.

2. See Johnson, *Purpose of the Biblical Genealogies,* 139–228; Brown, *Birth of the Messiah* 66–84, esp. 66–69, 587–96 and literature cited there.

3. Chatman (*Story and Discourse,* 19–26) would call this discourse. The *story* includes the chain of events, characters, and settings-the "what" in the narrative. *Discourse* is the form of expression, the "how" which involves the specific medium and presentation of the content (structure, point of view).

4. Throughout this chapter, quotations about identifying the functions of kernels and satellites are from Chatman, *Story and Discourse,* 53–56.

5. For the "kingdom of heaven" as partially present in Matthew, see R. Farmer, "The Kingdom of God in the Gospel of Matthew," in *The Kingdom of God in 20th-Century Interpretation* (ed. W. Willis;

Peabody: Hendrickson, 1987) 119–30; Kingsbury, *Matthew: Structure, Christology, Kingdom,* 128–60. See also N. Perrin, *Jesus and the Language of the Kingdom* (Philadelphia: Fortress, 1976). Perrin's argument (*Jesus,* 16–29) that a tensive symbol has a "set of meanings which can neither be exhausted nor adequately expressed by one referent" (*Jesus,* 30), but which requires attention to the context, is assumed here. W. Carter, "Challenging by Confirming, Renewing by Repeating: The Authorial Audience's Interaction with the Parables of 'the Reign of the Heavens' in Matthew 13 as Embedded Narratives," in *1995 SBLSP* (ed. E. Lovering; Atlanta: Scholars, 1995) 399–424.

6. See Carter, "Matthean Discipleship."

7. Chatman, *Story and Discourse,* 54.

8. Held, "Matthew as Interpreter of the Miracle Stories," in *Tradition and Interpretation,* 165–299.

9. Chatman, *Story and Discourse,* 54.

10. Note that these "deeds of the Christ" (11:2) correspond to the content of chs. 8–9: the blind (8:27–30), lame (8:5–13; 9:1–7), leper (8:1–4), deaf (8:32–34), and dead (9:18–26). Frequently such marginal people comprised the poor (cf. 5:3). The disciples are instructed in 10:7–8 to preach, "heal the sick, raise the dead, cleanse lepers, cast out demons."

11. For discussion, Davies and Allison, *Matthew,* 2.271–97, who in addition to wisdom material see Mosaic connections (Exod 33:12–14) as being more important; Harrington, *Matthew,* 166–70; D. Garland, *Reading Matthew* (New York: Crossroad, 1993), 130–34; M. J. Suggs, *Wisdom, Christology and Law in Matthew's Gospel* (Cambridge: Harvard University, 1970) 71–108, 129–30; C. Deutsch, *Hidden Wisdom and the Easy Yoke: Wisdom, Torah and Discipleship in Matthew 11.25–30* (JSNTSup 18; Sheffield: JSOT, 1987). For critique, M. D. Johnson, "Reflections on a Wisdom Approach to Matthew's Christology," *CBQ* 36 (1974) 44–64.

12. Davies and Allison, *Matthew,* 2.288–89.

13. Bar 3:9, 37–4:1; Sirach 24:3–25; 2 Bar 38:4; T. Levi 13:1–9.

14. The verb has been used in 2:2, 8, 11; 8:2; 9:18. It will appear again in 15:25; 20:20; 28:9, 17.

15. For discussion of chs. 19–20, Carter, *Households and Discipleship.*

16. The healing of the blind and lame is contrary to 2 Sam 5:8.

17. Garland, *Reading Matthew,* 211–13. See the earlier rejection of sacrifice (9:13; 12:7) and of the temple (12:6), also ch. 13 below.

18. See W. Carter, " 'To See the Tomb': A Note on Matthew's Women at the Tomb (28:1)," *ExpT* (forthcoming April 1996).

19. Chatman, *Story and Discourse,* 53.

20. Chatman, *Story and Discourse*, 85. Egan, "What Is a Plot?"

21. Burridge (*What Are the Gospels?* 149–52, 214–17) identifies seven possible "authorial intentions and purposes" for ancient biography: eliciting praise, providing a model, informing, entertaining, preserving memory, instructing, providing material for debate and argument (apologetic and polemic). For gospels, he particularly emphasizes the last two, along with providing a model. I have recast his material in terms of the audience's response (given his several references to audience and readers, Burridge seems to be discussing audience impact as much as authorial intention).

Chapter 12

Settings in Matthew's Gospel

The implied author of the Gospel of Matthew locates the events of the plot in various settings. The audience discerns various significances for these settings as it interprets the gospel.

Chatman notes that settings can function in diverse ways. They can provide a "minimally necessary backdrop 'against which' [a character's] actions and passions appropriately emerge." They might symbolize the action ("Tempestuous happenings take place in tempestuous places") or contrast it. They might exist in the character's imagination or rapidly shift back and forth between the imagination and the outside world.[1] The audience may understand a setting to reinforce the point of view or emphasize particular dimensions of the character's actions or connect an event with other events.

The explicit mention of a setting causes the audience to consider its importance. Some scenes lack a designated physical setting (1:18). Some connections between settings are vague (9:9). The author does not seem to assume that the audience has or needs a detailed knowledge of the geography of Galilee or Judea.

The gospel's author draws the audience's attention to some settings and interprets their importance. For instance, five times the opening chapters use scriptural citations to show the significance of a place.

2:1, 5–6	Bethlehem	Micah 5:2; 2 Sam 5:2
2:14–15	Egypt	Hosea 11:1
2:18	Ramah	Jer 31:15
2:23	Nazareth[2]	Judg 13:7; Isa 11:1, 42:6; 49:6
4:12–16	Capernaum/Galilee	Isa 8:23–9:1

The audience uses such references to understand that God is at work in these events. It also connects the events of Jesus with God's other liberating events like the exodus (2:14–15) and exile (2:17–18). God's action in Jesus belongs to this larger context.

As the audience moves through the gospel, it builds up diverse associations around each setting. Settings create expectations. They enable the audience to interpret and unify material. They underline themes and associations. We will selectively consider several settings.

The audience knows Galilee and Jerusalem to be two important locations because they provide the general settings for much of the story. Jerusalem figures in an important though brief way in chapter 2 and provides the setting for the fifth narrative block, the death of Jesus (chs. 21–27). Galilee provides the general setting for most of Jesus' ministry up to chapter 19 and for the final scene of the gospel (28:16–20).

GALILEE OF THE GENTILES: THE FIRST FOUR NARRATIVE BLOCKS

The audience first encounters Galilee in 2:22. It is a place of safety for Joseph, Mary, and Jesus in contrast to Jerusalem and Judea ruled by Archelaus. The author claims that Jesus' settlement in Nazareth fulfills the scriptures (2:23), though it is difficult to identify which ones.[3] Jesus' subsequent move to "Capernaum by the sea" is interpreted in a scriptural citation as a move to "Galilee of the Gentiles," and as a coming of light into a place of darkness and death (4:12–16). This citation reviews Jesus' commission (1:21, 23) to manifest God's saving presence and prepares for his public ministry beginning in 4:17.

Between 4:17 and 18:35 Jesus' ministry "throughout all Galilee" (4:23) centers on Capernaum (4:13; 8:5; 9:1; 17:24) and the Sea of Galilee (8:23–27; 13:1–2; 14:13, 22–33; 15:29–31, 32–39). Jesus seems to have a house in Capernaum ("the house," 9:10, 28, 32[?]; 13:1, 36; 17:25) as does Peter (8:14). Jesus' house may well be one of the places to which people, Gentiles as well as Galileans, come to see Jesus (8:5; 9:2, 14, 18, 28; 10:1[?]; 13:36; 17:24; 18:1).

Jesus also moves around Galilee, traveling to the other side of the lake (Gadarenes 8:28; 16:5), to the cities of Chorazin and Bethsaida (11:20–21), to Gennesaret and the surrounding region (14:34–35), to the region around Magadan (Magdala), and further north to Caesarea Philippi where Peter confesses Jesus' identity (16:13–20). Several summary statements indicate visits to other unnamed cities and villages (9:35; 11:1). He also visits the coastal Phoenician towns of Tyre and Sidon (15:21; cf. 11:20–24), and his fame is known in Syria (4:24). The audience gains a sense of Jesus' widespread movement and impact through general terms such as "country" (8:28), "neighborhood" (8:34), and "region" (14:35; 15:39).

He performs a variety of acts of ministry and receives a mixed reaction. Crowds from as far afield as Gentile areas such as the Decapolis and Syria as well as Jerusalem follow him (4:24–25). Several places are specifically condemned for rejecting him including his town of residence, Capernaum (also Chorazin and Bethsaida, 11:20–24), and his hometown Nazareth (13:53–58; 2:23; 26:69, 71).

Within Galilee several settings take on particular significance.

The Sea of Galilee

The location of Jesus' town of residence, Capernaum, is noted as being "by the sea" (4:13) so the audience builds up multiple associations around the Sea of Galilee. (1) Jesus calls the first disciples beside the sea (4:18–22). The shore is a place of decision and transition for them. If they refuse his call and return to fishing, the sea becomes a place of judgment. But in following his call, "beside the sea" is a place of encountering the light of God's saving presence in the midst of death and darkness (4:15–16; 1:21, 23). (2) In 8:23–27 the sea is a place of Jesus' revelation when he manifests God's power over the chaos-threatening power of the sea (cf. Gen 1:6–10). It is also a place for disciples to learn about discipleship and faith in stormy times. (3) In 8:32 it is a place of destruction for the pigs.

(4) In 13:1 the boat is a place for Jesus to teach while the crowd stands on the beach "beside the sea" (13:1–2). As in 4:18–22, this is a place of decision and division. Jesus' teaching divides the uncomprehending crowds from the understanding disciples (13:10–17). (5) The boat is a means of retreat (14:13). But Jesus sails to a place where significant ministry occurs (14:14–21; also 9:1). (6) In 14:22–33 events on the sea again disclose Jesus' identity as the one who manifests God's saving presence. This time the disciples recognize his identity. (7) In both 15:29 and 39 the sea is a backdrop as Jesus moves to another place. (8) The audience also identifies several metaphorical uses of sea images. In 13:47 the reign of God is likened to the act of fishing. In 18:6 the sea signifies a place of destruction and judgment for causing a disciple to sin.

The Mountain

The audience knows that throughout the biblical tradition mountains are important places on which people have met God. On Mount Moriah Abraham offers Isaac as a sacrifice (Gen 22:1–14). On Mount Horeb/Sinai, Moses meets God and the covenant relationship with Israel is secured (Exod 3; 19). Elijah witnesses God's power and presence on Mounts Carmel and Horeb (1 Kings 18–19). Mount Zion is the dwelling place of God (Ps 48; 125) associated with the covenant with David (Ps 132:11–13; 78:67–72). It is the place at which God gathers Jews and Gentiles in the future and provides a new revelation of God's will (Isa 2:2–3; Zech 8:20–23; Tob 14:5–7; 4 Ezra 13).[4]

In Matthew the mountain is a place of testing, authoritative revelation, and meeting with God. (1) In 4:8 Satan takes Jesus to a mountain to tempt him with the sight of "all the kingdoms of the world." Jesus refuses to give loyalty to Satan. He will instead faithfully proclaim God's saving presence, the "kingdom of heaven" (4:17). (2) Jesus teaches his disciples the will of God on a mountain (5:1; 8:1). Many interpreters have seen an echo of the story of Moses receiving the Ten Commandments on Mount Sinai.[5] Matthew 5:1 says that Jesus "went up on the mountain." This same phrase is used of Moses (Exod 19:3; 24:12, 13, 15 18). In the preceding chapters aspects of Jesus' birth (chs. 1–2) and temptation in the wilderness (4:1–11) echo the story of Moses and the exodus. In this sequence an echo in 5:1 of Moses' reception of God's revealed will on Mount Sinai is appropriate. In these terms the mountain emphasizes Jesus' authoritative teaching of the will of God in the tradition of Moses. It also raises the question of the relationship between Jesus' teaching and that of Moses, a question which is addressed in 5:17–48. (3) In 14:23 the mountain is Jesus' place of prayer. (4) In 15:29–31 crowds encounter God's healing presence and inclusive mercy on the mountain. (5) The transfiguration occurs on a mountain (17:1, 9). The mountain is the place for a revelation and vision of Jesus in heavenly glory. In this context God expresses approval for Jesus (17:5).

(6) The risen Jesus meets his disciples on a mountain in Galilee (28:16). This final scene in the gospel pulls together important threads: (a) The disciples obey Jesus, go to the mountain (vv. 10, 16), worship him, yet doubt (v. 17). This shows their ambivalence. (b) Jesus reveals that God has given him "all authority in heaven and earth" (v. 18). (c) Jesus shares God's cosmic rule and lordship (Ps 2:7–8; 110:1; Dan 7:13–14; cf. Matt 26:64). So he commissions the disciples to a mission for all people. They are to teach Jesus' words, baptize, and make disciples. This will enable people to encounter God's saving presence (Matt 28:19; cf. 1:21, 23) and to live according to God's will as revealed and interpreted by Jesus (7:24–27; 12:46–50; 24:35). This mission lasts until the end of the age (the judgment and completion of God's purposes). Finally, the disciples are promised the presence of the risen Jesus "to the end of the age" (28:20; 1:23).[6]

(7) The mountain also appears in Jesus' teaching. It provides an image of the visibility of the disciple's witness and mission (5:14). It signifies a large, fixed object in Jesus' teaching about powerful, transforming faith (17:20; 21:21). It provides a safe place for the ninety-nine sheep (18:12) and for disciples in future difficult times (24:16).

The House

Jesus seems to have had a house in Capernaum, the place to which people came to see him. The audience knows that the household is a basic unit of society.[7] Most aspects of Jesus' ministry take place in houses. It is a place of worship (2:11), healing (8:14–15; 9:28), raising the dead (9:23), eating with outsiders as a display of inclusive mercy (9:10), conflict (9:1–8, 11), revelation of his mission (9:12–13), teaching (13:36), and rejection (13:57). The foundations of houses and their fate in a storm provide an image of the responses of people to Jesus' teaching and their destiny in the judgment (7:24–27; see also 10:12–14; 10:6, and 15:24).

The audience understands that the house is more than an inconsequential backdrop. The actions performed in houses reflect the presence of God's saving reign which pervades all of daily life. It creates a new lifestyle and social interaction. The audience also incorporates references to Jesus' new family defined not by birth relationships but by commitment to do the will of God as revealed by him (12:46–50).[8]

Synagogues

The audience identifies four features associated with synagogues. (1) They are places where Jesus preaches, teaches (4:23; 9:35; 13:54), and heals (4:23[?]; 12:9–13). (2) Here opposition and hostility greet the disciples' mission and Jesus' healing activity (10:17; 12:9–14; also 23:34). (3) Synagogues are places of hypocrisy (6:2, 5; 23:6). (4) The use of the phrase "their synagogues" (4:23; 9:35; 10:17; 12:9; 13:54; 23:34 ["your"]) separates synagogues from Jesus and his community of disciples.

Desert Places

Several significant events occur in desert places or wilderness. (1) John the Baptist's ministry takes place in the desert area around the Jordan River (3:1; cf. 11:17). The citation from Isa 40:3 in Matt 3:3 explains the significance of this location. Isaiah's words recall the people's return from exile in Babylon (539 BCE). As with the exodus, the wilderness is the place of God's saving intervention, the place of deliverance. (2) Jesus' temptation occurs in the wilderness (4:1). The shared location allies John and Jesus as agents of God's saving presence. The wilderness is a dangerous place where Satan opposes God's action. The location also invokes the experience of Israel, God's son, after the exodus. In the wilderness Israel's loyalty was tested (Exod 15:22–16:3; 17:1–7; 32–33). Jesus successfully overcomes the temptation, remaining faithful to God's commission. (3) The miracles of the feeding of the five and four thousand take place in deserted places (14:13–21; 15:32–39). These events display Jesus' compassion for the hungry crowds as well as his miraculous ability to supply those needs. The setting recalls God's feeding of the people of Israel in the wilderness under Moses' leadership (Num 11:4–9). (4) Later in Jerusalem Jesus will warn that false Christs will appear in the wilderness (24:26).

Other Settings

The audience encounters other settings in Matthew. The grain field of 12:1 contributes an essential dimension to the conflict with the religious leaders over the issue of the Sabbath. The parables in chapters 13 invoke everyday familiar settings of the fields (13:3, 24, 31, 44), business (13:45), and fishing (13:47) in proclaiming the reign of God.

JERUSALEM

Between 19:1 and 21:1 Jesus travels from Galilee through Judea and Jericho to Jerusalem. Teaching, conflicts, healing, and anticipation of his death in Jerusalem mark these settings.

The audience gains knowledge of Jerusalem early in the narrative. Jerusalem appears briefly but significantly in chapter 2. Several aspects identify it as a center of religious, social, and political power. Herod is named as king (2:1). The Magi follow the star to Jerusalem looking to worship the one "born king of the Jews" (2:3). Here Herod assembles the religious leaders to inquire about the Christ's birthplace (2:4–6).

The audience also gathers several clues that suggest danger exists in Jerusalem. Neither the king nor the religious leaders respond to Jesus' birth as the Magi do. The Magi are warned not to return to Herod (2:12). Joseph, Mary, and Jesus flee to Egypt (2:13–14). Herod launches a murderous attack on children under two years in the region of Bethlehem (2:16). When Joseph, Mary, and Jesus return from Egypt during the reign of Herod's son Archelaus, they avoid Jerusalem, going instead to Galilee (2:22). Many "go out" from the city to be baptized by John as a sign of repentance (3:2, 5–6). The religious leaders receive a negative response from John (3:7–10).

From the outset the audience learns Jerusalem is a powerful and dangerous place. It does not welcome God's saving presence, though some from Jerusalem follow Jesus (4:25). This negative presentation is underlined by the description of Jerusalem as the "holy city" in 4:5 (also 27:53). The notion of holiness designates something or someone set apart for service to God. The city is not living up to its calling.

Several further references before the fifth narrative block reinforce this negative impression. (1) In 15:1 religious leaders *from Jerusalem* accuse Jesus' disciples of breaking "the tradition of the elders." (2) In 16:21 and 20:17–18 Jesus instructs the disciples that he must suffer many things and die *in Jerusalem*. (3) The audience also notices that cities in general are presented in a bad light in the second, third, and fourth narrative blocks (4:17–18:35). Often they are places of rejection (8:33–34; 10:14, 15, 23; 11:20–24) or conflict (9:1–8).

Once Jesus enters Jerusalem in the fifth narrative block (21:1–27:66), he clashes with the religious and political leadership in places central to their power. The temple (21:12, 14, 15, 23; 24:1–2), the palace of the high priest (26:3, 57), and the governor's headquarters (27:2, 11, 27) provide these locations, along with the Mount of Olives (24:3) and the Garden of Gethsemane (26:36).

His first act is to attack business in the temple. He attempts to restore it as a place of prayer and healing, and a place which includes the marginal members of society (21:12–16). The audience recalls that in 18:19–20 prayer takes place in a community gathered in Jesus' name, knowing his presence. In the temple Jesus conflicts with the religious leaders about his authority (21:23). He tells a series of parables condemning their negative response to his role as God's emissary (21:28–22:14). Two of these parables are set in a vineyard (21:28–46), invoking the familiar image of Israel as the vineyard planted by God but whose leadership is now rejected by God (Isa 5:1–7; Matt 21:45). Jesus warns them about what happens to a city that rejects a king's invitations (22:7). He laments Jerusalem's identity as a city with a tradition of "kill[ing] the prophets and ston[ing] those who are sent to it" (23:37). He passes judgment on the temple as abandoned and "desolate" (23:38).

Jesus then leaves the temple to teach from a mountain, the Mount of Olives (24:1–3). His teaching in chapters 24–25 concerns God's future actions, especially Jesus' return, and discusses how disciples are to live in the meantime. In his trial Jesus is charged, ironically, with claiming to be able to destroy the temple and build it in three days (26:61; 27:40). At his death the temple curtain tears (27:51). Through these chapters Jesus periodically withdraws from Jerusalem to nearby Bethany (21:17, 18; 26:6, 18).

JERUSALEM AND GALILEE IN THE SIXTH NARRATIVE BLOCK (28:1–20)

Jerusalem is the place of Jesus' death and burial, the first resurrection appearances (28:1–10; 27:51–53), as well as the attempts to resist God's action (28:11–15). The angel and the risen Jesus commission the women to be the first proclaimers of the resurrection (28:7, 10). They are to instruct the disciples to meet Jesus in Galilee (cf. 26:32).

This meeting occurs on "the mountain" (28:16). The positive associations about the mountain which the audience has built up from the earlier parts of the gospel are confirmed. The mountain is a place of worship and doubt (28:17), of revelation about Jesus and his authority (28:18), and of the commission and instruction for the mission community in whom God's presence is encountered (28:19–20). Garland sees this scene recasting Israel's expectations about Mount Zion.[9] In Isa 2:2–3 the prophet presents Mount Zion as the center of the world. He expects "many peoples" to come to Mount Zion to learn God's ways. But in these verses the important mountain is not Mount Zion in Jerusalem but one in lowly Galilee. The nations do not flock to this mountain but the disciples go out from it in worldwide mission. Israel no longer has a unique place in this mission. And while it is "the word of the Lord" that goes out, it is the word of the Lord as interpreted and taught by Jesus.

HEAVEN AND EARTH

In addition to Galilee and Jerusalem, and the settings explicit to each, the audience encounters two other important settings: heaven and earth.[10] The relationship between these two entities is crucial.

Jesus begins his ministry proclaiming that the reign of the heavens is at hand (4:17). Given his commission by God in 1:21, 23 to manifest God's saving presence in a world of sin, the audience understands "the heavens" as a reference to God. This is confirmed in the prayer which Jesus teaches in the Sermon on the Mount (6:9–13).

This prayer addresses God as "Our Father in heaven" (6:9). Disciples are then to pray "your kingdom come" (6:10a). This petition recognizes heaven as the source of God's reign. It assumes that earth, the abode of the petitioners, lacks this reign and needs it. In Jesus' ministry this kingdom "has come near" (4:17). Jesus mediates its presence which is the presence of God's will.[11] Accordingly, the prayer's next petition seeks a cosmic unity in asking that God's "will be done on earth as in heaven" (6:10b). These petitions recognize heaven as the sphere in which God's presence and will are known and enacted. It models the order which is to be realized on earth. Subsequently Jesus gives the church a role in maintaining this order (16:19; 18:18–19).

The unity of heaven and earth, marked by the observance of God's will, is challenged by three things. Sin is a failure to do God's will on earth. So disciples pray for forgiveness (6:12a), and extend it to others (6:12b, 14–15). Forgiveness restores relationships with God and also social bonds. Temptation offers a second challenge (6:13a) and Satan, the evil one, provides the third (6:13b; cf. 4:1–11). Disciples pray for God to enable them to overcome these powers and so maintain the unity of heaven and earth.[12]

Jesus announces at the close of the gospel that "all authority in heaven and on earth has been given to me" (28:18). Jesus'
authority unifies these two spheres. The passive construction
"has been given" indicates God's action. In raising Jesus, God
has given to Jesus universal authority over heaven and earth.
The audience recalls "one like a son of man" (lit.) in Dan 7:14
whom "all peoples, nations and languages should serve" (cf.
25:31–45; 26:64). The risen Jesus participates in God's universal authority over heaven and earth. At this point in the story
his authority is not widely recognized. So he commissions the
community of disciples to make it known to all nations in a
mission which teaches the will of God as interpreted by Jesus.
In the future his authority will judge people according to their
response to that mission.

TEMPORAL SETTINGS

Setting includes not only spatial concerns but also the
temporal location of events. We discussed this aspect in chapter
10, particularly the audience's attentiveness to the sequence of
events, so I will make only a few brief comments here.

The audience learns in the opening verses of Matthew that
the time setting of the gospel begins with Abraham and embraces Israel's history. Jesus comes as the Messiah in this context (1:1–17). Subsequently, Jesus extends this timespan back
to the creation of humankind (19:4) and of the universe
(13:35). In this way he reveals God's unchangeable will for the
present. Past is made present in Jesus as indicated by the
Scripture citations and allusions. The present is a special stage
in history precisely because of the special commission God has
given to Jesus.

The teaching of John the Baptist (3:11–12) and of Jesus
(7:24–27) indicate that his mission is not completed in the
present. He has a task in the future judgment (also chs. 13,
24–25). God's purposes will then be completed. There is continuity and discontinuity between present and future. The future
will bring the full establishment of God's reign which will
transform heaven and earth. But that future is already breaking
into the present in Jesus' ministry (cf. 12:28) and in the doing

of God's will as taught by Jesus (12:46–50; 25:31–46). Disciples live "in between" the time of their call, the time when they first encounter God's saving presence in Jesus and the future judgment and arrival of Jesus. Disciples must give account at that time as to whether they have lived God's will revealed by Jesus (24:45–25:46). Jesus' teaching provides the standard for this judgment. Extending beyond judgment there is either "eternal punishment" or "eternal life" (25:46).

Within this huge sweep of time particular moments are highlighted. The birth of Jesus is dated to the time of King Herod (2:1). Jesus' residence in Nazareth begins when Archelaus rules in Jerusalem (2:22–23). John the Baptist dies at the hand of Herod Antipas, Herod's son (14:1–12). Jesus dies when Caiaphas is high priest (26:57) and Pilate is governor (27:2).

The audience must also interpret what is appropriate to and significant about particular times. (1) Jesus conflicts with the religious leaders over the observance of the Sabbath (12:1–14). At issue is the authority to speak on God's behalf about how this day is to be used. (2) Times of sleep are important as opportunities for divine revelations and guidance through dreams (1:20; 2:12, 13, 19, 22). (3) Times of sleep, though, can be hindrances. The disciples are rebuked for sleeping instead of praying with Jesus (26:36–46). (4) The return of Jesus is a time for alertness and faithful watching, not sleep (24:42–44; 25:1–13). Disciples must be able to interpret the "signs of the times" (24:3), something Jesus has earlier condemned the religious leaders for not being able to do. To "interpret the signs of the times" means knowing the appropriate way to live. (5) The present is not the time to decide who belongs in the church and who does not. That task belongs to God, and will be carried out at the future judgment (13:24–30, 36–43, 47–50). (6) There is a time for initial ministry to Israel (10:6; 15:24) although it is an "evil and adulterous generation" (12:39; 16:4; 11:16–19; 23:34–36). The mission is broadened to all people in the time after the resurrection (28:19–20).

(7) Time determines the function of the Law and Prophets. Until the coming of John the Baptist the Law and Prophets prophesied and bore witness to God's will (11:13). Now that Jesus has come the Law and Prophets instruct disciples how to

live a life of love for God, others, and self (5:17–48; 22:36–40). Jesus does not abolish this tradition but instructs about its right interpretation and observance (5:17–20).[13] (8) Jesus' coming means that demons, emissaries of Satan, are overcome by the reign of God "before the time" of judgment (8:29).

The audience must interpret settings of place and time. Sometimes settings provide little more than background or sequence. But in other instances the place or the time may be central to the scene. They may symbolize the essence of the scene, or draw attention to crucial aspects of it. The audience utilizes clues about setting to interact with and interpret the text.

NOTES

1. Chatman, *Story and Discourse,* 138–45.

2. For discussion see the commentaries and Brown, *Birth of the Messiah,* 209–213, 218–19, 617.

3. Brown, *Birth of the Messiah,* 208–13; Davies and Allison, *Matthew,* 1.276–81.

4. Donaldson, *Jesus on the Mountain,* 35–83.

5. Davies and Allison, *Matthew,* 1.423–24, 192–95.

6. Garland, *Reading Matthew,* 265–69.

7. See M. Crosby, *House of Disciples: Church, Economics and Justice* (Maryknoll: Orbis, 1988); Carter, *Households and Discipleship,* 19–22.

8. Barton, *Discipleship and Family Ties,* 125–219.

9. Garland, *Reading Matthew,* 267–68; Donaldson, *Jesus on the Mountain,* 170–90.

10. K. Syreeni, "Between Heaven and Earth: On the Structure of Matthew's Symbolic Universe," *JSNT* 40 (1990) 3–13.

11. See further Carter, "Challenging by Confirming," 404–16.

12. W. Carter, "Recalling the Lord's Prayer: The Authorial Audience and Matthew's Prayer as Familiar Liturgical Experience," *CBQ* 57 (1995) 514–30.

13. Meier, *Law and History,* 82–89; idem, *Vision of Matthew,* 224–28.

Chapter 13

Characters: Jesus—Agent of God's Saving Presence

The author names Jesus in the gospel's opening verse. This is the first indication for the audience that he is the main character in the unfolding of the plot. Subsequently, the audience will learn that he is also the main representative of God's point of view.

CONSTRUCTION OF CHARACTERS

Just as the authorial audience works with clues in the text to construct a consistent point of view, formulate a coherent plot, and interpret settings, it does the same in constructing characters. The audience identifies traits or characteristics from a character's actions, words, relationships with other characters, and settings. Traits are consistent ways of being and doing which distinguish one character from another.[1] In presenting characters in this gospel, the author does more showing than telling but occasionally provides explicit comments or insight.

The authorial audience must combine these traits into a consistent pattern or picture of the character. As it moves through the text, it connects different elements, overturns, expands, or confirms previous conclusions, adds new insights, fills in gaps, resolves tensions or contradictions, leaves ambiguities open for further information. The audience builds the characters through the sequence of the gospel. It accumulates traits and integrates them to form a coherent character.[2]

Expectations

An audience brings certain expectations about characters to a text. Television viewers have different expectations of the characters in a sitcom than those in a murder mystery or psychological thriller. Likewise, the audience of an ancient biography carries expectations about its characters. We can identify three aspects of the expectations or knowledge assumed of the authorial audience.

(1) Readers of modern biographies and novels expect an author to provide insight into and analysis of the inner motivations and workings of characters. They expect to see characters develop and grow psychologically. Audiences of ancient biographies, however, generally do not expect an author to portray character development or offer internal or psychological analysis.[3]

(2) Audiences of ancient biography tend to evaluate characters morally as possessing good or bad qualities and as meriting praise or blame. There is some interest in how these qualities are formed (nature, upbringing and education, outside influences). There is also some recognition that people are responsible for their character and that character can change. The dominant approach, though, regards character as relatively fixed and stable.[4]

As a result there is a tendency to see a person's career and character in terms of a central trait or core of features. Sometimes attention focuses on the person's mature stage. This is the time when their major contributions to society were made and their character most evident. Sometimes this central trait or contribution is understood to extend over their whole lives.[5]

(3) The audience expects the author to portray character through actions, words, and relationships. It deduces the traits of the character from anecdotes, sayings, and comparisons with other characters (*synkrisis*). Sometimes the author will offer direct analysis by naming the trait to be admired or censored and by imputing thoughts or motives. Such presentations can lead to ideal or stereotypical characters with exaggerated description of positive or negative qualities.[6]

Burridge has demonstrated the applicability of these conventions and expectations to the gospels. The authorial audience is assumed to not be interested in Jesus' psychological processes, though the author of Matthew provides a few statements about his motivations, feelings, and inner knowledge. It is also assumed to have little interest in Jesus' childhood, upbringing, and youth. The emphasis falls on his adult life.

From the outset, the audience discovers the central trait which will be embodied in the subsequent public actions and teachings. Jesus is commissioned by God to manifest God's saving presence (1:21, 23). He embodies faithfulness to this task revealing God's presence and will through his words and actions. The audience deduces his character from his actions, words, and relationships.

I have suggested above that the audience builds its understanding of Jesus' character as it moves through the sequence of the story. While paying as much attention as possible to sequence and context, I will identify some of the ways in which the audience builds his character as well as the traits which the audience integrates to form a coherent character. In the rest of this chapter we will consider several conventions the author employs: terms or names used for Jesus, his actions and words, comparisons, and internal disclosures.[7]

NAMES OF ADDRESS FOR JESUS

Jesus

If the audience does not know in 1:1 that "Jesus" is the Greek form of the Hebrew name "Joshua" which means "God saves," it learns this meaning in 1:21. An angel of the Lord instructs Joseph to name Mary's baby Jesus, "for he will save his people from their sins." Jesus' naming is a divine commissioning. Two verses later another aspect is added to it. Jesus is Emmanuel, commissioned to manifest God's presence "with us." His name embodies his mission. Thereafter, as the audience encounters the name Jesus some 150 times, it recalls this statement of Jesus' role and observes how and if Jesus carries out the task. Around this name cluster the traits which the audience identifies through the narrative.

Characters in the gospel refer to or address Jesus by other names or terms. The audience must deduce what these forms of address say about Jesus and, at times, about those using them. The author does not stop to define these forms of address. The audience must supply meaning from their existing knowledge and from its use in the narrative (who uses it? in what circumstances?).[8]

The gospel opens with the implied author employing four names or terms for Jesus: "Jesus," "Christ" or "Messiah,"[9] "Son of David," and "Son of Abraham" (1:1). We have discussed the latter two in chapter 8; here we will look at "Christ."[10]

Christ (Messiah)

It is difficult to establish what the audience is assumed to understand when hearing the term "Christ." It is used in diverse ways in the audience's cultural world.[11]

At its root the term refers to someone commissioned by God to a task on God's behalf. Anointing symbolizes this commissioning. In the scriptures kings in the Davidic line were "anointed" or commissioned by God to rule God's people on God's behalf.[12] Priests were also set apart or "anointed" to lead the people in worship and to represent God (Lev 4:3, 5, 16). The Persian King Cyrus was called "anointed" because God commissioned him to return the exiles home from Babylon in 539 BCE (Isa 45:1, cf. 44:28–45:4).

Moreover, the term is used by various writers to refer to a figure whom God would send in the future. In Dan 9:25 an "anointed prince" will rebuild Jerusalem. The *Psalms of Solomon* (first century BCE) envisage a future ideal (human) king as God's anointed (Pss Sol 17:32; 18:5, 7; cf. 2 Sam 7). This king will expel the enemies (the Roman armies) by "the word of his mouth" (17:24) and restore God's righteous reign. Both the Qumran community (the Dead Sea Scrolls)[13] and the *Testaments of the 12 Patriarchs* (T. Sim 7:2; T. Jos 19:6) anticipate priestly and kingly Messiahs. 1 Enoch 37–71 identifies the anointed one or Messiah as a heavenly figure who will execute judgment on the day of judgment and vindicate the righteous

(1 En 48:10; 52:4). Fourth Ezra, written about the same time as Matthew, has several images of messiahs. One messiah (whose function is unclear) lives for four hundred years. His death is followed by seven days' silence before the new age of judgment, resurrection, and incorruptibility begins (7:28). Another messiah, a descendant of David, overthrows the wicked (Roman) rulers and makes the rest of the people joyful until the judgment (12:32). It should also be noted that many Jewish texts from the first century do not refer to a messiah at all.

Clearly the audience cannot supply a single, well-established understanding of "Messiah" or "anointed one" when it encounters the term "Christ" in Matt 1:1.[14] It must formulate that meaning from the ways in which the term is used throughout the narrative. The term in 1:1, "Son of David," guides the audience into an expectation of God's future ideal king from the line of David. This expectation is confirmed by the repetition of the term "Christ" in 1:16, 17, 18 and by the genealogy's emphasis on David (1:6–17). In 1:20 the angel addresses Joseph as "Son of David" further reinforcing the connection. The audience makes further connections with the Davidic kingly line in 2:2 when the Magi refer to Jesus as "King of the Jews."[15] Just two verses later in 2:4, King Herod inquires about the birthplace of "the Messiah." "King of the Jews" (2:2) and "Messiah" (2:4) are equivalent designations for Jesus. The modified citation of Micah 5:2 in 2:6 provides some general information about the King's/Christ's task expressed in 1:21, 23: He will shepherd or rule Israel on God's behalf.

The audience, though, identifies further clues which reshape the messianic expectation of a king in the line of David. In 1:1 "Son of David" is followed by "Son of Abraham." This sequence warns the audience against understanding the "Christ's" role as being restricted only to Israel. Abraham is the one in whom all the families of the earth are blessed (Gen 12:1–3). John the Baptist also warns the religious leaders against understanding descent from Abraham as an exclusive Jewish privilege (3:9).

Matthew 1:21, 23 makes the Christ's mission explicit. It does not consist of the use of military power or the exercise of political power in the place of Herod or the Romans. He is to save from sin and manifest God's presence. It is this reign of God over sin, death, and Satan that Jesus the Christ proclaims in 4:17 (the reign/kingdom of the heavens) and throughout his life.

Disciples are, with God's help (16:17), able to recognize and confess Jesus' identity from his actions and teaching (11:2; 16:16). They are, though, forbidden from proclaiming it until they are able to understand two things (16:20; 28:18–20): (1) Suffering and death are the means by which Jesus carries out God's commission to manifest God's saving presence (16:21). The use of the terms "Christ" (26:63, 68; 27:17, 22) and "King of the Jews" (27:11, 22, 29, 37) in the passion narrative associates them with suffering and misunderstanding (cf. 24:5, 23, 24), death and resurrection. (2) Jesus' messiahship or kingship also involves sharing in God's cosmic rule after his resurrection (28:18–20).

Non-disciples do not recognize this sort of messiahship. The term "Christ" is absent from the report of what "people" say about Jesus' identity (16:13–14). Jesus has to warn about the appearance of "false messiahs," especially those who perform miraculous deeds of power but do not suffer, or who do not return from heaven as he will (24:5, 23, 24). When the religious leaders use the term, they do so either as a question (26:63) or to mock (26:68). Nor do the crowds understand the inadequacy of the term "Son of David." In using "Son of David" and "prophet" when referring to Jesus they betray their lack of understanding (21:9, 11). The strange conversation between Jesus and the religious leaders in 22:41–46 demonstrates to the audience the limits of the Davidic tradition and of the religious leaders' comprehension.

Several traits emerge in the use of these terms. Jesus redefines Israel's expectations of a Davidic king causing many not to accept that he is God's commissioned agent. But disciples recognize that his God-given commission or "anointing" to manifest God's saving presence overcomes sin, includes Jew and Gentile, and extends over all cosmic forces in his resurrection and return.

Son of God

The audience encounters another term in the first narrative block (1:1–4:16), the term "my Son" (2:15), "my beloved Son" (3:17), the "Son of God" (4:3, 6). Future audiences, shaped by the creeds which emerged from the fourth and fifth century debates, understand this term as indicating Jesus' divinity. But the authorial audience brings different and diverse understandings to the text. As with the term "Christ," it must seek clarification from the narrative.[16]

In Jewish traditions "Son of God" could indicate a variety of roles and relationships with God. (1) The king, called to rule as God's agent, is addressed as God's Son (Ps 2:7). (2) The people of Israel in covenant relationship with God, chosen by God and bound to faithful obedience of God's will, are called "sons" or children of God (Hos 11:1). (3) So too are angels, "heavenly beings" who do God's will (Job 38:7). (4) The righteous individual who knows God, opposes the ways of wickedness, and abides by the laws of the covenant is called God's son (Wis 2:18). Rather than referring to a divine nature, the audience understands the term to indicate special relationships with God marked by loyalty to God's will. (5) In the Hellenistic world miracle workers, teachers, and kings were called sons of God.

The audience learns through the narrative that Jesus is God's Son in that he faithfully carries out the role God has called him to perform. He manifests God's saving presence or reign (1:21, 23; 4:17). The citation of Hos 11:1 in 2:15 invokes the exodus under Moses from slavery in Egypt to underline the liberating role Jesus will fulfill in covenant relationship with God. God expresses pleasure at Jesus' faithful commitment to this task in his baptism (3:17).

God's statement ("This is my Son, the Beloved, with whom I am well pleased") combines three scripture references to sketch important aspects of Jesus' sonship. In referring to Jesus as "my Son" God cites Ps 2:7 placing Jesus in the line of Davidic kings. Jesus is to be an agent of God's will and justice. God uses the word "beloved" when ordering Abraham to sacrifice his son Isaac (Gen 22:2). Invoking this story enables the audience to appreciate the intimate relationship between God and Jesus. It also links Jesus' sonship with the significance of Abraham in blessing all people, underlines the extent of obedience required by God, and connects Jesus' sonship with suffering. The last part of the verse derives from Isa 42:1 and 44:2, references to the suffering servant Israel, the covenant people, whom God delivers, blesses, and commissions to bear witness to the nations. Jesus' sonship comprises similar roles in a relationship of favor with God. Jesus' faithfulness to these roles is tested by Satan. As God's Son, Jesus remains loyal to God's commission (4:3, 6).

Through the subsequent narrative the audience learns: (1) Jesus' sonship is known by demons. They recognize him as the agent of God's judgment (8:29; cf. 3:12; 12:28). (2) Jesus' sonship involves the task of revealing God's purposes and saving presence. This task is grounded in Jesus' special and mutual intimate relationship with God (11:27). (3) His sonship is confessed by disciples who recognize the presence of God in Jesus' words and actions. This presence overcomes chaos and evil symbolized by the sea (14:33). (4) It is a synonym of "Christ" (16:16; cf. 26:63) and "Son of Man" (16:13). It can only be confessed by disciples as a result of God's revelation (16:17). (5) It is reinforced by God at the transfiguration in a repetition of the words of the baptismal scene (17:5). However, in the context of Jesus' disclosure that he must die (16:21), God's words emphasize to the disciples that Jesus' faithfulness to the divine will involves his suffering. (6) It is located in the context of salvation history (21:33–44, esp. 21:38). In this parable God (the landowner, 21:33) has made frequent efforts to have Israel (the vineyard) live according to the divine will. But Israel's leaders have rejected God's messengers (prophets, 21:34, 36) and Son (21:37, 38). Jesus' sonship involves his rejection and his death, but that rejection opens up the way for "other tenants" (21:41), the church, consisting of both Jews and Gentiles, to know God's favor and make it known to the vineyard, Israel. (7) Jesus' sonship is mocked by opponents of God's purposes (26:63; 27:40, 43). Ironically, in putting him to death, they carry out God's will. They ensure that in the resurrection and at his return as the eschatological judge ("Son of Man," 26:64) he will triumph over sin and death thus completing God's commission to "save people from their sins" (1:21). (8) It is recognized by a Gentile centurion (27:54, after 51–53) in Jesus' obedient death and in the eschatological sign of the raising of the saints.[17] (9) It involves his divinely given authority which extends throughout "heaven and on earth" (cf. Dan 7:14).

Disciples make known this authority and sonship in a universal mission (28:18–20).

The audience learns that "Son of God" not only discloses important dimensions of Jesus' role and relationship with God. It also indicates aspects of the identity of disciples. By "following" Jesus (4:18–22), by "welcoming" the presence of the reign of heaven (10:7, 40), by "believing" in Jesus (18:5), disciples become "sons" or "children" of God (5:9, 45; 13:38). They too bear witness to the saving presence and reign of God (cf. 10:7; 28:18–20). Disciples are brothers of Jesus (12:50; 23:8; 28:10). God is their father (5:16; 6:1, 4, 6, 8, 9, 14, 15, 18, etc.). Jesus' sonship, his special relationship with and task on behalf of God, provides the basis for disciples to encounter God's presence and to participate in the reign of God and God's saving work.

Several traits emerge with the term Son of God: Jesus' intimate and favored relationship with God, his faithfulness, obedience, power, revelatory actions, suffering, rejection, death, authority, and significance for Jew and Gentile.

Son of Man

Jesus uses this strange term some thirty times beginning at 8:20.[18] It is not clear what knowledge is assumed of the authorial audience. In the scriptures the term can refer to a human being,[19] or to a heavenly figure (Dan 7:13). In 1 Enoch this heavenly figure carries out the final judgment and is called "Christ" (1 En 46:3, 4). The audience engages the narrative to learn about Jesus as Son of Man.

Five of the first six uses of the term in the second and third narrative blocks (4:17–16:20) refer to Jesus' everyday life: his itinerancy and humble existence (8:20), his authority to forgive sin in accord with his divine commission (9:6; cf. 1:21), his opponents' misunderstanding of his compassion for those usually deemed beyond God's loving presence (11:19), his authority over religious traditions (12:8) and over evil spirits (12:32). Two more references complete statements about his authoritative action. In 13:37–38 he is active in "the world" proclaiming the "good news of the kingdom" (4:23; 9:35). In 16:13 he refers to himself as Son of Man in asking about people's reactions to him.

A cluster of references appears especially in the fourth narrative block (16:21–20:34) in relation to his death and resurrection (12:40; 17:9, 12, 22; 20:18, 28; 26:2). The audience learns of his betrayal, suffering, and death at the hands of religious leaders, as well as his resurrection. This giving of his life is a ransom, a means of serving and liberating "many" (20:28).

A third group of Son of Man sayings concerns Jesus' future advent, his *parousia*. This is the most numerous group, appearing in chapters 24–26. Jesus' imminent return (24:27) promotes urgency in the disciples' mission task (10:23). That return will be the occasion for a revelation of his power and glory (24:30; 25:31; 26:64). For some it will be an unpleasant surprise (24:37–39). The audience is warned to be ready by persevering faithfully (24:44). He will exercise judgment (16:27–28; 25:31), destroying evil doers (13:41) and vindicating those who have persevered to the end (19:28).

"Son of Man" covers every aspect of Jesus' history from his lowly human existence through his authoritative ministry carrying out God's commission, his rejection and death, his resurrection and exaltation, parousia and judgment, and dominion over all (26:64). Evident is the vast extent and powerful authority of his present and future roles in relation to sin (forgiveness) and judgment. A number of the references appear in polemical contexts as Jesus disputes and conflicts with his opponents (8:20; 9:6; 11:19; 12:8, 32, 40; 26:24, 64). Even in contexts where he is addressing his disciples he uses the term Son of Man in relation to negative or inadequate reactions of people to him (16:13, 21; 17:12, 22; 24:37–39).

From these observations emerges the central trait of Jesus as the Son of Man. The term denotes Jesus' relationship to the world. This conclusion partly explains why the term does not appear until 8:20 in the context of Jesus' public ministry. He is active in mission to the world in struggle with Satan (13:37–38), offering it forgiveness (9:6), divine presence (11:19), and his own life as its ransom (20:28). He relates to outsiders and enemies, suffers and dies as Son of Man. He is the cosmic judge, carrying out judgment of all the nations (25:31–32) in the sight of all (24:30).[20] "Son of Man" underlines his interaction with, frequent rejection by, and judgment of the world.

Lord

The audience finds that "Lord"[21] is used to address or refer to people in authority (Pilate, "sir," 27:63)[22] and to God.[23] Most often it is a term for Jesus. The audience notices it used particularly by people who approach Jesus recognizing his authority as the one commissioned to manifest God's saving presence and reign. In these instances "Lord" usually appears as a form of address (the vocative case).[24] Accompanying verbs such as "came," "approach"[25] and "kneel"[26] indicate the recognition of his authority. So too does the nature of their requests: for healing and mercy,[27] for saving,[28] and for instruction or direction.[29]

As Lord, Jesus does what he is authorized by God to do; to reveal God's saving presence, reign, and will. He heals,[30] casts out demons,[31] saves from nature,[32] and returns as judge of the world.[33] The term underlines his role to direct disciples (8:21; 17:4), to predict future betrayal (26:22), and to give commands (21:3).[34]

It also appears in teaching contexts. As Lord of the Sabbath he declares God's will (12:8), making an authoritative announcement concerning "right" interpretation of the tradition and scriptures (Exod 20:8–11; 1 Sam 21:1–16; Hos 6:6). Tradition and cultic practice are to be subjected to mercy (12:1, the hungry disciples). One who is greater than David and the temple, commissioned by God as Lord to reveal God's will, is able to exercise such authority.[35] Peter's question to the "Lord" about forgiveness provides the context for instruction on the forgiveness of sin (18:21).

The audience identifies several traits from the use of this term: Jesus' authority, the special relationship between Jesus and disciples, his mercy, his power over nature, disease, tradition and death, and his teaching role with disciples.

These various names and terms expand the name "Jesus." Generally, they highlight different aspects of Jesus' relationships and roles. "Christ" primarily denotes Jesus in relation to his divinely commissioned task. "Son of David" underlines his mission to Israel and his healing powers. "Son of God" sets him in relation to God. "Son of Man" denotes Jesus in relation to the world while "Lord" emphasizes his relation to disciples.

Inadequate Names

Other terms are used for Jesus, but the audience discerns from the context that these are inadequate designations. While it is accurate and positive to speak of Jeremiah (2:17), Isaiah (3:3), or John (11:9; 14:5; 21:26) as prophets, the term is not adequate for Jesus. The audience learns this in several ways. It is used by the crowds (16:14; 21:11, 46), those amazed by Jesus but not placing faith in him,[36] in contexts which indicate better understandings.[37] Moreover, several major differences exist between Jesus and the prophets. The fulfillment citations (e.g., 8:17: "This was to fulfill what had been spoken through the prophet")[38] indicate that prophets bear witness to the future life and acts of Jesus, the one who brings into being what they spoke about (cf. 13:17). Further, Jesus interprets the teaching of the prophets (5:17–20; 7:12; 22:37–40). In these respects Jesus is greater than, though in continuity with, the line of prophets.

Likewise, to address Jesus as "teacher" reveals an inadequate understanding. Religious leaders and non-disciples use this term for Jesus (8:19; 9:11; 12:38; 17:24; 19:16; 22:15–16, 23–24, 36).[39] The title "rabbi" is similar to this. Among the disciples only Judas calls Jesus "rabbi" (26:25, 49). Jesus forbids disciples to use it of each other, ensuring their distinction from the religious leaders and synagogue practice (23:2–8). Jesus' opponents call him "Beelzebul" (10:25), a name for Satan. They charge him with casting out demons by the prince of demons (9:34; 12:24). This charge, as Jesus points out, not only does not make sense (12:25–27) but is unforgivable blasphemy. It attributes the work of God's Spirit and presence of God's reign to Satan (12:28–32).[40]

No Names

Some scenes use no names or titles for Jesus, yet they make vital contributions to building his character. In part of the second kernel (4:18–22) in which Jesus calls the first disciples, no name, not even "Jesus," appears. The audience knows from 4:17 that the scene involves Jesus. It witnesses Jesus' authority to invade, disrupt, and reorient human existence and to call people to encounter the saving presence and reign of God. This scene, among other things, establishes Jesus' authority as an important trait. The audience will see his authority demonstrated again in the subsequent narrative as Jesus teaches with authority (7:29), has authority to forgive sin (9:6, 8), and gives disciples authority to cast out spirits and heal diseases (10:1; cf. 4:19, "fish for people"). God gives Jesus "all authority in heaven and on earth" (28:18). The religious leaders refuse to recognize his God-given authority (21:23, 24, 27).

ACTIONS AND WORDS

Through the gospel Jesus performs a wide range of actions. He calls disciples, teaches, conflicts with opponents, heals, casts out demons, overcomes nature, feeds hungry people, upsets religious leaders, forgives, offers hope and new life, suffers, prays, dies, and is resurrected. Throughout he reveals his mercy, power, concern for the outsider and the marginalized, and his unwavering commitment to God's will or justice.

One way in which the audience connects these diverse actions together is by relating them to the commission which God, through the angel, declares for Jesus at his conception (the first kernel, 1:18–25). Jesus is to save from sin and as Emmanuel he is to manifest God's saving presence (1:21, 23). Jesus' actions carry out this purpose.

The audience is reminded of this perspective throughout the narrative. In 8:17 the author uses part of the suffering servant passages from Isa 53:4 ("He took our infirmities and bore our diseases") to interpret Jesus' healings. Jesus displays the identity of the suffering servant in his actions. In his healings Jesus

> manifests his mercy, obedience and lowliness—the lowliness of the Servant who does not lose his might, but uses it not for himself, but in the service of the rejected (the leper, 8:1–4), the despised (the Gentile centurion's servant, 8:5–13) and the sick (Peter's mother-in-law and others, 8:14–16).[41]

More than this, the ancient world's view that sickness was punishment for sin (cf. John 9:2) may also indicate to the audience that healings are the taking away of sin. The combining of healing and forgiveness in 9:1–8 suggests this view. So too does the use of the verb "he will save," used for Jesus' commission in 1:21, to refer to healing or being "made well" (cf. 9:21, 22).

The author uses the verb "save" in a number of other contexts, reminding the audience of Jesus' purpose. Jesus "saves" disciples when the stormy waters, a symbol of the powers of chaos opposing God's created order, threaten to overwhelm them (8:25; 14:30; cf. Gen 1:6–10). Being "saved" has a present and future dimension. He instructs them that they, like him, must lose their lives (16:25; 19:25) and remain faithful to the end in order to be saved (10:22; 24:13, 22). The use of the verb on the lips of those mocking the crucified Jesus (27:40, 42 [2x], 49) enables the audience to connect the cross with Jesus' mission.

In 11:2–6 the implied author interprets the deeds of the Christ, his ministry since 4:17,[42] by using Isa 35:5–6. Jesus' healing and preaching actions enact God's saving will and manifest God's presence in fulfillment of Isaiah's hope (Isa 35:5–6). At 12:18–21 the author again uses a suffering servant passage (Isa 42:1–4) to interpret Jesus' actions. Jesus is God's chosen, beloved, and favored servant (cf. 3:15; 17:5). He gently proclaims God's saving presence ("justice") to all, including Gentiles. The quotation from Isaiah 42 reminds the audience that the driving power for Jesus' ministry is God's Spirit (1:18, 20; 3:12), a feature of the promised new age (Joel 2:28). It also presents

> the comprehensive sense of the saving work of Jesus directed towards the weak, the lost and the broken, those who are characterized elsewhere by Matthew alone as "harassed and helpless" (9:36) and "those who labor and are heavy laden (11:28). The vocation of the Servant, the goal of his activity, is the victorious establishment and carrying forward of God's justice, a justice which graciously and savingly seeks out and intervenes on behalf of the weak, the despised, the rejected and helpless, on behalf of their dignity and their rights. For this reason, the Gentiles, or the nations, will have cause to hope in his name, to hope for just judgment (cf. 21:31–46) and for a share in his saving mission (cf. 21:43; 24:14; 26:18–20).[43]

Several verses later at 12:28, in dispute with the religious leaders, Jesus interprets his casting out of demons as revealing the presence of God's reign and Spirit. In 13:10–17 he tells his disciples that the divisive impact of his teaching is in accord with Isa 6:9. He places his conflict with and rejection by the religious leaders in the context of the history of God's saving action (21:28–32, 33–45). In 22:37–40 he summarizes the heart of the law, Israel's teaching tradition. It consists of two commands, love for God and love for neighbor. Since he has already claimed to fulfill this tradition (5:17), his summary provides an interpretive key by which to understand his own life and actions. All of these actions manifest Jesus' identity as the one who faithfully and lovingly carries out God's saving will and purposes.

Jesus' teachings underline and reveal his compassion for the broken and needy and their inclusion in God's blessing (5:3–9); his awareness of and need to be resolute in opposition (5:10–12); his faithfulness to the traditions of the law and the prophets (5:17–48; cf. 8:1–4); his concern for reconciliation, purity, integrity, and inclusive love in relationships (5:21–48); and his concern for mission (10:5–42). But they also reveal his anger against disciples (23:1) who display false religious practice (6:1–18; 23), false motivation (23:3–12), neglect of the central matters of "justice and mercy and faith" (23:23), double standards and a lack of wholeness or integrity (23:25–28), being closed to God's initiative and purposes (23:29–39).

COMPARISONS (SYNKRISIS)

The author guides the audience to make comparisons between Jesus and other characters. This technique of *synkrisis* is a "form of speech which contrasts the better and the worse."[44] In each comparison Jesus is clearly the better, but his greatness is underlined not by denigrating the other character but by asserting Jesus' superiority to important and worthy characters.

This is most evident in chapter 12 where the audience encounters three comparisons. Jesus is: (1) greater than the temple (12:6); (2) greater than Jonah (12:40–41); (3) greater than Solomon (12:42).

The claim to be greater than the temple appears in the context of Jesus justifying his disciples' actions on the Sabbath by pointing to the actions of David and the priests. If their actions are "guiltless," so are Jesus' for "something greater than the temple is here." The claim to be greater than Jonah (12:40–41) is made in response to the religious leaders' request for a sign to authenticate Jesus' claims. Since he has already produced many such signs (cf. 11:2–6), Jesus points to the forthcoming sign of his resurrection. The comparison with Jonah claims a similarity between Jesus' resurrection and Jonah's "three days and nights in the belly of the sea monster" (12:40). Jesus and Jonah are allies as God's agents. But whereas Gentile Nineveh repented at Jonah's preaching and will be vindicated in the judgment, most of Israel has not so responded to Jesus (12:41). Since he is greater than Jonah, their lack of responsiveness and destiny are proportionally worse.

The comparison between Israel's rejection of Jesus and the accepting response of the Gentile queen of Sheba (1 Kings 10:1–13) to Solomon (12:42) makes a similar point. Jesus and Solomon are linked in that both are kings and are associated with wisdom. But Jesus is greater. He shares God's reign (12:28) and embodies wisdom (11:28–30).

Other comparisons are not as explicit. The audience notices that Jesus, John the Baptist, and the disciples proclaim the nearness of God's reign (3:2; 4:17; 10:7). They suffer rejection, even death, in their similar missions (10:16–31; 11:7–19; 14:1–2; 27:50). Both John and Jesus condemn the religious leaders as a "brood of vipers" (3:7; 12:34). Both are buried by their disciples (14:12; 27:57–61). The disciples, like Jesus, perform miracles (10:8) and relate to God as God's "children" (5:9), yet Jesus' sonship, like his death, has some unique dimensions (cf. 11:25–30).

Other comparisons rely on the audience's knowledge outside the narrative. For instance, chapter 2 cites Hos 11:1 and its reference to Egypt (2:15). Several other clues recall aspects of the story of Moses and the exodus of the people from Egypt: (1) The presence of Magi (astrologers) and the star (Matt 2:1–12; cf. Exod 1:15); (2) Herod's attack on the infant boys (Matt 2:16–18; cf. Exod 1:22); (3) The infant Jesus lives in the shadow of death but is protected (Matt 2:13–23; cf. Exod

2:1–10); (4) Jesus' departure from Bethlehem because of Herod (Matt 2:13; cf. Exod 2:15); (5) Joseph, Mary, and Jesus return to Israel after Herod's death (Matt 2:19–23; cf. Exod 4:19–20).

Such connections are the beginning of numerous echoes throughout the gospel. Recalling Moses serves to illumine Jesus. Jesus is presented as a liberator, prophet, and teacher in continuity with the authoritative, divinely commissioned Moses. But as one who is Emmanuel, Son of God, and Lord, Jesus is greater.[45] He offers the definitive interpretation of the tradition from Moses (5:17–48; 22:34–40). He is sure that his words will never pass away (24:35). Obedience to them is the standard by which people are judged (7:24–27). His death and resurrection require a role exceeding that of Moses. But the audience does not find an attack on Moses. He is part of the story of God's dealings with Israel into which Jesus enters.

DISCLOSURE

On rare occasions, the implied author discloses Jesus' inner knowledge, motivations, and emotions. Twice, for example, the audience learns that Jesus is hungry (4:2b; 21:18). It also learns something about his religious experiences. The author discloses that Jesus sees the Spirit descend like a dove at his baptism (3:16). It also discloses Jesus' inner struggle with God's will in his prayer at Gethsemane (26:37, 39, 42, 44). In these instances, the audience learns directly from the author without having to deduce traits from actions, relationships, and comparisons. Uspensky identifies the use of inner disclosure as the psychological aspect of expressing point of view.[46]

Jesus' Knowledge

On at least four occasions the implied author indicates that Jesus knows the evil thoughts or efforts of the religious leaders (9:3–4; 12:14–15, 25; 22:18). He knows, without being told, of the disciples' failure to understand (16:8–9; 26:10), of their fear (17:7) and little faith (17:20). He rightly predicts their imminent betrayal of him (26:21, 23–24, 31). He knows the crowds do not understand (13:10–17). The disclosure of this knowledge reinforces Jesus' authority, provides opportunities for confrontation or instruction, and, in exposing evil and unbelief, reinforces God's point of view.

Jesus' Motivation

At least three times the implied author notes Jesus' compassion for those he is healing (9:36; 14:14; 20:34). The repeated use of the same verb (σπλαγχνίζομαι, *splanchnizomai*) draws the audience's attention to his motivation. This disclosure makes explicit the basis for Jesus' mission and actions, including sending the disciples out to heal (10:7–8). It shows Jesus to be acting consistently with his own teaching about mercy and love (5:43–48; 9:13; 12:7; 22:37–39). The audience also learns Jesus' motivation for reproaching the cities of Chorazin, Bethsaida, and Capernaum: "they did not repent" (11:20). He does few mighty works in his hometown "because of their unbelief" (13:58).

Jesus' Emotions

The audience gains rare insight into Jesus' emotions. At 8:10 the implied author relates Jesus' response of amazement at the Gentile centurion's recognition of his authority. In the Garden of Gethsemane the audience learns that Jesus is "grieved and agitated" (26:37).

SUMMARY

In this chapter we have discussed four ways the author employs to enable the audience to learn about Jesus: the titles or terms of address, his actions and words, comparisons, and direct disclosure. From these narrative conventions the audience identifies traits or characteristics which it combines to form a coherent understanding of Jesus as the one commissioned by God to manifest God's merciful, saving presence.

NOTES

1. Chatman, *Story and Discourse,* 121–26.

2. See Chatman, *Story and Discourse,* 107–38; F. W. Burnett, "Characterization and Reader Construction of Characters in the Gospels," *Semeia* 63 (1993) 3–28; J. Darr, "Narrator as Character: Mapping a Reader-Oriented Approach to Narration in Luke–Acts," *Semeia* 63 (1993) 43–60.

3. Burridge, *What Are the Gospels?* 121, 124; Burnett, "Characterization and Reader Construction," 6–15; C. Gill, "Character-Development in Plutarch and Tacitus," *Classical Quarterly* 33 (1983) 469–87; C. Pelling, ed. *Characterization and Individuality in Greek Literature* (Oxford: Clarendon, 1990).

4. Gill, "Character-Development"; Burnett, "Characterization," 10–15.

5. Cox, *Biography in Late Antiquity,* 56–7; G. H. Polman, "Chronological Biography and *AKMĒ* in Plutarch," *Classical Philology* 69 (1974) 169–77.

6. Burridge, *What Are the Gospels?* 121, 124, 143–44, 148–49, 175–77, 182–84, 205–6; Polman, "Chronological Biography," 176–77; Cox, *Biography in Late Antiquity,* 57–65.

7. Recall the discussion of "Narrative Conventions" in ch. 7 of Part One.

8. L. Keck ("Renewal," 362–77) notes limitations of a titular approach to Christology. It ignores the wider literary context which informs the content and use of a title. It overlooks passages which do not use a title.

9. "Messiah" is an anglicized form of the Hebrew word *mashiah* which means "anointed." "Christ" is an anglicized form of the Greek word χριστός *(christos),* also meaning "anointed."

10. There is some debate about whether "Christ" is a title or a proper name in 1:1. Either way it elicits a variety of understandings from the audience.

11. For its use in Matthew, Kingsbury, *Matthew: Structure, Christology, Kingdom,* 96–103; for the wider context, O. Cullmann, *The Christology of the New Testament* (Philadelphia: Westminster, 1963) 111–36; R. Fuller, *The Foundations of New Testament Christology* (New York: Charles Scribner's Sons, 1965); F. Hahn, *The Titles of Jesus in Christology* (New York: World, 1969) 136–278; G. E. Ladd, *Theology of the New Testament* (Guildford and London: Lutterworth, 1974) 135–44; J. Neusner, W. Green, E. Frerichs, eds., *Judaisms and Their Messiahs at the Turn of the Christian Era* (Cambridge: Cambridge

University, 1987); J. Charlesworth, ed., *The Messiah: Developments in Earliest Judaism and Christianity* (Minneapolis: Fortress, 1992); M. de Jonge, "Christ," *ABD*, 1.914–18; idem, "Messiah," *ABD*, 4.777–88; for some texts, G. W. E. Nickelsburg and M. E. Stone, *Faith and Piety in Early Judaism: Texts and Documents* (Philadelphia: Fortress, 1983) 161–87.

12. See the royal Psalms: 2:2–9; 18:50; 89:20, 38, 51.

13. CD 19:10–11; 20:1; 1QS 9:11–12; 1QSb 5:20; 4Q 161 (Pesher Isa); 4Q Florilegium. See L. Schiffman, "Messianic Figures and Ideas in the Qumran Scrolls," in *The Messiah* (ed. Charlesworth) 116–29.

14. In addition to 1:1, the term appears in 1:16, 17, 18; 2:4; 11:2; 16:16, 20; 22:42; 23:10; 24:5, 23, (24); 26:63, 68; 27:17, 22.

15. Subsequently, "Son of David" will be used in 15:22–24 and 21:5, 9 to emphasize Jesus as the Messiah, the "lowly" King, sent to but not received by many in Israel. It should also be noted that "Son of David" is used in accounts of Jesus' healing those on the margins of society (9:27; 12:22–23; 15:22; 20:30). The audience may be assumed to know traditions about Solomon, son of David, as a healer, exorcist and magician. See D. Duling, "Solomon, Exorcism, and the Son of David," *HTR* 68 (1975) 235–52; Kingsbury, "The Title 'Son of David,' " 591–602; Duling, "The Therapeutic Son of David," 392–410; Loader, "Son of David," 570–85.

16. Cullmann, *Christology*, 270–305; Hahn, *Titles*, 279–346; M. Hengel, *The Son of God* (Philadelphia: Fortress, 1976); J. D. G. Dunn, *Christology in the Making* (Philadelphia: Westminster, 1980) 12–64; Kingsbury, *Matthew: Structure, Christology, Kingdom*, 40–83; J. Fossum, "Son of God," *ABD*, 6.128–37.

17. D. Senior, *The Passion of Jesus in the Gospel of Matthew* (Wilmington: Michael Glazier, 1985) 141–49.

18. U. Luz, "The Son of Man in Matthew: Heavenly Judge or Human Christ," *JSNT* 48 (1992) 3–21; Kingsbury, *Matthew: Structure, Christology, Kingdom*, 113–22; Davies and Allison, *Matthew*, 2.43–52; for wider discussion, Cullmann, *Christology*, 137–92; Fuller, *Foundations*; Hahn, *Titles*, 15–67; Dunn, *Christology*, 65–97; J. Donahue, "Recent Studies on the Origin of 'Son of Man' in the Gospels," *CBQ* 48 (1986) 484–98; G. W. E. Nickelsburg, "Son of Man," *ABD*, 6.137–50.

19. For example Ps 8:4; 146:3 translated as "mortals," and Ezek 2:1, 3, 6 etc. (over 90 times) translated as "(O) mortal" and indicating Ezekiel's suffering in the service of God.

20. Davies and Allison, *Matthew*, 2.51; Kingsbury, *Matthew: Structure, Christology, Kingdom*, 117. Kingsbury designates this term "a public title." However, that is sometimes misleading given that Jesus uses it on a number of instances when the disciples are his audience (10:23; 13:37, 41; 16:13, 27, 28; etc.). Kingsbury's description is

helpful if it is remembered that the title is "public" in that Matthew's
Jesus employs it to refer to his interaction with the world. Luz, "Son
of Man," 18.

21. Kingsbury, *Matthew: Structure, Christology, Kingdom*, 103–13;
Bornkamm, "End-Expectation and Church," 41–43; Cullmann, *Christology*, 195–237; Hahn, *Titles*, 68–135; Fuller, *Foundations*. Jesus also
uses this term to refer to his own present (12:8; 21:3) and future
(24:42) activity.

22. Also 10:24–25; 15:27. This usage is common in the parables
(13:27; 18:25, 27, 31, 32, 34; 20:8; 21:30, 40; 24:45, 46, 48, 50; 25:11,
18, 19, 20, 21, 22, 23, 24, 26). Given the context of the parables and
polyvalent nature of language, the term also becomes a referent for
God and Jesus.

23. For example, 1:20, 22, 24; 2:13, 15, 19; 3:3; 4:7, 10; 5:33; 9:38;
11:25; 21:9, 42; 22:37, 43, 44, 45; 23:39; 27:10; 28:2.

24. 7:21–22; 8:2, 6, 8, 21, 25; 9:28; 14:28, 30; 15:22, 25, 27; 16:22;
17:4, 15; 18:21; 20:30–31, 33; 25:37, 44; 26:22.

25. Προσέρχομαι (*proserchomai*, "come") 8:2, 5–6, 25; 17:14–15;
18:21. See Edwards, "Use of προσέρχεσθαι," 65–74. Edwards argues
this verb has cultic connotations and denotes recognition of Jesus'
authority.

26. Προσκυνέω (*proskyneō*, "worship," "kneel") 8:2; 15:25; γονυ-
πετέω (*gonypeteō*, "kneel") 17:14–15.

27. 8:2, 6; 9:28; 15:22, 25; 17:15; 20:31.

28. 8:25; 14:30.

29. 8:21; 14:28; 17:4; 18:21; 25:37, 44.

30. 8:2, 6, 8; 9:28; 20:31, 33. As a synonym for "Son of David" in
9:27–28; 15:22; 20:30–31, 33.

31. 15:22, 25, 27; 17:15.

32. 8:25; 14:28, 30.

33. 7:21–23; 24:42; 25:37, 44. The usage in 7:21–22 by the
"evildoers" indicates that the term can be misused by those who appear
active but who do not do the "will of my Father in heaven."

34. As a synonym for "king" (21:5), "Son of David" (21:9), and
"prophet" (21:11).

35. Garland, *Reading Matthew*, 134–37; Davies and Allison, *Matthew*, 304–16.

36. W. Carter, "The Crowds in Matthew's Gospel," *CBQ* 55
(1993) 54–67.

37. Cf. "Messiah, the Son of the living God," 16:16; "king," 21:5;
"son," 21:37, 38.

38. 1:22; 2:5, 15, 17, 23; 3:3; 4:14; 8:17; 12:7; 13:35; 21:4–5;
26:56; 27:9.

39. It should be noted that Jesus uses it of himself in 23:8 as a synonym for Christ the instructor (23:10). To address Jesus as teacher without confessing him to be the Christ is inadequate. In 10:24–25 he uses it to draw an analogy between his experience of rejection and that of the disciples (persecution). There is another self-reference at 26:18.

40. Stanton, *Gospel for a New People*, 169–80.

41. D. Hill, "Son and Servant: An Essay on Matthean Christology," *JSNT* 6 (1980) 2–16, esp. 9.

42. Healing the blind (9:27–31), the lame (9:1–7), the leper (8:1–4), the deaf (9:32–34), raising the dead (9:18–26), and preaching to the poor (4:17, 23; 5:3; 9:35; 10:7).

43. Hill, "Son and Servant," 12.

44. Stanton, *Gospel for a New People*, 78–84.

45. See Allison, *New Moses*, 137–270.

46. Uspensky, *Poetics*, 81–100. See ch. 8 above.

Chapter 14

Characters: Jesus—Crucified and Risen

The climactic events in the plot of the Gospel of Matthew are Jesus' death and resurrection. These are explicitly narrated in chapters 26–28 in the fifth and sixth narrative blocks, though anticipated by the rest of the gospel. These events confirm many of Jesus' traits identified in the previous discussion. These traits continue to be apparent as the audience learns about the multiple meanings of these events.[1]

JESUS' DEATH: THE WORK OF HIS OPPONENTS

The audience first learns that Jesus' death is the work of his opponents. It exhibits their negative response to Jesus' teaching and actions.[2] After Jesus claims authority to interpret the Decalogue's command about the Sabbath, the religious leaders "conspired . . . how to destroy him" (12:14). Subsequent scenes reveal the leaders plotting and achieving their goal (21:46; 26:3–5, 14–16, 47–57, 59–68; 27:1–2, 11–44). In the important trial scene the high priest asks Jesus if he is "the Messiah, the Son of God" (26:63). The audience knows that these two terms express major elements of Jesus' identity. Jesus neither confirms nor denies the question. He uses Ps 110:1 ("seated at the right hand") and Dan 7:14 ("coming on the clouds of heaven") to confess his exaltation and return as Son of Man to judge the world (26:64). The claim to such relationship with God and participation in God's power and purposes brings cries of "blasphemy" (26:65) and the judgment of death (26:66). The religious leaders' efforts to destroy Jesus place them in the long line of those who have rejected God's messengers (21:33–46; 22:1–14; 23:29–39).[3]

JESUS' DEATH: GOD'S WILL

The audience also learns that Jesus' death is God's will. The first clue comes with the designation of Jesus as "Son of God" (2:15; 3:17). This term invokes God's instruction to Abraham to sacrifice Isaac,[4] as well as the suffering servant material in Isa 42. Both passages identify suffering as the locus for God's actions of vindication.

In 16:21, the fourth kernel, Jesus teaches that he *must* (δεῖ, *dei*) go to Jerusalem to die. Given that Jesus' focus has been on God's will, the audience understands his compulsion as a reference to God's will.[5] The repeated use of the passive construction ("is to be delivered") in Jesus' three subsequent predictions of his death indicates God at work in the midst of the actions of the religious leaders (17:22–23; 20:17–19; 26:1–2).[6]

On other occasions Jesus refers explicitly to God working through the opposition of the religious leaders. Quoting Ps 118:22 to the religious leaders, Jesus refers to himself as "The stone that the builders rejected [which] has become the cornerstone; *this was the Lord's doing* . . . " (21:42). Later Jesus declares that "all this has taken place that the scriptures of the prophets may be fulfilled" (26:56, also 26:54). Though this statement is made in the context of his arrest, the "all" of the statement indicates a broader sweep, that the whole passion is in accord with the divine will.

Both the overall structure of and details in the passion narrative conform to the scriptures. Some scholars have seen Isaiah's suffering servant (cited in 8:17; 12:18–21) as informing the presentation of Jesus as the righteous sufferer whom God vindicates in resurrection.[7] Others have seen a reflection of a lament Psalm such as Ps 22 in which the righteous sufferer seeks (Ps 22:1–21) and finally experiences (Ps 22:22–31) God's deliverance.[8] Numerous details in the narrative invoke Ps 22 for the audience:

Ps 22:6–8	mocking	Matt 27:29–31, 39–44
Ps 22:6–8, 12–13	surrounded by enemies	Matt 26:47–68; 27:11–26, 39, 43, 44
Ps 22:7b	shaking their heads	Matt 27:39
Ps 22:16	surrounded by evildoers	Matt 27:38, 44
Ps 22:18	dividing clothing	Matt 27:35
Ps 22:1	the cry that God has forsaken him	Matt 27:46
Ps 22:28	Gentiles worship	Matt 27:54
Ps 22:16c	"They have pierced my hands and feet" (LXX)	Matt 27:35

Several direct citations remind the audience of the divine will pervading the events. Jesus describes his abandonment by the disciples in 26:31 as carrying out Zech 13:7.[9] The author informs the audience that the purchase of the field with the "blood money" returned by Judas fulfills words of Jeremiah (27:3–10; Jer 19:1–13).[10]

Other events recall the audience's knowledge of the scriptures. The offering to Jesus of wine (27:34, 48) echoes another Psalm of lament (Ps 69:21).[11] Pilate's washing of his hands (27:24) invokes a ritual which, after the discovery of a murdered body, proclaims innocence of the murder and seeks protection from any further consequences (Deut 21:1–9). Ironically, his actions imply that Jesus' death is a murder.

JESUS' DEATH AS SELF-GIVING

The audience learns that Jesus' death is a voluntary self-giving. While it is God's will, Jesus consents to that will. His willing compliance is reflected in his journeying to Jerusalem and his repeated instruction to the disciples about his coming death (16:21; 17:22–23; 20:17–20). At 20:28 he describes his death as an act of service, of giving his life.

Throughout the passion narrative Jesus appears in control. His life is not being taken from him as much as he is giving it up. Before reaching Jerusalem he accurately predicts what will happen to him (16:21; 17:22; 20:17–20).[12] The one-to-one correspondences, which allow his passion predictions to function for the audience as plot summaries, underscore the reliability of his word and the sense of his control over the events. Even while the religious leaders plot his death Jesus reminds his disciples that he will be crucified (26:1–5). He displays a certainty that "my time is near" (26:18) in very deliberate preparations for the Passover, the time of his death (26:1–2). The notion of "my time" recalls the audience's knowledge that this term expresses the final age of God's salvation (8:29; 13:30; cf. 13:40). He accurately identifies his betrayer (26:25). In the garden he urges Judas to "do what you are here to do" (26:50). He refuses to resist arrest (in contrast to the violent actions of one of those with him, 26:51–52) or call on the legions of angels who might free him (26:53). Steadfastly, on the cross he rejects the repeated temptations of the passers-by, the religious leaders and the bandit to come down from the cross (27:39, 40, 41–44). Their use of the phrase "If you are the Son of God . . . " (27:40) recalls the devil's words at the temptation (4:3, 6). Jesus actively and faithfully consents to God's will and dies trusting that God will raise him.

One scene presents Jesus struggling with God's will. In Gethsemane the implied author informs the audience that Jesus is "grieved and agitated" (26:37). Jesus himself repeats the information in the next verse. The repetition and the unusual direct disclosure of his emotional state underline his struggle. This disclosure recalls the prayers of lament of a righteous sufferer in the face of oppressive enemies (Pss 42:5–6; 43:5; also Pss 22, 69). Jesus prays three times that God will "let this cup pass from me" (26:39, 42, 44) but each time expresses his willingness to do God's will.

JESUS' DEATH AS A MODEL FOR DISCIPLESHIP

The audience observes important aspects of discipleship from Jesus' death. Jesus displays faithful and steadfast commitment to do the will of God, a quality which disciples are exhorted to emulate (7:24–27; 12:46–50; 24:45–51; 25:14–46). In this he evidences consistency in living what he teaches. Jesus is not one of the hypocrites against whom he often speaks who say one thing and do another.[13] Jesus demonstrates the wholeness, the integrity of love which marks God's way of being, and which he instructs disciples to imitate (5:43–48).[14]

Consistent with his instruction about his forthcoming death, Jesus welcomes the anointing for burial performed by the unnamed woman (26:6–13). In praying to do God's will (26:36–46), Jesus echoes the words of the prayer he taught his disciples (6:10). In his arrest (26:47–56) he refuses to resist with violence—consistent with his teaching in the Sermon on the Mount (5:38–42). Before the council (26:59–68) and Pilate (27:11–14) Jesus shows no fear (cf. 10:28–31) or anxiety about what to say, combining bold confession and silence in accord with his instructions to his disciples about their likely persecution and arrest (10:16–23). Even though the high priest uses an oath to compel him to answer, Jesus refuses to swear an oath (26:63–64; cf. 5:33–37; 23:16–22). Throughout, Jesus faithfully perseveres in his God-given task consistent with his teaching that the one who "endures to the end will be saved" (10:22b; 24:13). He knows that to save one's life is to lose it and to lose it is to find it (16:25).

JESUS' DEATH ACCOMPLISHED FOR OTHERS

The audience learns that Jesus' death involves more than the opposition of the religious leaders and Jesus' faithful example as a suffering righteous person compliant to God's will. His death is a death *for others* just as his life has been.[15] In 20:28 Jesus describes the giving of his life as a ransom "for many." Most scholars think that the "many" reflects a semitic way of talking about "all." The preposition translated "for" (ἀντί, *anti*) means "in place of" or "on behalf of" another who benefits by the event. It denotes a substitution or an exchange.[16]

A similar phrase appears in Jesus' words at the Last Supper. The cup is "my blood of the covenant, which is poured out *for many*" (26:28). Again the "many" indicates "all"; the preposition "for" changes from *anti* to *peri* (περί). However, *peri* has the same meaning of an action "on behalf of" another and beneficial to them.[17] Jesus' death is on behalf of and for the benefit of others.

JESUS' DEATH TO SAVE FROM SIN

The audience understands that Jesus' death and resurrection carry out his divinely given commission to save from sins (1:21).[18] Four elements contribute to this understanding:

(1) *Jesus dies as one who is innocent and righteous.* The religious leaders must find false testimony with which to condemn him (26:59–60). Judas, having witnessed the results of his betrayal, repents and returns the thirty pieces of silver to the religious leaders with the words "I have sinned by betraying innocent blood" (27:4). The Gentile Pilate has his doubts about the religious leaders' motives. He thinks the action against Jesus says more about their jealousy than about Jesus (27:18). Pilate's wife is convinced of Jesus' innocence as the result of a disturbing dream (27:19). The audience knows from the presence of dreams in the birth narrative that they are important sources of divine communication (1:20; 2:12, 13, 19–20). Pilate's Gentile wife functions as a spokesperson for God's point of view on Jesus. Moreover, the word she uses to describe Jesus ("righteous") is a cognate of the word "righteousness" (δικαιοσύνη, *dikaiosynē*) used by Jesus in 3:15 to express his commitment to doing God's saving will. God bears witness that Jesus does not die for his own sins but dies while carrying out God's saving will for others.

(2) *Jesus' death is a sacrifice on behalf of and for the benefit of the sins of others.* The audience knows that Jesus is commissioned to save from sin in 1:21 and that he has been faithful to this task throughout the gospel. For example, he successfully resists the devil's efforts to turn him from God's will (4:1–11). The implied author describes his ministry as bringing light, a metaphor for God's saving presence (Ps 27:1), into the arena of darkness and death (4:15–16). He begins his public ministry by calling people to repent as part of their encounter with God's saving power (4:17). He instructs his disciples to pray for forgiveness of sin (6:12), aware that in seeking it from God they must extend it to others (6:14–15; 18:21–35). His miracles of healing indicate saving from sin. In 9:1–8 he heals and forgives sin. In an acted parable he eats with "tax collectors and sinners" (9:10–13). He tells the puzzled religious leaders that this act embodies mercy (in accord with Hos 6:6) and expresses his

mission of calling not the righteous but sinners (9:10). He effects the liberation of others from Satan's power by casting out demons (cf. 12:28). In chapter 13 he discloses that the Son of Man will overcome Satan's current opposition to God's will and purposes in the final judgment at the end of the age (13:36–43). In 15:1–20 he names the human heart as the source of evil.

What, then, does Jesus' death accomplish? Why is it necessary or significant if in his life and ministry Jesus is able to forgive sin? The ransom saying in Matt 20:28 provides a partial answer. The first part of the verse asserts a basic perspective on Jesus' life: Jesus comes to serve. The second part of the verse ("to give his life as a ransom for many") places his death in that context. His life and death are a unity marked by service and self-giving. His death is not a different act which relegates the rest of his life to insignificance. Nor is his death of no importance. Within this unity his death makes a particular contribution.

The ransom saying in 20:28 offers some explanation of this contribution. The audience must use its cultural and religious knowledge to make sense of the ransom image. In general usage it referred to the means of releasing someone from captivity. In the scriptures it belongs to a larger group of sayings concerning redemption in which paying a price or making a sacrifice obtains the freedom or deliverance of someone (slave, prisoner). Often the act of liberation is stressed rather than the price. This emphasis is especially present in references to God redeeming Israel from captivity in Egypt and from exile in Babylon because of God's love and faithfulness to the covenant (Deut 7:8; Isa 41:14; 43:3; 47:4). God also redeems or rescues individuals from danger (Pss 31:5; 72:12–14). In the centuries immediately before the time of Matthew, accounts of the Maccabean martyrs interpreted their faithful, suffering deaths as a ransom (4 Macc 17:21). Their deaths caused God to intervene mercifully and redeem or liberate Israel from the Seleucid tyranny (2 Macc 7:37–38). They were also the means of purifying Israel's sin and taking Israel's punishment, thereby ending the foreign tyranny (4 Macc 1:11; 6:27–8; 17:21–22).[19]

The use of this ransom image for Jesus' giving his life "for many" (for all) means that the audience understands his death to be one through which God works to liberate others. In the context of his commission to save from sins (1:21), his death liberates all people, Jew and Gentile, from sin's power and destructive consequences (personal, political, social, economic, etc). In the specific context of 20:20–28, sin is manifested in self-seeking actions and through the oppressive use and structures of power (20:21–22a, 25). By contrast, God's will calls for actions which seek the benefit of others.[20]

The Last Supper scene (26:26–29) provides further confirmation for the audience. This meal is the Passover, the celebration of God's liberating or redeeming or ransoming of Israel from slavery in Egypt (26:17–19). Jesus supplies self-referential meanings for elements used in the meal. He breaks bread and distributes it to the disciples to eat, declaring it to be his own broken body (26:26). The offering of the broken bread represents his offering of his own life in death (cf. 20:28b).

In inviting the disciples to drink from the cup he designates it as "the blood of the covenant." The shedding of blood in Exodus 24 confirms the covenant between God and Israel, requiring each party to be faithful to its obligations (Exod 24:7–8). The giving of the blood of Jesus, Emmanuel, renews and reconfigures this covenant. Jesus explains that his "blood of the covenant" is "poured out for many [for all] for the forgiveness of sins" (26:28). This phrase invokes several parts of the scriptures:

(a) The offering of blood sacrifices on the Day of Atonement, for instance, was understood as a way of removing the barrier of sin (Lev 16). The animal was offered as a representative of and in the place of people. An exchange took place: The sinless animal died, taking away sin, in order that the people might partake of a new life in covenant relationship with God.

(b) The word "for" in the phrase "for many" appears twice in Isa 53, in verses 4 ("for us") and 10 ("for sin"). The righteous servant suffers on behalf of others in order to make many (all) righteous (Isa 53:11). The completing of Jesus' God-given mission is through suffering and death.

(c) Jeremiah looks beyond exile to a time when God will make a new covenant with God's people marked by heartfelt obedience, the presence of God, and forgiveness of sin (Jer 31:31–34).

(d) The covenant was widely celebrated as a distinctively Jewish possession which signified God's favor for Israel, and excluded Gentiles. But the inclusion of "for many" (for all) signifies the absence of any ethnic privilege in Jesus' action. Its benefits are available to all.[21]

From these associations the audience understands that Jesus' death is a sacrifice to take away sin (1:21). He suffers on behalf of all sinners in order that Jew and Gentile might share new life in which the presence of God is known and God's will is done. The confession of the Gentile centurion that Jesus is Son of God (27:54), the actions of Joseph in providing a tomb (27:57–60), and the presence of the faithful women (27:55–56, 61) indicate the universal scope of Jesus' death.

(3) *Jesus' death "for many" is a punishment, the judgment for the sin of all.* Liberation from sin involves another dimension. Constantly through the scriptures sin brings punishment and judgment.[22]

The audience combines seven clues to reach this conclusion: (a) At least nineteen times the author uses the verb "being handed over to" or "betrayed" to refer to Jesus' crucifixion and death.[23] It is assumed that the authorial audience knows that this verb appears in the prophets as an image of God's judgment (Jer 21:10; Ezek 11:9–11). The passive construction in Matt 17:22; 20:18; 26:2 points to God handing the innocent Jesus over to judgment in his death for others.[24] (b) Jesus prays in Gethsemane for God to "let this cup pass from me" (26:39). In 20:22, just two verses after speaking of his coming death (20:17–20) and five verses before speaking of it again (20:28, a ransom), Jesus also uses the image of a cup to express his destiny. The image assumes the audience's knowledge of the cup as a common image for judgment.[25] Jesus' death is his cup, God's judgment on sin. (c) In 26:31 Jesus speaks of the desertion of the disciples by quoting Zech 13:7, "I will strike the shepherd, and the sheep of the flock will be scattered." While the second part of the verse indicates the actions of the disciples, the first part refers to Jesus the shepherd (cf. 2:6d) who will be struck by God, the "I" of the passage.[26] (d) The Barabbas scene (27:15–23) underlines the point that Jesus' death takes the punishment of another. At the urging of the crowds and religious leaders, Pilate releases Barabbas and crucifies Jesus in his place. (e) Jesus' cry from the cross, "My God, My God why have you forsaken me?" (27:46) is the cry of one from whom God's presence has been withdrawn, the experience of judgment. (f) Jesus' death is accompanied by darkness (27:45), a symbol of God's judgment (Exod 10:21–27; Isa 13:9–13; Joel 2:2, 10–11; cf. Matt 4:16). (g) Jesus' death on a cross recalls Deut 21:23, "anyone hung on a tree is under God's curse."

This discussion has identified a number of aspects which clarify the significance of Jesus' giving of himself in his death for others. His death redeems or liberates from sin, it renews covenant with God, it is a sacrifice to remove sin, he suffers to offer Jews and Gentiles a new life marked by God's presence and will, and he takes the judgment for sin in the place of others. The audience understands through this narrative that atonement for sin, the removal of sin's destructive hold on human life, and relationship with God, is possible through Jesus' death. But this understanding raises a question about other ways of atonement such as the temple's sacrificial system.

(4) *Jesus, Son of God, is the temple of God where people encounter God's forgiving presence and atonement for sin.* In the scene before the Jewish council, two witnesses accuse Jesus of claiming "I am able to destroy the temple of God and to build it in three days" (26:61). The charge is repeated by the passers-by in 27:40. The audience has not heard Jesus make this claim previously, though in 23:38 he observed that the temple ("your house") is "desolate." In 24:2 he predicted that the temple will be destroyed.

At issue in the reported statement of 26:61 is not an intention ("I will destroy . . .") but Jesus' claim to have the power to determine the temple's future ("I am able to destroy"). Such a claim is a serious threat given the understanding of the temple as the place in which God's presence was known on earth (1 Kings 8:27–30; Ps 68:35; 76:2) and the close alliance between Jesus' opponents, the religious leaders, and the temple. But the reference to three days for its rebuilding alerts the audience to a further layer of meaning because in his passion predictions Jesus spoke of his resurrection "on the third day" (16:21; 17:23; 20:19).

The audience recalls the anticipation of this identification through the gospel. Jesus is identified as Emmanuel, God with us, the one in whom God's presence is manifested (1:23). In two places (9:13; 12:7) Jesus cites Hos 6:6 in which God says "I desire mercy and not sacrifice," a criticism of the temple's sacrificial system. In 12:6 in claiming to be lord of the Sabbath, Jesus identifies himself to be "greater than the temple." In 18:20 he promises his disciples that they will encounter his presence, the presence of God, when two or three gather in Jesus' name.[27] On entering Jerusalem (21:1–11) Jesus immediately judges the temple (21:12–17). His actions of throwing out those who exchange money and sell doves for sacrifice are an attack on its sacrificial worship. People exchanged money in order to purchase animals for sacrifice. Jesus' actions prevent the temple's function as a place of sacrifice. Instead, Jesus cites Isa 56:7 in calling it to be a house of prayer (21:13). He welcomes and heals those usually excluded from the temple (21:14). They encounter God's saving presence and accepting, inclusive mercy.

These actions indicate that the temple's sacrificial system is no longer needed. He is the ransom (20:28), the sacrifice poured out for the forgiveness of sin (26:28). His death splits the temple curtain covering the holy of holies, the place associated with the ark, the locus of God's faithful presence and forgiveness (27:51; cf. Exod 26:31–35). This act of tearing it "from top to bottom" is an action of God, probably an act of judgment (27:45, darkness; 27:46, Jesus' cry). Jesus is the one in whom God's presence is encountered through worship by Jew and Gentile (27:54; 28:17–20). Instead of the temple on Mount Zion being the focal gathering place for Jews and Gentiles in the new age (Isa 2:2–3), the risen Jesus gathers his disciples to himself on a mountain in Galilee. From there he sends them out to the nations to teach his words.

The authorial audience knows that the Jerusalem temple was destroyed by the Romans some 10–15 years earlier, around 70 CE. This presentation of Jesus as the new temple does not require the audience to choose between Jesus or the Jerusalem temple since the latter no longer exists. Rather, the presentation of Jesus as the place of atonement for sin and the locus of God's presence, the new temple, is made in the context of post-70 Jewish debates about how God's presence and atonement were experienced now that the temple worship was ended (see chs.

5–6 above). The gospel presentation of Jesus confirms these aspects of the audience's experience of God.[28]

JESUS' DEATH UNITING JEWS AND GENTILES AS THE PEOPLE OF GOD

Jesus' commission is to "save his *people* from their sins" (1:21). The audience knows that in the Septuagint the word λαός (*laos*, "people") usually designates God's covenant people Israel. In the context of the history narrated by the genealogy (1:2–17), the audience may understand Jesus' commission to be limited to Israel. However, even by 1:21 several clues point the audience to a much greater extent for God's purposes. The reference to Abraham (1:1), through whom all the families of the earth will be blessed (Gen 12:1–3), and the inclusion of four Gentile women in the genealogy (1:3, 5–6) indicate Gentiles are also in view. The appearance of the worshipping Magi from the East in chapter 2 confirms this. John the Baptist warns the religious leaders that God's power to create "children" is not restricted to ethnicity. Such a relationship requires a lifestyle of faithful obedience to God's will (3:9–10).

While Jesus' ministry centers on Israel (10:5; 15:21–28), Gentiles are also affected by it. Frequently, they respond positively to Jesus in contrast to many in Israel who do not believe (4:12–16, 24a; 8:5–13; 10:18; 12:18–21; 13:37–38; 15:21–28). The crucial exchanges, though, come in the parables of chapters 21–22. The parable of the vineyard, a symbol of Israel (Isa 5), narrates a history of Israel's leaders rejecting the messengers (prophets) and son (Jesus) sent by the landowner (God). God's verdict is announced in 21:43, "the kingdom of God will be taken away from you and given to a people producing the fruits of the kingdom." This utterance redefines the basis for encountering God's reign. No longer is it on the basis of ethnicity or nationality. What counts is response to God's son (cf. 22:1–14).[29]

The passion narrative shows the final rejection of Jesus by the religious leaders. By contrast it is the Gentile Pilate and his wife who defend Jesus' innocence (27:19, 24). A Gentile centurion confesses that Jesus is "God's Son" (27:54), agreeing with God's point of view (cf. 2:15; 3:17) and contrasting with the mockery of the religious leaders (27:38–44). The risen Jesus gives his disciples the commission to "make disciples of all nations" (28:19).[30] As a result of the rejection of Jesus, Israel loses its exclusive claim to God's reign. In Jesus God's purposes open up to Jew and Gentile. God's saving will creates a nation, the church, consisting of those who actively embrace God's purposes as manifested in Jesus (4:17–22; 9:9; 10:1–4). It is these people, all people, that Jesus is commissioned to save from sin.[31]

JESUS' DEATH AND RESURRECTION AS THE BEGINNING OF THE NEW AGE

The audience understands Jesus' death and resurrection (along with his life) as the inauguration of the promised new age.[32] In overcoming sin and taking its judgment for others, Jesus also overcomes sin's consequence, death, in his resurrection. His death and resurrection, along with the rest of his life and ministry, show the establishment of God's reign over death (cf. 4:16, darkness and death; 4:17; 12:28).

Jesus' death has cosmic effects. We have noted that the darkness of judgment (27:45) and tearing of the temple curtain (27:51) express the inclusion of Gentiles in the people of God. Earthquakes (27:51) figure prominently in scenes in which God judges enemies and sin before establishing God's reign and will.[33] This event precedes the opening of the tombs, the raising of the bodies of those who had died, and their appearance to many in Jerusalem (27:53b) after Jesus' resurrection (27:53a).

This latter material recalls the audience to several scenes from the scriptural tradition. In Ezek 37, Ezekiel pictures the restoration of God's people from exile as God resuscitating a valley of dry bones. Daniel associates resurrection with the final judgment in Dan 12:1–2, with some being raised to everlasting life and others to condemnation. Resurrection is one of the events that belongs to the new age, that signifies God's action in bringing this age marked by sin, death, and Satan's power to an end with the establishment of God's reign and will.[34]

Jesus' resurrection precedes that of the saints (27:53a). The scene emphasizes his resurrection as the first in the new age, enabling the resurrection of others. The attempt by the religious leaders to secure the tomb against Jesus' prediction (27:64,

62–66) recalls Jesus' previous predictions (12:40; 16:21; 17:23; 20:19; 26:32). Jesus' resurrection overcomes the sinful plans of the religious leaders in putting him to death. Their mocking of the crucified Jesus is in turn mocked by God's display of power. Their symbols of oppressive, death-bringing power—a scarlet robe (27:28), a crown (27:29), their kneeling before him in mock homage to address him as "King of the Jews" (27:29b), their feeble attempt to place a guard on the tomb (27:62–66) and to spread a false story (28:11–15)—are no match for God's lifegiving action. God's will, not sin and death, determine Jesus' existence and that of those who follow him.

The victory to which Jesus' resurrection attests is also reflected in the new future that opens up for him and his followers. Jesus' resurrection means his participation in God's reign as God's authority over heaven and earth (28:18). His predictions of exaltation to this participation in God's reign (26:29, 64) are fulfilled. His resurrection demonstrates the reliability of his other teachings which are yet to be enacted: his return as Son of Man and Lord to judge the world (25:31–46), to vindicate his followers (19:28; 24:13), and to condemn the wicked (13:37–43). That God's purposes are "not yet" complete means Jesus' continuing presence will be with his disciples (1:23) in their worship (18:20) and mission activity among the poor and suffering of the world (25:31–45; 28:20) until the completion of those purposes.

SUMMARY OF TRAITS

We can summarize our discussion of Jesus by listing some of the central traits or characteristics of Jesus that we have observed. (a) Jesus is commissioned by God to carry out God's purposes, to manifest God's saving presence in his words and actions (including his death, resurrection, and return). (b) Jesus faithfully and authoritatively carries out his task, giving his life, trusting that God will raise him. (c) Jesus exhibits compassion, mercy, and love. (d) Jesus displays power over human lives, nature, disease, sin, death, Satan, the present and future. (e) Jesus has integrity, doing what he teaches. (f) Jesus is a disturbing presence, confronting the status quo and witnessing to the new reality of God's reign (saving presence). (g) Jesus seeks to extend God's mercy to all, Jew and Gentile, male and female, rich and poor. (h) Jesus exhibits courage and steadfastness in his actions and teaching. (i) Jesus' death and resurrection save from sin, opening up a new future in God's presence available for all people.

As followers of Jesus the authorial audience understands and experiences these traits exhibited in Jesus' life, death, and resurrection. Its identity and lifestyle are shaped by his commission to manifest God's merciful, lifegiving, saving presence. An actual audience may experience all or some of these realities, or may conclude that they cannot live the role required of the authorial audience.

NOTES

1. In addition to the commentaries, see H. Hendrickx, *The Passion Narratives of the Synoptic Tradition* (London: Geoffrey Chapman, 1984); Senior, *Passion of Jesus;* F. J. Matera, *Passion Narratives and Gospel Theologies* (New York: Paulist, 1986) 80–149; R. E. Brown, *The Death of the Messiah* (2 vols.; New York: Doubleday, 1994).

2. See ch. 15 below. Brown, *Death*, 2.1424–34.

3. Connections between John the Baptist and Jesus underline and foreshadow this rejection motif for the audience. The religious leaders reject John and Jesus (11:16–19). Fear of the crowd (14:5; 21:46; 26:3–5) and manipulation of other parties (14:6–10; 27:11–26) figure in both deaths.

4. Brown, *Death*, 2.1435–44; D. Moo, *The Old Testament in the Gospel Passion Narratives* (Sheffield: Almond, 1983) 325–28.

5. This understanding is confirmed by the use of δεῖ *(dei)* in 24:6 to refer to Jesus' revelatory teaching about the end, and in 17:10 and 26:54 to refer to scriptural predictions.

6. 16:21, "be killed," "be raised"; 17:22, "to be betrayed"; 20:18–19, "will be handed over," "to be mocked and flogged and crucified, and on the third day he will be raised"; 26:2, "will be handed over to be crucified"; 26:32, "after I am raised up." "Being raised" is an action that God performs.

7. B. Gerhardsson, *The Mighty Acts of Jesus According to Matthew* (Lund: C. W. K. Gleerup, 1979) 88–91; Hill, "Son and Servant;" J. Neyrey, "The Thematic Use of Isa 42, 1–4 in Matthew 12," *Biblica* 63 (1982) 457–73; Moo, *Old Testament*, 79–172, esp. 163–64; Brown, *Death*, 2.1448–49.

8. Senior, *Passion of Jesus*, 127–30; Moo, *Old Testament*, 225–300, esp. 285–86; Brown, *Death*, 2.1455–65.

9. For the use of Zech 9–14, Moo, *Old Testament*, 222, 173–224.

10. The exact link here is difficult to locate. Some scholars point to Jer 18:2–3 or 32:6–9, while others think that Zech 11:13 is more appropriate. Either way, the implied author has made a free adaptation.

11. Brown, *Death*, 2.1452–55.

12. 16:21: to Jerusalem (19:1–2; 21:1–11), suffering from religious leaders (26:47–68), killed (27:50), raised (ch. 28); 17:22: delivered (26:57), killed and raised (as above); 20:17–20: handed over to religious leaders and condemned to death (26:47–68); delivered to Gentiles (27:1–2, 11–26), mocked (26:63–68; 27:27–31, 37–44), scourged (27:26), crucified (27:31–50), raised (ch. 28). Verbal similarities are extensive.

13. 6:2, 5, 16; 7:5; 15:7; 22:18; 23:13, 15, 23, 25, 27, 29; 24:51.

14. The word translated "perfect" (τέλειος, *teleios*) is better understood as wholeness or integrity. The integrity consists of living God's way of love. See the commentaries. The image of "fruit" expresses the same notion of wholeness. If fruit evidencing repentance is lacking, judgment follows (3:8, 10). Also 7:16–20; 12:33–37.

15. On death for others in the Greco-Roman world, M. Hengel, *The Atonement* (Philadelphia: Fortress, 1981) 2–32.

16. BAGD, 73; Louw and Nida, *Lexicon*, 1.803, no. 90.37.

17. BAGD, 644(f); Louw and Nida, *Lexicon*, 1.803; no. 90.39.

18. For discussion of the larger issues, Hengel, *Atonement*, 33–75; Moo, *Old Testament*, 301–30.

19. S. Williams, *Jesus' Death as Saving Event: The Background and Origin of a Concept* (HDR 2; Missoula: Scholars, 1975).

20. Garland, *Reading Matthew*, 208. Sin is defined more broadly and specifically: Herod's murderous resistance to God's will (ch. 2); the failure of religious leaders to act on what they know (2:5–6); the failure to repent (3:8); the presumption of those who equate ethnic descent with God's favor (3:9); the failure to show obedience to God's will (3:10); Satan's opposition to God's will (4:1–11). Sin includes the misuse of political power (Herod in ch. 2, the oppressive Roman forces in 5:38–42, the Gentile rulers in 20:25) and destructive social patterns (the hierarchical patriarchal households of chs. 19–20). I do not completely agree with Davies and Allison (*Matthew*, 1.210) when they claim about Jesus' mission to "save people from their sin" (1:21) that "This underlies the religious and moral—as opposed to political—character of messianic deliverance. Liberation removes the wall of sin between God and the human race; nothing is said about freedom from the oppression of governing powers (contrast Pss. Sol. 17)." While Jesus

is not a nationalistic deliverer, I would argue that his deliverance from sin has profound social, political, and economic consequences, consequences for the sin affecting human relationships (cf 5:21–26; 18:21–35).

21. See J. D. G. Dunn, *Romans 1–8* (WBC 38A; Dallas: Word, 1988) lxiii–lxxii; E. P. Sanders, *Paul and Palestinian Judaism* (London: SCM, 1977).

22. For example, Gen 2:15–17; 3:1–24; Deut 29–30, esp. 29:20–29; 30:15–20; Jer 25; Amos 1:3–4:13.

23. The verb is παραδίδωμι *(paradidōmi)*; see 10:4; 17:22; 20:18, 19; 26:2, 15, 16, 21, 23, 24, 25, 45, 46, 48; 27:2, 3, 4, 18, 26.

24. In other instances it refers to Judas, the human agent of God's will.

25. Ps 11:5–6; 75:7–10; Isa 51:17–23; Jer 25:8–31, esp. 15, 17, 28–9, 31; 49:12; Ezek 23:25–35, esp. 31–34.

26. In the LXX the verse begins with an imperative "Strike the shepherd." The context refers to judgment that God is bringing on the people.

27. The difficult text of 17:24–27 should be noted. Jesus and his disciples are free from such a payment which upheld the sacrificial system. "One greater than the temple" is here. I understand Jesus' payment of the temple tax to be a gesture of choice so as not, at this stage, to give offense. He demonstrates the concern for others which he teaches in ch. 18. See Garland, *Reading Matthew*, 186–87; Davies and Allison, *Matthew*, 2.737–49.

28. For other views of the temple including post–70 responses, Nickelsburg and Stone, *Faith and Piety*, 51–88, esp. 75–77, 85–87.

29. J. D. Kingsbury, "The Parable of the Wicked Husbandmen and the Secret of Jesus' Divine Sonship in Matthew: Some Literary-Critical Observations," *JBL* 105 (1986) 643–55.

30. I understand this to be a command which includes mission to Israel as well as Gentiles ("all the nations"). There is no final and absolute rejection of Israel. See Meier, "Nations or Gentiles," 94–102. Meier responds to an earlier article by Hare and Harrington, "Make Disciples," 359–69.

31. N. Dahl, "The Passion Narrative in Matthew," in *Interpretation of Matthew* (ed. Stanton) 42–55, esp. 48–52.

32. I do not agree with J. Meier ("Salvation-History in Matthew: In Search of a Starting Point," *CBQ* 37 [1975] 203–15) that Jesus' death-resurrection event is the "single eschatological event signifying the passage of the old and the breaking-in of the new" (207). Certainly the death-resurrection is a significant part of this transition, but some of the supporting evidence that Meier cites (the breaking in of the *basileia* [reign], the Son of God confession [209–10]) points to the

whole of Jesus' life and death as inaugurating the new age. Already in his actions (12:28) and teaching (21:43) God's reign is present. Because of these actions and teaching, disciples are able to confess him to be "Son of God" (14:33; 16:16). Again it should be noted that God's commission to Jesus to manifest God's saving presence stands over the whole of his life (1:21, 23; 4:12–16).

33. Judg 5:4–5; 2 Sam 22:8; Ps 68:7–8; Isa 13:13; 24:17–23; Jer 10:10; Ezek 38:17–23; Amos 8:7–14; 4 Ezra 6:13–28, esp. 14, 16; 9:1–13, esp. 3; 2 Bar 32:1–7, esp. 2; 70:1–10, esp. 8.

34. G. W. E. Nickelsburg, *Resurrection, Immortality and Eternal Life in Intertestamental Judaism* (Cambridge: Harvard University, 1972); idem, "Resurrection: Early Judaism and Christianity," *ABD*, 5.684–91; D. Senior, "The Death of Jesus and the Resurrection of the Holy Ones," *CBQ* 38 (1976) 312–29; idem, *Passion of Jesus*, 143–47; P. Perkins, *Resurrection: New Testament Witness and Contemporary Reflection* (Garden City: Doubleday, 1984) 37–69, 124–47.

Chapter 15

Characters: The Religious Leaders—Opponents of God's Will

Chapters 13 and 14 discussed the audience's task of identifying traits of the gospel's central figure, Jesus, and formulating his character. Responses to Jesus and to God's saving action manifested in Jesus determine the role that other characters play. Jesus provides the standard by which the audience evaluates all other characters, their actions and words.

In this chapter and the next we will discuss the responses to Jesus of two groups, the disciples and the religious leaders. Though individuals stand out from each group at times (e.g. Peter, or "a scribe of the Pharisees"), both groups essentially function as single characters. We will identify the traits of each group that emerge as the audience moves through the sequence of the story forming coherent characters. The religious leaders demonstrate how not to respond to Jesus. The disciples exhibit the identity and lifestyle required of the authorial audience.

THE RELIGIOUS LEADERS

As a single character the religious leaders combine several groups which share similar traits.[1] Two of these groups appear first in chapter 2. After hearing of Jesus' birth, Herod asks "all the chief priests and scribes of the people" where "the Messiah was to be born" (2:4). Several factors underline for the audience the religious identity and leadership function of these people: (1) the audience's assumed knowledge of the function of "priests" and "scribes," (2) King Herod's use of them as advisors, (3) the religious nature of Herod's question concerning the Messiah's birth, (4) their citation of the scriptures in answering (2:5–6). Nevertheless, the audience perceives something is amiss. These religious leaders show no recognition that in Jesus' birth the Christ has come.

Two further groups appear in 3:1–11 when John the Baptist calls people to confess their sins in baptism in preparation for the reign of God. The "Pharisees and Sadducees" come for baptism only to receive a sharp rebuke (3:7–10, "brood of vipers"). It is assumed that the audience knows of the Pharisees' and Sadducees' religious roles and beliefs. These characters, like the chief priests and scribes in 2:4, respond to John's announcement of God's word in an inadequate way. Like the "priests and scribes" they seem to be on the wrong side of what God is doing. This trait, their inadequate responses, along with their religious duties, allies these four entities (priests, scribes, Pharisees, Sadducees) in the audience's mind as a single group: religious leaders.

The audience's sense of this group's common identity is confirmed by their third and fourth appearances. In 5:20 Jesus instructs the disciples to display a righteousness or justice which exceeds that of "the scribes and the Pharisees." The audience notices that again these religious figures receive an unfavorable mention. But significantly this verse refers to a new combination from the four groups mentioned in the last two references, the scribes from 2:4 and the Pharisees from 3:7.

In 7:29, at the end of the Sermon on the Mount, the author reports the response of the crowds to Jesus' teaching. They are astonished that he teaches with authority and not like "their scribes." Here the scribes appear on their own, but again in poor light. They also appear as an entity distinct from the crowds. The crowds' openness to Jesus' teaching underlines the negative presentation of the religious leaders.[2]

This "mix and match" approach in which the religious leaders appear in various combinations continues throughout the gospel:

- The Pharisees
- The Sadducees
- Pharisees and Sadducees
- The scribes
- The scribes and Pharisees
- The chief priests
- The elders
- The chief priests and elders
- The chief priests and Pharisees
- The chief priests and scribes
- The scribes and elders
- The elders and chief priests and scribes.[3]

In our discussion we refer to the "religious leaders" and any of these combinations interchangeably.

THE RELIGIOUS LEADERS: OPPONENTS OF GOD'S ACTION IN JESUS

The audience notices that in the first four references the religious leaders appear in bad light. The audience must account for this negative trait. It learns important information from the scene in 2:2–6.

The religious leaders respond to Herod's question about the birthplace of the king of the Jews, the Messiah, by naming "Bethlehem of Judea" (2:5). To support this they cite Mic 5:2. They are knowledgeable about the scriptures. They can quote chapter and verse. But the audience is surprised that they draw no connection with the birth of Jesus. Their inaction contrasts graphically with the Magi's journey and worship (2:1–2, 7–12) and Herod's fear-driven interest (2:3–7).

The audience can suggest at least two possible factors to account for the religious leaders' behavior: (1) The religious leaders do not recognize Jesus as God's commissioned agent, the Messiah. They do not accept the author's claims to this effect (1:1, 16, 17). That would mean they do not accept God's revelation of Jesus' identity and mission, to save from sins and manifest God's saving presence (1:21, 23). The audience, however, does not yet know whether they willfully refuse to accept God's work. Perhaps they are simply uninformed and will respond differently as they learn more about Jesus.

(2) The religious leaders may know the scriptures but they do not know how to interpret them. The audience knows from the use of Isa 7:14 in 1:23 that the scriptures bear witness to Jesus. His life brings into being what they predict. The religious leaders, it seems, do not know this. They know Mic 5:2, but they do not know to interpret it in relation to Jesus. If they did know how to interpret it properly, they would act on what they know. They would journey to worship, like the Magi. Again the audience does not know if they deliberately misinterpret the scriptures. The audience needs to press on to confirm or modify its attempt to explain the religious leaders' behavior.

The exchange between John the Baptist and the religious leaders offers some clarification (3:7–11). John shows little respect for them, calling them a "brood of vipers." They are not "worthy" of a baptism of repentance because their lives do not show they have repented. Rather, they presume to be God's people because of their ethnicity as descendants of Abraham. John declares that lives based on presumption rather than active obedience to God's will deserve condemnation in the judgment (3:9–10).

Two negative traits emerge from this scene: (1) They presume, arrogantly and falsely, to be God's children by birthright. Instead of trusting God, they trust their inheritance. (2) They lack integrity. They do not live in accord with God's will. The negative comparison in 5:20 also suggests they have progress to make in this area. So too does the negative reference to the inadequate piety of the "hypocrites" in the synagogues (6:1–18).

The audience adds another trait from the brief negative comparison in 7:29. Jesus teaches with authority, claiming that conformity to his words is the very standard required by God in the cosmic judgment (7:24–27). In comparison, the crowds observe the lack of authority in the scribes' teaching. The audience knows that Jesus' authority is God-given. It derives this from his commission as the authorized agent of God (1:21, 23). By implication the scribes lack a similar authorization and authority.

The audience observes that the issue of authority is important in chapter 9. Jesus and the religious leaders have direct contact with each other for the first time. In three scenes they conflict over Jesus' authority to act as he does. The leaders fail to recognize his identity and the source of his actions.

In 9:1–8 the scribes interpret Jesus' words of forgiveness as blasphemy (9:2–3), as an unauthorized attempt to claim a role that belongs only to God. Their charge, which would be correct for any other person, rebounds on them. It indicates that they do not recognize Jesus' God-given role to save from sins and to manifest God's presence (1:21, 23). Jesus labels their wrong interpretation "evil" (9:4), suggesting it is something other than a well-intentioned but uninformed mistake.

A similar situation develops in 9:10–13 over Jesus' eating with outsiders. The religious leaders ask why Jesus associates with the marginal tax collectors and sinners. Jesus responds in terms of his mission, to call sinners (9:13; 1:21), and in terms of God's motivation, mercy. Their question and his answer indicate that they do not understand his mission or the purposes of God as being merciful and inclusive of all. His citation of Hos 6:6 with the words "Go and learn what this means . . . " (9:13) also underlines their inability to interpret scripture.

A third scene raises the same issues of Jesus' authority and how to interpret his actions (9:32–34). The religious leaders interpret his casting out of a demon as indicating his allegiance to and empowerment by "the ruler of the demons." Their analysis demonstrates to the audience that they do not understand or accept Jesus' authority to act. They misinterpret it, attributing the action of God to Satan.

The audience recognizes that through this threefold sequence the religious leaders show no ability to learn or to change their minds about Jesus. The author passes judgment on the leaders in 9:36 with an unusual disclosure of Jesus' inner motivation. His compassion for the crowds reflects their situation of being "sheep without a shepherd." The audience knows that "shepherd" is a common term for a leader (Ezek 34). The religious leaders are supposed to be the shepherds or leaders.

But their responses to Jesus—not being able to recognize the action of God or interpret the scriptures—display their inadequacies. They have not and cannot lead the people properly. They have forfeited their leadership. Though they do not recognize or accept it, God has anointed Jesus the Messiah to "shepherd" the people (cf. 2:6). The audience discerns in the echo of 2:6 a repeated condemnation of the leaders for not interpreting Scripture properly.

THE THIRD NARRATIVE BLOCK (11:2–16:20)

As we observed in chapter 11, the central issue of this block concerns responses to Jesus. Can people recognize Jesus as God's commissioned agent? A cluster of six scenes involving Jesus and the religious leaders provides an important, and negative, contrast to the positive responses of the disciples.

In the four scenes of chapter 12 conflict between Jesus and the religious leaders intensifies. In contrast to the more indirect conflict of chapter 9 in which the leaders *think* about Jesus negatively (cf. 9:3–4) or confront his disciples (9:10–13), they now confront him directly (12:2) to accuse him (12:10). The consequence of the exchanges is more serious. At the end of the second exchange they leave, plotting to destroy him (12:14). The audience must identify what in the exchanges causes the religious leaders to plot his death.

The first two scenes (12:1–8, 9–14) involve disputes over the Sabbath. The audience knows that observing the Sabbath was required by the Ten Commandments, being rooted in either creation (Exod 20:8–11) or the exodus (Deut 5:15). This observance distinguished Jewish people from others. There was a deep conviction about its importance as well as a long tradition of debate over its use.[4]

The religious leaders complain that Jesus' disciples work and thereby break the law when "harvesting" grain to eat (12:1–2). The religious leaders present themselves as the defenders and right interpreters of the Mosaic tradition, the will of God. Jesus argues that merciful deeds (feeding the hungry disciples, 12:1–2) and actions of worship (the priests, 12:5) are legitimate actions on the Sabbath.

But more than identifying criteria for deciding what is permissible, Jesus' comments make a greater claim. Three times he assumes the authority to interpret the Mosaic teaching about the Sabbath: (1) In verse 6 he asserts he is greater than the temple, having authority to regulate the house of God and the actions of its priests. (2) He claims to interpret the scriptures accurately, thereby revealing the will of God for the use of the Sabbath (mercy not sacrifice, 12:7). His insight contrasts with the ignorance of the religious leaders. (3) He exerts his own identity in the exalted God-like terms of "Son of Man" and "Lord" (12:8). Only someone who is commissioned by God to save from sin and manifest God's presence as Emmanuel (1:21, 23), who has intimate relationship with God, and has been given the privileged charge of revealing God (11:25–27) can make such claims. The surface issue is the use of the Sabbath. The larger issue for the religious leaders is Jesus' claim to have the God-given authority to interpret Moses' teaching, to reveal the will of God. The leaders claim it for themselves but do not accept that Jesus has such a commission.

The next exchange repeats the issue but in relation to a healing (12:9–14). The audience is aware that the mood of the religious leaders is more intense. Whereas the last scene concerned the actions of the disciples, this scene concerns Jesus' actions. And the implied author makes the audience aware of the leaders' motivation, to accuse him (12:10). Jesus repeats the divine will for the Sabbath, "it is lawful to do good" (12:12; cf. 12:7). For the religious leaders his teachings and actions not only violate the commandment to rest on the Sabbath, but are based on what they regard as a false authority to interpret the tradition. They must destroy him (12:14).

The third scene makes clear to the audience how mistaken the religious leaders are and increases the hostility. Two points of view collide. The author cites Isa 42:1–4 (12:17–21) to emphasize God placing the Spirit upon Jesus as the basis and empowerment for his merciful and inclusive ministry. Then the religious leaders offer their interpretation of the source of Jesus' actions. They repeat their view from 9:32–34 that Jesus is the agent of Beelzebul (Satan, 12:24). They position themselves as the ones who speak and act on God's behalf. But the placement of the Isaiah citation immediately before the scene and the repetition of 9:32–34 indicate to the audience how mistaken the leaders are. Jesus reasserts his Spirit-led task in which his acts of power manifest the presence of God's reign (12:28, 31). He condemns the leaders for their "evil" (12:34) and repeats John's condemnation of them as a "brood of vipers" (cf. 3:7). His condemnation challenges their presumption to act on God's behalf.

The fourth (12:38–45), fifth (15:1–11), and sixth (16:1–4, 5–11) confrontations emphasize the same themes and the irreconcilable gap between the leaders and Jesus. Jesus identifies their request for a "sign," a confirmation that God has commissioned him (12:39), as evidence that they are an "evil and adulterous generation." His whole life has been a sign of God's commission, but they have not recognized it. Their failure to repent will be condemned at the judgment (12:38–45), the ultimate validation of Jesus' condemnation of them for not carrying out God's will.

Their charges in chapter 15 against Jesus' disciples for failing to wash their hands in accordance with purity rules (15:1–2; Lev 15:11; Exod 30:17–21) bring a sharp response. Jesus accuses the religious leaders of confusing tradition with the commandment of God, honoring the former and breaking the latter. As an example he cites their avoidance of one of the Ten Commandments, honoring one's parents. They take money which should support parents and instead offer it in a vow to the service of God. Observing the vow appears to be God's will (cf. Deut 23:21–23) but in fact it "make[s] void the word of God." As in chapter 12 the religious leaders exhibit the traits of not interpreting scripture accurately and failing to exercise mercy toward their parents. Jesus further condemns them as hypocrites with Isaiah's words (15:8–9; cf. Isa 29:13). They lack integrity. Their words mask the real commitment of their hearts. They read their own wishes into the divine will. They do not act on God's behalf. They misinterpret Scripture.

The disciples report that the Pharisees take offense at Jesus' condemnation of them (15:12). Jesus declares to the disciples, "Every plant that my heavenly Father has not planted will be uprooted" (15:13). His comment emphasizes that (1) the religious leaders have no commission from God and do not belong to Israel. God did not "plant" them (15:13). (2) God will judge ("uproot") them since (3) they originate from the evil one. The audience recalls from the parable of the weeds that the weeds planted by Satan, the evil one, will be uprooted (13:29, 38b–42). The use of the same image in 15:13 ("will be up-rooted") discloses the religious leaders' identity and origin as "children of the evil one" (13:38), planted by Satan. The use of the adjective "evil" for the religious leaders (12:34, 39, 45) and for the devil (the evil one, 6:13; 13:38–39) makes the same connection. (4) In 15:14 Jesus declares that the leaders are blind because they cannot interpret the scriptures and cannot discern God's saving presence and reign in Jesus. They lead others to disaster. The use of the adjective "blind" contrasts with the earlier use of the image of "seeing" to denote the disciples' acceptance of and understanding of Jesus as commissioned by God to manifest God's saving presence and reign (13:10–17).

Their final scene in the third narrative block reinforces several traits, namely their evil motivation and allegiance to Satan. They come to test Jesus (16:1). The audience knows that the verb "test" describes Satan's role in his temptation of Jesus in 4:1–11 (4:1, 3). The religious leaders are allied with Satan in opposing God's will and in trying to divert Jesus from his allegiance to God. Their request for a sign in 16:1 repeats their demand from 12:38. It exhibits both their lack of comprehension and their unwillingness to accept Jesus' answer. Jesus again refuses to give them a new sign but repeats the enigmatic reference to Jonah (12:39–40).

THE FOURTH (16:21–20:34) AND FIFTH (21:1–27:66) NARRATIVE BLOCKS

The religious leaders make a few appearances in the fourth narrative block (16:21–20:34). In Jesus' predictions of his forth-coming death he names the leaders as those who will put him to death (16:21; 20:18). In 19:3–12 they challenge Jesus with another question about interpreting the tradition, this time Moses' teaching about divorce. Jesus' emphasis on God's will "from the beginning" (19:4–6; cf. 13:35) contrasts with their adherence to Moses' provision for divorce. Jesus charges them with being hard-hearted (19:8) since they refuse to accept his authority to advocate the creator's will "from the beginning."

In the fifth narrative block Jesus enters Jerusalem. The conflict with the religious leaders in chapters 21–23 increases and they put him to death (chs. 26–27). While they continue to see themselves as the legitimate leaders of Israel and right interpreters of its scriptures and traditions, Jesus declares them to be excluded from God's saving purposes and to have brought punishment on Israel.

In 21:23–27 they return to the issue expressed in their requests for signs. "By what authority are you doing these things, and who gave you this authority?" As in each of these exchanges, Jesus' response reveals their inadequate understanding. The questioners, inquiring about Jesus' identity and authority, become the questioned and their own falsehood is exposed. Jesus questions them about the origin of John's baptism, is it "from heaven or . . . of human origin?" (21:25). The audience knows that the reference to John addresses the issue of recognizing Jesus' God-given authority because John has borne witness to Jesus (3:1–12). Also Jesus previously lamented that both he and John have been rejected (11:7–24).

The leaders debate the two possible answers to Jesus' question about John's baptism. If they answer "from heaven," Jesus will ask them why they did not act on their knowledge and believe John (21:25). By implication they would have to account for not believing Jesus. Nor are they willing to answer "from human beings" because that will upset the crowds. They answer untruthfully, "We do not know" (21:27) and thus betray their unwillingness to accept Jesus' claims. This confirms that they do not have their origin in God and exposes their allegiance to the devil (cf. 15:13–14).

Jesus responds with three parables condemning the leaders. The first (21:28–32) condemns their refusal to change their minds and believe, even though they have seen God at work in Christ. The audience recalls the very first appearance of the religious leaders in 2:5–6 when they did not act on what they knew.

The next parable (21:33–46) is an allegory of Israel's history with God. Those responsible for the vineyard (the leaders) fail consistently to meet their obligations to the landowner (God, 21:34–36). Even when God sends God's son, they violently reject him (21:37–40). Jesus' parable places the religious

leaders in this history of rejection. God is now giving responsibility for the vineyard to those who respond positively to
God (21:41–44). The leaders understand that Jesus is speaking
about them, but they refuse to hear this as God's word (21:45).
Instead they seek to arrest him (21:46).

The third parable (22:1–10) makes the same point about
the relationship between the religious leaders and the kingdom
of God. A king has prepared a wedding banquet, an image of
joy in God's presence (22:2). Those invited find excuses not to
attend and kill those bearing the invitations (22:3–6). The king
responds by destroying their city as punishment[5] and inviting
outsiders to attend (22:8–10). But these are warned that if
they do not "dress" appropriately for the banquet they will be
thrown out (22:11–14).

Now the judged attempt to judge the judge—the religious
leaders respond by plotting "to entrap him" (22:15). Four
scenes follow in which various combinations of the religious
leaders (Pharisees and Herodians, 22:15–16; Sadducees, 22:23;
Pharisees and Sadducees, 22:34–35; Pharisees, 22:41) try to
trap Jesus by asking him difficult questions about religious
matters. Should one pay taxes to Caesar (22:15–22)? If a woman
has had numerous husbands, to whom is she married in the
resurrection (22:23–33)? Which is the greatest commandment
(22:34–40)? Then Jesus asks them a question about the Messiah, "Whose son is he?" (22:41–46). Jesus exposes their malice
(22:18) and bests them in each exchange (22:22, 33) so that no
one dared "to ask him any more questions" (22:46). Always
aware of their standing before the crowds (21:15–16, 26, 46),
the leaders' limits and evil intentions are exposed (22:33). Jesus
sums up two traits that have been evident throughout this
conflict, "You know neither the scriptures nor the power of
God" (22:29). Chapter 23 follows with its summary of their
faults as hypocrites and blind guides—a means of instructing
the disciples not to emulate them (23:3).

The religious leaders reappear in chapter 26 and, true
to Jesus' prediction (26:1–2), plan Jesus' arrest "by stealth"
(26:3–5). Their method of stealth reveals their desperation and
character. They do not arrest Jesus openly but employ betrayal
by a disciple (26:14–16, 47–56). They hide behind a large
crowd which they send to secure the arrest (26:47). Jesus'

comment about teaching the crowds day after day in the temple underlines their manipulation (26:55). In the trial they employ false testimony and false witnesses (26:59–60). They judge Jesus to have blasphemed and be deserving of death (26:65–68). In so doing, they claim to speak God's will when God has already excluded them from God's reign (15:13–14; 21:32, 41). They refuse to hear Judas' anguish about his betrayal of Jesus (27:4) and stir up the crowds to call for Barabbas' release rather than Jesus' (27:20). They mock Jesus on the cross using the terms "King of Israel" and "God's Son" (27:41–43).

Even in his death and resurrection the religious leaders continue to resist God's purposes. With a futile gesture they seek to thwart the resurrection by sealing and guarding the tomb. Ironically, they claim to be guarding against the disciples' possible deception (27:62–66). After hearing of the resurrection they resort again to stealth, commissioning the soldiers to proclaim falsely that while they were asleep, the disciples stole Jesus' body (28:11–15). The contrasts in chapter 28 between the leaders' acts of resistance and God's vindication of Jesus, giving him all authority, and the commissioning of the disciples to worldwide mission are obvious.

CONCLUSION

Clearly, the religious leaders are presented in unfavorable light from the beginning to the end of Matthew. They have no redeeming traits. They learn nothing. Their sole purpose is to oppose God's will actively and destructively by putting Jesus to death. They refuse to acknowledge Jesus' God-given authority, attributing it to the devil (9:34; 12:24). In turn Jesus accuses them of being children of the devil (13:38–39; 15:13–14). They have no God-given mandate to lead the people. They cannot interpret the scriptures accurately. They cannot recognize the power and presence of God in Jesus (22:29). They consistently reject God's initiatives in the history of salvation (21:43). They are deemed responsible for the destruction of Jerusalem (22:7). In leading the people astray, they cause them to utter a curse, "His blood be on us and on our children" (27:25). Their point of view is not endorsed in the story. They exhibit for the authorial audience how not to respond to Jesus. They manifest an identity and way of life which the authorial audience is not expected to adopt.

By way of contrast, the disciples demonstrate a very different response. They are the subject of the next chapter.

NOTES

1. Van Tilborg, *Jewish Leaders;* J. D. Kingsbury, "The Developing Conflict between Jesus and the Jewish Leaders in Matthew's Gospel: A Literary-Critical Study," *CBQ* 49 (1987) 57–73; idem, *Matthew as Story,* 17–24, 115–27; Saunders, *"No One Dared Ask Him Anything More"*; Anderson, *Matthew's Narrative Web,* 97–126.

2. Carter, "Crowds."

3. The Pharisees, 9:11, 14, 34; 12:2, 14, 24; 15:12; 19:3; 22:15, 34, 41; 23:26; the Sadducees, 22:23, 34; Pharisees and Sadducees, 3:7; 16:1, 6, 11, 12; the scribes, 7:29; 8:19; 9:3; 17:10; the scribes and Pharisees, 5:20; 12:38; 15:1; 23:2, 13, 15, 23, 25, 27, 29; the chief priests, 26:14, 59; 27:6; 28:11; the elders, 15:2; the chief priests and elders, 21:23; 26:3, 47; 27:1, 3, 12, 20; 28:11–12; the chief priests and Pharisees, 21:45; 27:62; the chief priests and scribes, 2:4; 20:18; 21:15; the scribes and elders (with Caiaphas the high priest), 26:57; the elders, chief priests, and scribes, 16:21; 27:41. Van Tilborg, *Jewish Leaders,* 1–6.

4. Jub. 2:30; 1 Macc 2:38–41; 2 Macc 5:25–26. For the Sabbath as a marker of Jewish identity and distinctiveness (along with circumcision and food laws), G. G. Hasel, "Sabbath," *ABD,* 5.849–56, esp. 853–54; Dunn, *Romans 1–8,* lxiii–lxxxii.

5. Many have seen a reference to the destruction of Jerusalem by the Romans in 70 CE. The verse interprets this destruction as punishment of the religious leaders for not accepting Jesus.

Chapter 16

Characters: The Disciples—Prototypes of Believers

Throughout the gospel the audience encounters the disciples, the special group of twelve called by Jesus (10:1–4). Sometimes several individuals from this group receive attention: the call of Peter and Andrew, James and John (4:18–22), the call of Matthew (9:9), Peter's confession (16:16). Generally the disciples appear as a group in the story. The gospel also includes characters not belonging to the twelve who respond positively to Jesus. These we can call the "other 'disciples.' " They interact with and respond positively to Jesus in brief scenes. Though not explicitly identified as "disciples," these characters are often portrayed with traits that the audience recognizes as appropriate to disciples. Frequently they contrast with the struggling disciples. Often they are people from the margins, outsiders who experience God's inclusive and transforming mercy and presence.

THE OTHER DISCIPLES

In 1:18–25 Joseph, on hearing of Mary's pregnancy, plans to follow the religious tradition of Deut 22:23–27 and divorce her (although, displaying mercy, he will do so quietly, 1:19). But the angel's revelation that Mary is pregnant by the Holy Spirit and that Joseph must marry her requires of him an action that appears strange and unconventional to others. God's will rather than social and religious conventions shapes Joseph's action. In 2:1–11 the Gentile Magi exhibit the worshipful reception of God's saving purposes desired of all people. In 8:5–13 a Gentile centurion exhibits a type of faith which Jesus has not found in Israel. A ruler, a sick woman, and two blind men also exhibit life-transforming faith in reliance on Jesus' mercy and power (9:18–31). A Canaanite woman who as a foreigner, a woman, and the mother of a demon-possessed daughter does not seem to have any claim on a man like Jesus, shows persistence with her repeated pleas for a miracle (15:21–28). As one of the poor in spirit (5:3), she encounters God's saving presence (12:28). A woman recognizes Jesus' divinely appointed mission to die and anoints him for burial as the Christ (26:6–13). While the disciples flee, a group of women from Galilee witness the crucifixion (27:55–56) and wait opposite the tomb (27:61). After the Sabbath they go to see the tomb (28:1). Since "seeing" is a metaphor for believing knowledge (13:10–17), the audience knows that their presence at the tomb does not signify grief. The women are there because they expect that Jesus will be raised as he had taught.[1]

The audience recognizes in these characters, and others like them, the traits of disciples even though they are not identified as such. Often they display a trait which, ironically, the disciples themselves fail to produce. The appearance of these characters assists the audience to recognize the identity and lifestyle that mark discipleship. The "other disciples" are part of the audience's educative process in hearing the narrative of this gospel.

THE DISCIPLES

An important dimension of the audience's understanding of the disciples involves their inconsistency. The audience encounters the disciples as they are, and, in Jesus' teaching, as they should be. The audience must account for the inconsistencies between these two dimensions. Some inconsistencies are due to the disciples' growing understanding. Some result from their failure to live out their identity and required way of life. Some reflect high points, moments of insight and faithfulness.

THE SECOND NARRATIVE BLOCK (4:17–11:1): DISCIPLES CALLED AND INSTRUCTED

Disciples first appear in the kernel of the second narrative block (4:17–25).[2] Jesus begins his public ministry and the task of manifesting God's saving presence. In 4:18–22 he calls two sets of brothers, Simon Peter[3] and Andrew, and James and John, from their family fishing businesses. This act identifies the first trait of disciples. They are a consequence of Jesus' ministry. They exist because of what Jesus is commissioned to do. People do not volunteer to be disciples (cf. 8:19–20). Discipleship begins with the call of Jesus which invades everyday life and separates disciples from nondisciples (4:18–22; 9:9; 10:1–4).

Disciples are those who commit to "follow" Jesus.[4] In dramatic and immediate style, the brothers leave their families (their social structure) and businesses (the means of their economic livelihood; 4:20, 22). Their commitment to Jesus, expressed in such decisive and costly actions, seems admirable. Yet the audience must make sense of Jesus' authoritative call and the fishermen's instant response in terms of the narrative world of 1:1–4:16. In consenting to Jesus' call, "follow me," the fishermen encounter God's saving presence, the reign of God. The call of Jesus is God's call. In following Jesus they begin a reoriented existence characterized by Emmanuel, "God with us."[5] To follow him means not only to accompany him, but to be loyal participants with him in his mission.

Disciples live in permanent transition. Discipleship has a temporal structure. Having committed to follow Jesus, their destiny is caught up with his. The audience already knows that John has revealed the goal of Jesus' mission to be his role in the future judgment (3:12). Disciples follow Jesus in transition to vindication in this judgment.

The call scene of 4:18–22 raises questions for the audience about how disciples are to live between their calling and the judgment day. The scene gives conflicting messages. On one hand the fishermen seem to abandon their social and economic structures, their fishing business and family (4:22), to follow Jesus. They seem to form a new family. Yet Jesus will not allow them to abandon society. He commissions them to "fish for people" (4:19). This image indicates mission work which requires involvement in society. The new disciples embark on an ambivalent existence, neither fully in social structures nor fully cut off from them. Theirs is an existence on the social margins.

The audience must read on to learn more about these and other aspects of the disciples' identity and lifestyle. In chapters 5–7 Jesus, while on a mountain,[6] instructs the new disciples[7] in the Sermon on the Mount.[8] This lengthy instruction, the first of five in the narrative, indicates that disciples are learners. Jesus' teaching identifies important traits of disciples:

(1) Disciples are participants in the reign of God revealed by God's action in Jesus. The Sermon begins with nine Beatitudes, statements of blessing (5:3–12). These statements reveal the divine blessings that disciples have already encountered in Jesus. They also assure disciples of their participation in the future completion of God's purposes.[9] (2) Disciples live in uneasy relation with society, experiencing social harassment (5:11) as they carry out their mission duties in everyday life (5:10–16). (3) Disciples are called to a life of greater righteousness (5:17–20). This life displays God's saving presence and reign in their actions, relationships, and words (5:21–48).[10] These actions include reconciling and faithful relationships (5:21–26, 27–32), honoring one's word (5:33–37), nonviolent resistance to evil (5:38–42),[11] and love and prayer even for one's enemies (5:43–48). (4) Disciples give charity, pray, and fast, motivated by their desire to please God (6:1–18; 7:7–11). They are people of integrity whose external actions truly express their inner commitment (cf. 5:48). (5) Disciples are not focused on or anxious about material wealth (as the Gentiles are, 6:32). Rather their primary focus is on God's saving presence and will (6:33, 6:19–34). They are to trust God to supply the needs of daily life. (6) Disciples do not judge (7:1–5). (7) Disciples are to treat others as they wish to be treated (7:12). This means foregoing violent retaliation (5:38–42) in the practice of love that includes even an enemy (5:43–48). (8) Disciples do the will of God as taught by Jesus (7:15–23, 24–27) knowing that they are accountable to God in the future judgment

(7:24–27). (9) Disciples live an alternative existence. They do not follow religious traditions (5:21–48 "you have heard that it was said . . . but I say") or social customs ("do not . . . as the Gentiles do," 6:7, 32). The words of Jesus establish an alternative reality (5:21–48; 7:24–27). (10) Having left their families to follow Jesus, disciples enter a new family as children of God (5:9, 45), with God as their Father (5:45, 48; 6:1, 4, 6, 9, 14, 15, 18, 26, 32; 7:11) and other disciples as their brothers and sisters (5:22–24; 7:4–5).

The next two scenes show disciples involved in continuing education. A disciple asks Jesus if he may bury his father (8:21–22). The audience understands this to be a reasonable request according to social and religious conventions (the fourth commandment to honor one's parents). But Jesus shockingly forbids it, calling the disciple to follow him. The disciple must learn the harsh lesson that to "strive first for the kingdom of God and his righteousness" (as Jesus teaches in the Sermon, 6:33) means following Jesus' disruptive, nonconventional word, not social conventions. Disciples are to live a marginal existence in relation to social norms and structures.

The next scene depicts the disciples in a storm on the lake (8:23–27). This presents two areas for their further learning. The stormy waves, a common image of the powers of chaos (Pss 74:12–17; 107:23–32), terrify the disciples (8:26). The disciples awaken Jesus asking him to save them. Their "little faith" has at least enabled them to turn to him. Their fear, though, indicates they have yet to learn not to be anxious (6:19–34) and to trust God even through storms (7:24–27). Further, their question of 8:27, "What sort of man is this?" betrays the need for more insight. Jesus' God-like actions of calming the storm reveal him as Emmanuel, God with us (cf. 1:23). But while the audience knows this, the disciples do not.

Jesus commissions the disciples to "fish for people" (4:19). The audience must wait until chapter 10 for clarification of this task. Chapter 10 is the next major teaching unit after chapters 5–7. It begins with a summary call and naming of the twelve disciples (10:1–4). The author identifies the twelve as "apostles" (10:2), a word that indicates their function as people sent to do a particular task. Jesus entrusts to them a share in his ministry to cast out demons (cf. 4:24; 8:16, 28–34; 9:32–33) and heal

(4:24; 8:1–4, 5–13, 14–17; 9:1–8, 18–31, 35). In 10:7–8 Jesus adds preaching to their tasks (10:7). Their mission to Israel (10:5–6) is a participation in Jesus' mission. Jesus instructs them again about the need to trust God (10:9–10), warns about the divisive effect of their ministry (10:11–15) and reassures them of God's presence even in hostile persecution (10:16–31; cf. 5:10–12). They also learn that the response to their mission carries eschatological implications. It determines destiny in the judgment. To receive the disciples (to embrace their message) is to receive Jesus and God (10:32–42).

THE THIRD NARRATIVE BLOCK (11:2–16:20): THE DISCIPLES AS RECIPIENTS OF REVELATION; THEIR STRUGGLE, AND CONTRASTS WITH THE RELIGIOUS LEADERS

This section concentrates on the recognition of Jesus as the one commissioned to manifest God's saving presence. It establishes three important traits of disciples: (1) They receive the revelation of God's saving presence and reign in Jesus. (2) They stand in increasing opposition to and contrast with the religious leaders who reject Jesus' claims. (3) They have much to learn and are very inconsistent in their discipleship.

In 11:6 the audience is reminded of the blessing that disciples experience as the "infants" who have embraced God's revelation in Jesus (11:25). The term "infants" assumes the audience knows of its use in the Septuagint to refer to the righteous or simple who trust and obey God.[12] It contrasts with the worldly wise, those who rely on their own skills and knowledge. Such people, like the religious leaders, have no place for or openness to God's revelation. In contrast to the religious leaders, the community of disciples constitutes a new family in relation to Jesus and each other. This is distinct from their birth families and is marked by doing the will of God (12:46–50).

In chapter 13 Jesus again blesses the disciples for seeing and hearing the secrets of the kingdom in contrast to the crowds (13:10–17). The disciples' knowledge results from God's revealing action; it "has been given" to them. By contrast the secrets of the kingdom have not been given to the crowds

(13:11). The audience interprets the "secrets of the kingdom" in relation to Jesus, in whom God's reign, God's saving presence, is being manifested (12:28; 4:17; 1:21, 23). The "parables of the kingdom" in chapter 13 (13:18, 19, 24, 31, 33, 44, 45, 47) confirm and thereby challenge, repeat and thereby renew, the audience's experience of the reign of God.[13] The disciples, though, do not understand everything. They have to ask for an explanation of the parable of the weeds of the field (13:36). But by the end of the section they are willing to answer yes when Jesus asks if they have understood (13:51).

Their confidence, though, seems misplaced as the audience follows the disciples through a rollercoaster ride in the next three chapters. They witness Jesus' power in healing the sick crowds (14:14), but they want to send the hungry crowds away because they cannot conceive of feeding them (14:15–16). After Jesus miraculously supplies food, the disciples join with Jesus in feeding them (14:17–19). This carries out what will later be revealed as an important aspect of God's will (cf. 25:31–46). Immediately after this, the disciples embark on another boat journey (14:22–33). A storm again inspires great terror, recalling their fear and failure from the previous boat and storm incident in 8:23–27. But this time the incident ends differently. Instead of puzzled questions about Jesus' identity (8:27), the disciples worship and confess, "Truly you are the Son of God" (14:33). In doing so, the disciples agree with God's point of view (2:15; 3:17). This shows they are recipients of the divine revelation (11:25–27).

Yet in the next chapter they seem to have learned nothing. Another crowd, this one smaller than the last, needs food (four thousand not five thousand, 15:38; cf. 14:21). The disciples recognize they are "in the desert" (15:33). The audience knows the desert to be the place of God's feeding of the children of Israel in the exodus from Egypt, and the place of the previous feeding miracle (cf. 14:13, 15), but they do not look to Jesus for another miracle. Instead, they display their lack of understanding and trust with the question, "Where are we to get enough bread in the desert to feed so great a crowd?" (15:33). Further misunderstanding follows in 16:1–12 as, rather comically and pathetically, they do not grasp Jesus' warning about the teaching of the religious leaders (16:1–12).

The rollercoaster ride continues in the final scene of the third narrative block. Jesus asks the disciples who people say he is (16:13). They report various erroneous verdicts before Peter, the group's spokesperson, repeats the confession of 14:33 and God's point of view, "You are the Messiah, the Son of the living God" (16:16). Jesus blesses him for this understanding, recognizing its origin in the revelation of God (16:17). Peter's confession is foundational for the community that Jesus will build (16:18–19). Surprisingly, though, Jesus charges them not to proclaim this revelation (16:20). The audience learns from the next narrative block that there is further crucial information which the disciples must understand before they can proclaim this revelation.

THE FOURTH NARRATIVE BLOCK (16:21–20:34): THE DISCIPLES STRUGGLE WITH THE WAY OF THE CROSS

Here Jesus presents the disciples with new teaching about his mission (16:21). It is God's will that he go to Jerusalem to die. In a surprising turnaround Peter, who but a few verses earlier had by God's revelation confessed Jesus as Son of God, now rejects Jesus' teaching and thus God's point of view. "This must never happen to you," he says (16:22). Jesus responds to this by identifying Peter as Satan, the arch opponent of God's will. Peter is not on God's side, he does not share God's point of view but that of the people who do not understand who Jesus is or what he is about (16:22–23; cf. 16:13).

Jesus, nevertheless, instructs the disciples about their discipleship in the light of his death: Until the judgment disciples must take up their cross. Jesus' words call them to a self-giving life of living for others as the life-giving will of God (16:24–28). This is reinforced by God's voice from heaven in the revelatory transfiguration scene (17:1–8). God proclaims again that Jesus is God's Son and appeals to them to "listen to him" (17:5).

Yet faith comes hard for the disciples. While they understand that John the Baptist is Elijah (17:13), they struggle to exercise faith in casting out a demon (17:14–20, esp. 16). They thereby fail at the mission task which Jesus has commissioned them to do (10:1, 8). More than this, Jesus' comments indicate that they fail because of their little faith (17:17, 20).

Again Jesus instructs them about his forthcoming death (17:22). This time no disciple directly opposes it (cf. 16:22–23). Instead, they are greatly distressed. If they cannot trust God to deliver from demons, how could they believe God can raise Jesus from the dead?

They also seem not to have heard Jesus' instruction about the way of the cross as the giving of one's life for others. Instead, in 18:1 they are concerned with their own status and preeminence. They ask Jesus about being the greatest in the kingdom. In reply Jesus outlines further traits of the community of disciples: (1) Disciples are children. The audience knows that in the ancient world children were generally regarded as insignificant marginal beings, the least in the household. Jesus calls all the disciples to this humble identity (18:2–4). This shows that disciples do not seek great status or elevation over others. All disciples share one status as children who depend on others and on God.

(2) Jesus affirms how valuable and vulnerable disciples are. To receive a disciple is to receive Jesus (18:5). To cause another disciple, "one of these little ones," to sin is to risk condemnation in the judgment (18:6–9). To despise one of them is equally risky (18:10). Rather, like an ever-vigilant shepherd for whom even one sheep is valuable, God values every disciple, not wanting any to perish. God's will provides the model for the way disciples treat each other (18:10–14).

(3) The community of disciples must practice reconciliation (18:15–20) and forgiveness (18:21–35). The basis for their forgiveness from the heart (18:35) is God's forgiveness and mercy to them (18:21–35). The audience knows that mercy and forgiveness are not widely valued traits in the ancient world. Jesus' instruction creates an alternative, out-of-step community in tension with its surrounding society.[14]

More radical instruction follows in chapters 19–20.[15] The audience encounters teaching which opposes the hierarchical patriarchal structure of households. Jesus calls for an alternative, more egalitarian pattern. Husbands and wives are to form a union of "one flesh," an image of mutuality and permanence (19:3–12). Children are welcomed, not marginalized

(19:13–15). Wealth is not to be used to define one's identity (the "rich person" [19:23]) but is to be redistributed to the poor in seeking a more egalitarian and just society (19:16–30, esp. 21). Disciples are to be slaves and servants like Jesus, in contrast to the Gentile way of ruling over others (20:17–28). Throughout, Jesus resists male domination and hierarchy. He offers disciples images and roles as the marginalized: eunuchs (19:12), children (19:14), servants and slaves (20:26–27). There are no separate instructions for parents or masters in this community of equals. The parable of the householder (20:1–16) demonstrates to the audience God's different values. To be able to "see" (to understand) this new way of life requires crying out for God's empowering mercy (20:29–34). The disciples, though, struggle with this difficult and radical teaching and its vision of social transformation (19:10, 13, 25; 20:20–24).

THE FIFTH NARRATIVE BLOCK (21:1–27:66): THE DISCIPLES' FAILURE

As Jesus enters Jerusalem, conflict with the religious leaders increases in chapters 21–22. Here the disciples have a minimal role. They help provide the donkey (cf. 21:1–7) and ask the key question about the fig tree which enables Jesus to explain further about prayer and faith in relation to the temple (21:20).

The disciples reappear in 23:1 to witness Jesus' attack on the religious leaders. This role alerts the audience to the purpose of Jesus' harsh words in chapter 23. They are a warning to the disciples not to repeat the sins of the religious leaders.[16] This is not a theoretical warning since the audience has seen the disciples display unacceptable behavior and attitudes through the narrative. This chapter, therefore, provides an important perspective on some of the traits already named as being required of or forbidden to disciples:

23:3–4	The gap between doing and saying (the repeated epithet "hypocrites" in 23:13, 23, 25, 29)	7:15–23
23:5–7	Desire for places of honor	18:1–4; 20:20–28
23:8–10	Egalitarian relationship	12:46–50; 19:13–15; 20:20–28

23:11–12	Being a servant	20:26–27
23:13–15	Shutting people out of the kingdom	18:6; 19:13
23:16–22	The use of vows	5:33–37
23:23–24	Neglecting the weightier matters of justice, mercy and faith	5:38–48; 8:23–27; 17:14–20; 19:13
23:25	Greed	6:19–21, 24
23:25–28	Hypocrisy	6:1–18; 7:15–23
23:29–39	Rejection of God's purposes and messengers	16:22; 19:10, 13, 25; 20:20–24

In chapters 24–25 Jesus instructs the disciples on the signs which anticipate the destruction of the temple and his return as Son of Man at "the end of the age" (24:1–3). Jesus highlights traits required of disciples until he returns: (1) Disciples are in transition until the return of the Son of Man. This event provides the goal or destiny of their existence. (2) Jesus recognizes that disciples are vulnerable to being lead astray (24:4–8, 15–28). He acknowledges the power of persecution to weaken the community of disciples through betrayal, hatred, and love that grows cold (24:9–12). (3) He urges disciples to endure to the end (24:13). (4) Disciples are to continue in mission throughout the world (24:14). (5) Disciples must remain alert and watchful for the return of the Son of Man since they do not know its time (24:42–44; 25:1–13). (6) Wise and faithful disciples continue in service until the end (24:45–51; 25:14–30). (7) In the meantime disciples continue actively in mission, living as people who feed the hungry, give drink to the thirsty, welcome the stranger, clothe the naked, and visit the sick and the imprisoned (25:31–46). In active compassionate service among the broken and poor, disciples encounter the presence of the Son of Man (25:40, 45), just as they encounter him in prayer, worship (18:20), and in proclamation of the gospel (28:18–20).[17]

The passion narrative (chs. 26–27) indicates how little of this instruction the disciples understand. Jesus' teaching and companionship seem to have little impact on how they conduct themselves in this last difficult week of Jesus' life. Even though they want to be loyal (26:19, 21–22, 35, 41), repeated failure seems inevitable.

Though Jesus reminds them that he must die (26:2), they resist the woman who recognizes his divinely authorized role in anointing him for burial (26:6–13). One of them, Judas, offers to betray Jesus for thirty pieces of silver (26:14–15). In eating the Passover meal with them, Jesus predicts the betrayal by one of them (26:21–25) and the flight of all of them (26:31–35). Given their previous fickleness, their protests of fidelity seem empty. This sense is confirmed as they prefer sleep to watchful prayer in Gethsemane (26:36–46, esp. 40, 43, 45) as Judas carries out his task (26:47–50). "One of those with Jesus" (26:51) draws his sword to resist, indicating he has not understood either Jesus' instruction about nonviolent resistance (5:38–42) or about his death as the will of God (16:21). As Jesus predicted, they all flee (26:56). Peter follows at a distance (26:58) only to betray him three times as Jesus had predicted (26:69–75, cf. 26:34). The chapter ends with Peter weeping bitterly (26:75).

The disciples are conspicuously absent from chapter 27. Judas' suicide is noted at the beginning (27:3–10) and the religious leaders fear the disciples will steal Jesus' body from the tomb and proclaim him risen (27:64), so they seek to guard the tomb.

THE SIXTH NARRATIVE BLOCK (28:1–20): RESTORATION AND COMMISSIONING

In chapter 28 both the angel and the risen Jesus instruct the women to proclaim to the disciples that he is risen (28:7, 10). Although the disciples have failed Jesus, he does not abandon or reject them. They are sent to Galilee to meet him. They obey (28:16a) but, typically, respond ambivalently to him. Some worship (28:17a; cf. 2:2, 8, 11; 8:2; 9:18; 14:33; 28:9), while others doubt or hesitate.

The use of the word "doubt" raises further concerns for the audience. The audience recalls Jesus' use of it in 14:31 after he has pulled the sinking Peter out of the water. Jesus addresses Peter as "man of little faith" and asks, "Why did you doubt?" The use of the same verb in 28:17 suggests that, despite all that has happened since chapter 14, the disciples have made little progress beyond the "little faith" they previously exhibited. Yet immediately after Jesus' address to Peter and his action of calming the storm, the disciples exhibit great insight "worshipping" (same word as 28:17) and confessing him as "Son of God" (14:33). While the verb "doubt" in 28:17 disturbs the audience, it offers hope that in these circumstances the disciples may also show understanding and faithfulness.

In the final scene of the Gospel of Matthew Jesus recommissions the disciples. They are to go, make disciples, baptize, and teach (28:16–20). Again the audience senses positive and negative responses. The disciples are supposed to have learned enough from Jesus to provide the basis for their teaching and discipling mission. But the audience is very aware of the disciples' inadequacies for this task. The audience also recalls Jesus' teaching that the missionary activity committed to the "infants" and the "little ones" (11:25; 18:1–6) frequently encounters opposition and hostility (5:10–12; 10:16–32; 24:9–14). Yet Jesus' faith in them, despite their uneven past and ambivalent present (worship and doubt), as well as his promise to be with them offer reasons for hope. The audience knows that, like the previous narrative, the future of the community of disciples, the church (16:17: 18:17), includes insight and confusion, faithlessness and faithfulness, fear and courage. So in this way disciples must live until the coming of the Son of Man.

THE IDENTITY AND LIFESTYLE OF DISCIPLES

The traits which the audience associates with the disciples form a vision of the identity and lifestyle of the audience's discipleship. Several features combine to form this vision of what can be called a *liminal* existence:[18]

(1) Disciples are in transition. Discipleship begins with the disruptive call of Jesus and ends in the final judgment. Disciples live faithfully between these two events.

(2) Disciples live an alternative existence. Committed to following and obeying Jesus and his teaching, the community or new family of disciples lives an existence marked by different values and social structures.

(3) Disciples live a marginalized, alternative social existence, though they cannot withdraw from society. They are in mission to it, following Jesus in the midst of everyday life. Their commitment to Jesus, their different identity and lifestyle, place them in tension with conventional social values and structures. Accordingly they live on the edge, as participants in society, yet detached from it by their different orientation. Theirs is a difficult, ambivalent, marginal existence until Jesus returns.

NOTES

1. Carter, "To See the Tomb," forthcoming.
2. For studies on disciples, U. Luz, "The Disciples in the Gospel According to Matthew," in *Interpretation of Matthew* (ed. Stanton) 98–128; R. A. Edwards, "Uncertain Faith: Matthew's Portrait of the Disciples," in *Discipleship in the New Testament* (ed. F. Segovia; Philadelphia: Fortress, 1985) 47–61; Kingsbury, *Matthew as Story*, 13–17, 129–45; M. J. Wilkins, *The Concept of Discipleship in Matthew's Gospel as Reflected in the Use of the Term Mathētēs* (Leiden: E. J. Brill, 1988); Carter, *Households and Discipleship*, 15–29.
3. The audience must account for the significance of calling Peter first. Subsequently, it will notice that he is listed first in the twelve (10:2), that he often functions as spokesperson on behalf of the group (16:16–18; 18:21; 19:27), and that he often has preeminence in the group (14:28–31; 26:33–35). Scholars have proposed several options: (1) Peter has a unique role as the guarantor and transmitter of the tradition from the Matthean Jesus; (2) Peter is a typical or representative disciple, a model (both positive and negative) for others; (3) Peter is first among equals, having salvation history primacy as the first to be called, but as in the second view, he is typical of disciples. See Kingsbury, "Figure of Peter," 67–83; Anderson, *Matthew's Narrative Web*, 90–97.
4. Kingsbury, "ἀκολουθεῖν," 56–73.
5. Carter, "Matthean Discipleship," *CBQ*, forthcoming.
6. Does the audience recall Moses on Mount Sinai, or Mount Zion? For the former possibility, D. Allison, "Jesus and Moses (Mt 5:1–2)," *ExpT* 98 (1987) 203–5; idem, *New Moses*, 172–80; for the latter view, Donaldson, *Jesus on the Mountain*, 105–21.
7. This is the first time the word "disciple" (μαθητής, *mathētēs*) is used. Using the distinction between "crowds" and "disciples" in 5:1,

and the identification of "crowds" in 4:25, the audience identifies "disciples" with those called in 4:18–22.

8. Carter, *Sermon on the Mount*; Kingsbury, "The Place, Structure, and Meaning of the Sermon on the Mount within Matthew," *Int* 41 (1987) 131–43; L. Cahill, "The Ethical Implications of the Sermon on the Mount," *Int* 41 (1987) 144–56; R. Lischer, "The Sermon on the Mount as Radical Pastoral Care," *Int* 41 (1987) 157–69.

9. R. Guelich, "The Matthean Beatitudes: 'Entrance-Requirements' or Eschatological Blessings?" *JBL* 95 (1976) 415–34; idem, *The Sermon on the Mount* (Dallas: Word, 1982) 109–11.

10. Scholars debate the meaning of "righteousness" or "justice" (3:15; 5:6, 10, 20; 6:1, 33; 21:32), whether it primarily denotes God's saving action, or human ethical action in accord with God's will, or a combination of both senses. See Meier, *Law and History*, 76–80. Meier follows the third possibility, arguing that some refer to disciples' way of life (5:10, 20; 6:1), some refer to God's saving action (3:15; 5:6; 6:33), and one includes both 21:32. For 5:20, Guelich (*Sermon on the Mount*, 157–61, 170–74) sees soteriological, ethical, and eschatological dimensions; Kingsbury ("Place, Structure and Meaning," 136–37) understands love towards God and neighbor as the heart of this greater righteousness. Davies and Allison (*Matthew*, 1.499–500) highlight "character and conduct in accordance with the demands of Jesus."

11. See W. Wink, "Beyond Just War and Pacifism: Jesus' Nonviolent Way," *RevExp* 68 (1992) 197–214.

12. LXX Ps 18:7, NRSV 19:7 "making wise the *simple*"; LXX Ps 114:6, NRSV 116:6 "the *simple*"; LXX Ps 118:130, NRSV 119:130.

13. Carter, "Challenging by Confirming."

14. For the limited and quite different notions of mercy in the ancient world, see Harris, "Idea of Mercy," and Judge, "Quest for Mercy," in *God Who Is Rich in Mercy* (ed. O'Brien and Peterson) 89–105, 107–21; Stark, "Antioch," in *Social History* (ed. Balch) 189–210, esp. 198–202.

15. Carter, *Households and Discipleship*.

16. The issue of anti-Judaism and anti-Semitism in relation to Matthew's presentation of the religious leaders will be addressed in the next chapter.

17. For discussion, M. A. Powell, *God With Us: A Pastoral Theology of Matthew's Gospel* (Minneapolis: Fortress, 1995) 113–14, 145–48, and the literature cited there.

18. The term derives from anthropologist Victor Turner. See Carter, *Households and Discipleship*, 52–55.

PART THREE: AFTER READING

Chapter 17

Conclusion: The Content of Matthew's Gospel

In Part Two we saw the way in which the audience utilizes the author's narrative conventions and its assumed knowledge and experience to formulate the gospel's point of view (chs. 8–9), plot (chs. 10–11), settings (ch. 12), and characters (chs. 13–16). In performing these tasks it constructs a world of significant realities, actions, and values. The world constructed by the interaction of audience and text contains affirmations about life and human society. It presents human identity and lifestyle in the light of God's saving presence in Jesus. This final chapter looks back over the authorial audience's experiences of reading Matthew, notes some aspects of its identity and way of life, and offers some brief reflections on connections between this gospel and contemporary religious experience.

THE IDENTITY AND LIFESTYLE OF MATTHEW'S AUDIENCE

(1) Central to the world of Matthew's gospel is the affirmation that human identity and lifestyle exist in relationship to God. Human existence is not viewed as autonomous. It consists of more than the material and physical realms. It consists of more than the present. More is happening than the eye can see.

God created the world and human beings (13:35; 19:4). God shapes history (1:1–17; 11:12–13; 21:33–43) and controls human destiny (13:40–43; 19:28). God blesses the present with life (5:45) and with accountability, disclosing God's presence (1:21; 14:22–33; 18:20; 28:20) and will to human beings (5:17–48; 12:46–50). Central to human life is worship and love for God (2:2, 11; 4:9–10; 22:37). Of supreme importance is that God's "will be done, on earth as it is in heaven" (6:10). This is to be the central focus of the human heart. The gospel warns about other claimants which seek to shape human identity and daily living: the devil (4:1–11), wealth (6:24; 13:22; 19:16–30), family (8:21–22), "the cares of the world" (13:22), and power (20:20–28). To live without reference to God's presence and will is to sin (1:21). It is to prefer darkness and death to the light and life of God's saving presence (4:12–16).

(2) God's presence among and claim on human beings is actively manifested in Jesus (1:21, 23). God has previously been known in Israel's history (1:1–17). The scriptures include important figures like Moses, Isaiah, and Jeremiah who have made God's will known and witnessed to what God will do in the coming of Jesus (11:13; 13:17). Historically, God has been encountered in the Jerusalem temple. Throughout history God has been present to bless, to judge, and to recall people to their central purpose (21:33–46).

But now, in this context, God has mercifully initiated a further attempt to deal with God's people. God has commissioned Jesus to save from sin. As Emmanuel he manifests God's saving presence and reveals God's will among people (1:21, 23; 11:25–27; 13:35). Jesus discloses the reign of God as the gift and demand of God's saving presence (4:17; 12:28). His words and actions, his death and resurrection embody God's merciful, forgiving call to people to turn from sin and Satan and to live a life in God's will (12:46–50). In the resurrection God raises Jesus, demonstrating that nothing can thwart God's purposes for wholeness. Jesus participates in God's complete authority "in heaven and on earth" (28:18–20).

(3) God's calling creates an identity and lifestyle for the community of disciples of Jesus. Disciples trust Jesus' call to follow. They repent. They believe and enter the reign of God. They receive Jesus and the God he reveals. They know Emmanuel, God with us. They constitute a new family or household which does the will of God as interpreted by Jesus. They

form a community of worship, prayer, and mutual care (12:46–50; 18:1–35). Identity and lifestyle are constituted by commitment to Jesus.

This community, guided by the words of Jesus and assured by his promised presence "to the end of the age" (28:20), embodies God's presence in its daily living. Centered on Jesus, this community is merciful, inclusive of all people regardless of ethnicity, race, gender, social class, economic means, or age. Shaped by the story of God's action in Jesus, it lives against the grain of its society. It is suspicious of the values of a society that does not acknowledge God's presence. It embodies God's forgiving love in its own relationships. It is an open and mission community, actively seeking others to join it. It knows solidarity with the marginal and unlovely, among whom it serves and encounters God's presence. It is the community of righteousness or justice, the community which evidences God's saving presence and will in its actions. It has integrity, living its confession. It knows struggle and inconsistency.

(4) The disclosure of God's saving presence brings division. Jesus disturbs as well as comforts. He challenges misplaced loyalties, false identities, and sinful lifestyles. He calls for realignment and a new center. He questions commitments, goals, and the use of power. He confronts political and religious authorities. Part of the present reality is that conflict with sin, death, and Satan accompanies the manifestation of God's presence in Jesus and in the community committed to him.

The audience knows that God's efforts bring two responses, acceptance and rejection. More often than not, rejection dominates. It can be expressed by the crowds who do not understand or who do not resist evil plans. It can be expressed in name-calling (5:11) or beatings (10:17). It can be expressed in the violent, life-depriving actions of the Herods, of Pilate, of the religious leaders, or of a disciple like Judas. But despite the prevalence of rejection, the minority and marginal community of disciples must sustain one another and persevere in the mission task, strengthened by Jesus' presence.

(5) The past and present are not the sum of God's purposes. The identity and lifestyle of the present are open to God's future. This future, when God will complete God's purposes, casts its light and its shadow on the present. God will establish

the new world in its fullness at the return of Jesus in glory. Response to Jesus in the present determines destiny in the judgment, either vindication or condemnation. Active acceptance of and obedience to Jesus' teaching provided the standard by which judgment is carried out.

Human existence remains accountable to God. The repeated instruction about the forthcoming judgment unsettles disciples' securities and spurs them to active witness and faithful perseverance. It reminds them that they are in transition until that unknown time. It offers hope and reassurance that their loyalty will be rewarded. It warns those who reject Jesus in the present that they will have their decision confirmed by God in the future judgment.

In sum, the good news in the world constructed by the interaction of the audience and Matthew's gospel concerns God's merciful presence among human beings. The life, words, death, resurrection, and future advent of Jesus invite sinful people to encounter God's saving presence and to form a new community of justice. In its worship and mission, its faithfulness and failures, its fear and hope, this community knows the comforting and challenging, forgiving and judging, summoning and commissioning, disturbing and inclusive presence of God. Though often confronting and colliding with cultural values, it continues its steadfast and hopeful mission until the completion of God's purposes in the future and certain advent of Jesus. This is its identity and lifestyle.

MATTHEW AND CONTEMPORARY RELIGIOUS EXPERIENCE

We have attempted to read Matthew as if we were the authorial audience, restating and redescribing its content. But such a role requires consideration of two further dimensions: (1) What do we make of the roles, identity, and lifestyle we have been asked to adopt in reading the gospel? (2) Does understanding this gospel have any implications for how we live at the beginning of the twenty-first century? In this section I want to raise some issues in relation to these two questions. I will use the five categories set out in the last few pages as a base. My comments are suggestive and illustrative, not comprehensive.

No doubt there are many other issues to be explored. I recognize that it is simply impossible here to incorporate every way in which audiences might respond to this work. These few pages are a small contribution to an ongoing conversation.[1]

Central to the world of Matthew's gospel is the affirmation that human life exists in relationship to God

Such a claim seems strange in our post–Enlightenment, cause and effect, world of rational explanation. Materialism, the pursuit of happiness, rugged individualism, and self-sufficiency (to name but a few) often exclude any recognition of God's presence, gift, or claim on human life. Even among communities of faith, there is a strong proscribing of the experience of God. Some branches of contemporary Christianity, especially Pentecostal churches, openly recognize God's presence and power. Other churches, North American mainline churches for example, frequently suffer embarrassment at such experience and talk. Matthew's gospel challenges us to consider our received cultural understandings of reality and to be open to experiences of divine power and presence which systems of closed, rational, cause and effect logic do not embrace.

Moreover, we have observed that for Matthew, a relationship with God involves gift and demand. God's merciful initiative and gift to human beings is the possibility of a new existence which trusts and enjoys God's mercy and love. But such a life brings with it the difficult demand to do and live God's will. The interweaving of these themes through the actions and teachings of Jesus means that Matthew's God is neither an eternal Santa Claus handing out "goodies" nor a fierce, punishing judge. Our reading of Matthew's gospel requires us to reflect on life in relation to the God who defies either category, and about how and what sort of God we might experience.

God's presence among and claim on human beings is actively manifested in Jesus

For Matthew, while God does act apart from Jesus (1:1–17; 5:45), God is particularly known through Jesus. Jesus' birth, life, actions, words, death, and resurrection provide the means by which God's saving, loving, merciful power and presence are encountered by believing, following, learning disciples. Such a claim can seem uncompromising and rigid in a world of relativity and an age of interfaith dialogue. Some are ready to surrender it in the name of tolerance. Others affirm their experience of and commitment to this reality of God's saving presence, without thereby dismissing other religious traditions.

One area in which this claim of God's revelation through Jesus has caused particular problems is the gospel's presentation of the Jewish religious leaders' rejection of Jesus. This was outlined in chapter 15.

Throughout the church's two-thousand-year history, actual audiences have responded in several ways to the sustained negative presentation of the religious leaders. Some have seen this as representing all Jews for all time. Jews are "Christ killers," forever excluded from God's mercy and saving purposes. Others see it as an accurate presentation and justified indictment of the dead legalistic state of first-century Judaism, a religion of display that had no interest in an encounter with God. Some have not thought much about it and have absorbed it without reflection. Others have been puzzled by Matthew's presentation and have been left pondering why the religious leaders do not receive Jesus. Others have been embarrassed or shocked by it. The Jesus who teaches love even for enemies in 5:43–48, who continually holds out mercy and forgiveness as central aspects of knowing God's presence, seems strangely unforgiving, merciless, and condemnatory with regard to the religious leaders. Some readers regret deeply the attitudes and actions of Christian anti-Judaism and anti-Semitism that have been fed by this characterization through the centuries.

Several comments are in order.[2] (1) Recent research on first-century Judaism makes it impossible to understand Matthew's presentation as an indictment of Judaism as a dead and lifeless religion. What emerges in this research is a picture of first-century Judaism as a very vibrant and diverse community of faith. The Maccabean traditions show a passionate concern for faithfulness to God. A number of prayers and Psalms (including Qumran material) indicate deep piety. The Pharisees sought to understand and live all of life as worship and service to God. We cannot confuse the characters in Matthew's gospel with the general religious practice of the time. The gospel is a story with Jewish religious leaders as the characters in it. They serve the purposes of the story. They do not represent all Jews. The gospel does not present a historically accurate portrait of first-century religious life.

(2) Other scholars recognize that in the ancient world there were conventions or typical ways of talking about opposing religious groups. These conventions marked them as opponents and indicated disagreement with them. D. Allison notes examples of Jewish groups accusing other Jewish groups of being "hypocrites," "blind," guilty of various sins, false teachers, destined for eschatological condemnation, and much else besides.[3]

Contemporary politics, of course, shows similarity in its use of such narrative conventions. One party does not agree with the other. Almost on principle their policies are too limited, too expensive, too late, too little, too hasty, too ill-informed, etc. Opposing characters are marred by greed or lust or selfishness or lack of concern or remoteness. The author of Matthew presents the religious leaders in conventional ways to show that they are opponents of Jesus.

The period after the fall of the temple in 70 CE was a time of much soul-searching and debate among Jewish people. They sought to interpret the past, including the fall of Jerusalem and destruction of the temple. They tried to define present and future religious practice without the temple, the sacrificial system, and traditional authorities such as priests. Books like 4 Ezra and 2 Baruch originate from the same time as this gospel. These books struggle mightily with such vital questions as the cause of and responses to the disasters of 70 CE. Some texts see the fall of Jerusalem and the temple as punishment.[4] Matthew's gospel is part of this large "in-house" debate among the Jews. Matthew's presentation of the religious leaders is not made by a self-righteous Gentile gloating over Jewish misfortunes. It is made by and for Jewish people in the midst of a time of disaster and confusion. Its characterization of the religious leaders is not an indictment of all Jews at that time or for all time. Some Jews in the story do believe (the disciples and others); others such as the crowds indicate openness; the religious leaders do not.

(3) Throughout the Hebrew scriptures the prophetic tradition constantly called people to repentance. This self-critique was a means of renewal, of maintaining integrity and faithfulness. Matthew's author clearly knows the prophetic tradition and places Jesus within it. In this he is not unique or unusual.

(4) We noted in Matt 23 that the condemnation of the religious leaders is addressed to Jesus' disciples. We saw in chapter 22 that the parable of the Wedding Feast is concerned not only with the fate of those who do not accept the invitation (22:1–10) but also with the guests inside the party (22:11–14). So the author uses the critique of the religious leaders to warn disciples about the same mistakes. Disciples are also prone to hypocrisy and lack of integrity. A similar fate awaits them if they do not repent. The religious leaders function throughout as a warning to the authorial audience which identifies with the disciples.

(5) I have suggested that this gospel is not anti–Jewish in the way that this term has often been understood. However, there is no doubt that the text can have that destructive impact. While the author probably did not intend to foster anti–Jewish attitudes,[5] they can result when readers of a different ethnic identity and in different circumstances hear the text. The major difficulty with this material comes because the majority of the gospel's contemporary audience is no longer Jewish (as it was when it was produced). Gentile Christian readers can understand a condemnation of the religious leaders, a group distinct from ourselves, as an address *across* ethnic boundaries, rather than as part of an "in-house" family debate. This causes unjustified negative images of (and actions against) Jewish people which contradict the gospel's vision of inclusive mercy and love.

When working with the Gospel of Matthew, whether in proclamation or study or daily life, it is crucial that contemporary audiences identify and adopt reading strategies that do not allow this negative impact, these misunderstandings, to continue. This can be accomplished by: (i) Understanding the use of the religious leaders as examples for the disciples. (ii) Understanding the circumstances of the text's origin and the nature of the authorial audience. (iii) Having the humility to recognize that the failings of our own lives and religions provides a point of solidarity. (iv) Substituting different language for terms like "scribes," "priests," and "Pharisees." The use of "religious leaders" allows the language to function for "us" rather than against "them."

Because of its circumstances of origin, this text places the authorial audience over against other Jewish groups. Contemporary audiences, however, can refuse that role and find other roles and relationships. Christians and Jews can respect one another, including their differences. They can recognize common ground and heritage as well as honor different paths taken. They can be partners and friends in a future of cooperation rather than condemnation. Actual audiences can agree with the gospel's claims about Jesus without unfortunate repercussions for relationships with other communities of faith.

God's calling creates a community of disciples of Jesus

Matthew's gospel recognizes that life in relation to God cannot be lived apart from relationships with others. The gospel challenges some contemporary understandings that faith or discipleship comprise only "Jesus and me." It affirms the presence and mission of the community of disciples, the church (16:18; 18:17), which was called into being by God's merciful actions. It presents a powerful and demanding vision of the church as a community with an agenda of justice, mission, and mercy. To be a disciple of Jesus is to live life in a community which knows the presence of God in Jesus and which actively does the will of God as taught by Jesus. This community lives against the grain. In God's presence members sustain one another to live as an alternative community. It questions the status quo. It opposes and resists the barriers and values of its society by upholding the inclusive mercy of God. It is a mission community with the task of transformation. It is a community of justice which speaks and does the will of God.

Such a vision questions the enculturation of many contemporary churches. It challenges any understanding of the church which elevates worship over service or vice versa. It corrects any church which thinks it exists for itself, is comfortable with the status quo, or takes upon itself the task of excluding any people. For contemporary audiences who belong to churches, reading Matthew is often a paradoxical experience. We hear the good news of a powerful vision of what the church might be, along with the bad and disillusioning news of what we frequently recognize to be our reality. Such a vision can encourage, challenge, correct, discourage, and frustrate.

It should be remembered, though, that Matthew does not present the community of disciples as perfect. Disciples fail and fear. They deny their calling. The gospel recognizes that faithfulness and faithlessness coexist. So do demand and mercy, challenge and comfort, rebuke and affirmation. As much as the community bravely and energetically engages in mission, it also offers a haven to the weak and broken, the overlooked and excluded, the socially unlovely and the marginal.[6]

The disclosure of God's saving presence disturbs as well as comforts

For some actual audiences Jesus' words and actions will have no lasting significance. They do not find in this text any convincing or life-giving material. Some find it full of judgment with little mercy or grace. Some observe that the grace evident in the gospel's opening is quickly overwhelmed by its subsequent demands. For others Jesus' teaching contained, for instance, in the Sermon on the Mount functions to continually shape their identity and lives of faithful discipleship. It provides basic principles or values which shape relationships, devotional activity, acts of mercy, and witness.

The past and present are not the sum of God's purposes. The present is open to God's future

Some contemporary audiences find the cosmic scenario of Jesus' return and future judgment to be unconvincing. The extreme actions and predictions of some sectarian groups, the disrepute of "fire and brimstone" preaching, a distaste for talk of judgment in a society that sanctions freedom to do one's own thing, a focus on the now, and the foreignness of this scenario with its claim of such dramatic divine intervention may, for some, render this aspect of Matthew's world obsolete or unacceptable. Frequently, these sections are simply ignored or omitted from study of the gospel. Others find this eschatological approach to ethics, the promise of future reward for present actions, to be a crass basis for ethical decisions. Some theologians have sought to deconstruct this mythological world to recover basic affirmations such as God as the one who always comes to human beings, or as the possibility of a new future with authentic existence.

Others, though, find much of value here. The vision of God's coming intervention underlines human accountability to God, an unpopular notion in a society that so often thinks it, rather than God, controls its future destiny. The fundamental claim of Matthew's vision that the heavens and the earth, the past, present and future, belong to God unmasks human pretensions and relativizes the power of other claimants who do not recognize any such context. Such a vision has particular power for those who experience daily life as crisis, who know the margins as home, who live in powerlessness, injustice, and hopelessness. Others find in this vision an affirmation of the value and significance of the present in relation to this future. That realization energizes actions of mercy and justice which seek to transform the present to harmonize with God's future.[7]

Whatever our responses, this eschatological material, so pervasive in the gospel and its worldview, raises important questions about human accountability, about the future and destiny of the human community, about attempts to circumscribe and/or control the present, and about our understandings of a life lived in the presence of God.

Matthew's gospel: A resource for the identity and living of contemporary Christian communities

On one hand the Bible is frequently dismissed as being too difficult or irrelevant. On the other hand, reading the Bible is carried out in the way prescribed by a bumper sticker: "The Bible says it, I believe it, that settles it." But our discussion has shown that "it" is never self-evident. Biblical material requires interpretation and the active role of the audience in formulating its meaning. Reading and understanding this gospel, or any biblical material, is not a passive receiving but involves recognizing conventions or clues in the material, filling in gaps, supplying assumed knowledge and experiences from the time of writing.

The approach used in this book offers a way of understanding not only Matthew's gospel but any part of the biblical material. Reading as the authorial audience means taking up the roles of the audience which an author had in mind when writing. Doing so does not result in a privileged or unassailable reading which is to be unquestioningly accepted or instantly rejected. Rather, it provides the basis for further reflection and dialogue concerning biblical material in relation to contemporary situations and experiences. To read the Bible only with contemporary concerns in mind is to turn a possible dialogue into a monologue. It can swamp the biblical material with our agenda. Conversely, to read the Bible with a focus only on the ancient world from which it originated is to be detached from the present. To read as the authorial audience, however, begins a dialogue between the text and our contemporary world. It means hearing the text in all its strangeness and unconventional perspectives in the midst of our world. This allows that voice to converse with our issues and experiences, and to make its distinctive contribution. In that dialogue our identities and ways of life can be challenged, confirmed, shaped anew, modified, or left untouched.

UNDERSTANDING MATTHEW'S GOSPEL

To understand Matthew's gospel as the authorial audience involves two dimensions: (1) to restate its content in words and (2) to embody it in an appropriate identity and lifestyle as disciples of Jesus (7:24–27; 12:46–50; 13:10–17, 51–52). The former task has been our concern in this book. Actual audiences, if they do not immediately and unthoughtfully accept everything in the gospel as determinative for their existence, or dismiss the gospel as irrelevant or unimportant, face both challenges. The latter dimension, formulating an appropriate identity and lifestyle, requires continuing communal reflection and action in the midst of the complex realities of daily societal living.

NOTES

1. It may help for me to identify a little of my own social location in this conversation. I am a member of a USA, mainline Protestant denomination and teach New Testament studies in a seminary of a mainline denomination. I am also a relative newcomer to this culture, having lived most of my life in another country.

2. The discussion of this matter is extensive. See L. T. Johnson, "The New Testament's Anti–Jewish Slander and the Conventions of Ancient Rhetoric," *JBL* 108 (1989) 419–41; F. W. Burnett, "Exposing the Anti–Jewish Ideology of Matthew's Implied Author: The Characterization of God as Father," *Semeia* 59 (1992) 155–91. The commentary by D. Harrington, *The Gospel of Matthew* (Sacra Pagina 1: Collegeville: Michael Glazier, 1991) pays particular attention to the post-70 Jewish origin of the gospel throughout; see also 20–22. Also Garland, *Reading Matthew*, 227–29. See D. Allison's review of Harrington's commentary in *Biblica* 75 (1994) 115–18.

3. Allison, Review, 117–18.

4. Josephus, *Jewish War* 2.539; 5.412; 6.110, 250; 2 Bar 1:4.

5. Recall the discussion in ch. 1 above about authorial intention.

6. See, for example, Lischer, "Sermon on the Mount."

7. For further discussion, Carter, *Sermon on the Mount*, 103–26, and the literature cited there; also Keck, "Ethics in the Gospel According to Matthew;" Cahill, "Ethical Implications"; J. C. Beker, "The Challenge of Paul's Apocalyptic Gospel for the Church Today," *Journal of Religious Thought* 40 (1983) 9–15; J. Gustafson, "The Place of Scripture in Christian Ethics: A Methodological Study," *Int* 24 (1970) 430–55.

Appendix: Redaction and Narrative Approaches

Throughout this book we have employed two methods (or criticisms) for understanding Matthew's gospel. Our main method has been a form of narrative or literary criticism known as audience-oriented or reader-response criticism. We have also used a subsidiary method, redaction criticism, particularly in chapters 2–6. This appendix discusses the purposes, strengths, and limitations of each method or approach. I suggest that both methods ask questions appropriate to different aspects of Matthew's gospel and so contribute in different ways to our understanding of the gospel.

REDACTION CRITICISM

In the last thirty years, redaction criticism has been the main method for studying Matthew's gospel. It asks three questions: (1) What sources does the author use? (2) How does an author shape sources to express his theological perspectives? (3) What are the circumstances of the community which the author addresses? Redaction critics focus on the changes an author makes to these sources. The changes are understood to be reflective of the author's own theological agenda and of the circumstances of the community being addressed. We have adopted this method of redaction criticism to investigate not so much the author as the experience and knowledge assumed of the authorial audience, thereby subsuming it to our central approach of audience-oriented criticism.

Particularly useful has been redaction criticism's concern with sources as a means of identifying some of the religious knowledge and experience of Jesus assumed of the audience. We cannot assume that the audience shares the detailed knowledge of this material demonstrated by the gospel's author. It is fair, though, to posit that the authorial audience is assumed to be generally familiar with these traditions. Texts such as Q and Mark functioned as identity-shaping documents for Matthew's community before the writing of Matthew's gospel. The authorial audience is assumed to be familiar with them.

Likewise, redaction criticism identifies the author's contribution to these sources by attending to the author's changes to the material. Some redaction critics such as Ulrich Luz argue convincingly that Matthew's redaction of these sources generally reflects the theological understandings of his community. That is, the author assumes his authorial audience is essentially familiar with and in agreement with his presentation. On this reading the author largely derives his theological understandings from the community for whom he writes. Redaction criticism has enabled us to identify some of this shared knowledge.

Redaction criticism's focus on the circumstances of the community being addressed also enables us to gain insight into the social/religious experience assumed of the authorial audience. The author's impression of these circumstances constitutes the authorial audience. The authorial audience thus bears some correspondence to the actual community being addressed. We observed four characteristics of its social experience from the way in which the author shapes and presents the story of Jesus. That is, redaction criticism assists in identifying further aspects of the social and religious knowledge and experience assumed of the authorial audience.

Redaction criticism has been useful in the service of the central concerns of this study. Its particular set of questions, focusing on the author, sources, and community of the gospel, has helped us to fill in some of the historical, cultural, social, and religious knowledge and experiences assumed of the authorial audience. But as with any set of questions, this method has its limits. Further questions, not part of this method, open up other dimensions of understanding Matthew's gospel.[1]

LIMITATIONS OF REDACTION CRITICISM

(1) Redaction criticism has generally focused on the author and the author's work in producing the gospel text. Our use of it has been somewhat unusual in that we have employed it to investigate the authorial audience. Redaction criticism has generally not been concerned with the audience or reader's role in interpreting the text. It has paid little attention to the roles of actual audiences in different situations. It has often overlooked the different readings that result in these situations.

(2) Redaction critics read Matthew in a somewhat unusual way. As we have seen, comparison between one gospel and another is fundamental to redaction criticism. Redaction critics have frequently worked with sections of the gospel and read them "sideways." That is, they have compared Matthew with the parallel texts in Mark and Luke to observe and explain Matthew's changes to his sources. The three-columned gospel synopsis is a basic tool for this work.[2]

But such work, while producing detailed, comparative readings of particular sections, has often neglected the place of a section within the gospel of which it is a part. More particularly, this approach has often ignored the observation that reading is not usually a comparative, sideways act centering on one short section. The act of reading is, more often, a temporal event. Audiences generally move in sequence through a narrative from beginning to end.

(3) Redaction criticism concentrates on the changes that Matthew the redactor made to the traditions. It regards these changes as especially reflective of his theological agenda and the situation he addressed. However, reading from change to change pays minimal attention to the parts of his sources which Matthew chooses to retain and include in his gospel without change. To assume that these are of lesser or of no significance fails to explain why the author includes them. To assume that

retained material does not change when used in new literary contexts overlooks basic dynamics of interaction with a text. Reading from change to change loses sight of the finished form of the whole text with which audiences interact and from which they make meaning.

(4) Redaction critics have viewed the text as a window to view the life of the community for which it was produced. But it has not always been easy for redaction critics to determine when a feature of the text reflects a particular situation in the life of the redactor's community.[3] For instance, we noted Barth's claim that the references to breaking the law (the noun ἀνομία, *anomia*) in 5:17–19, 7:15–23, 13:41, and 24:11–13 (all unique to Matthew) indicate a particular group within Matthew's community who believe that the law should in no way shape how the community lives.

But how does Barth know this material assumes and addresses such a group? Could it not offer general instruction to the gospel's hearers about not neglecting to do God's will? The text does not indicate a specificity of address to one subgroup. As many scholars have noted, the phrase that opens 5:17 ("Do not think") is added by Matthew in 10:34 to reject a theoretical possibility, rather than address a specific group. 13:41 includes the word "all" ("all causes of sin and all evildoers") which may suggest an inclusive reference rather than a particular group. Deciding when a change reflects specific community conditions has presented redaction critics with a challenge.

AUDIENCE-ORIENTED CRITICISM

Audience-oriented or reader-response criticism, a subset of narrative criticism, asks a different set of questions. This is a more recent approach to studying the gospels.[4] Influenced by literary theory as well as by limitations in redaction criticism, it has concentrated more on the role of the audience in making meaning of the gospel.[5] This has been our basic method throughout, appropriate for our purpose of attempting to read Matthew as the authorial audience. I will briefly sketch six general emphases in audience-oriented criticism.[6]

(1) This approach understands the audience's interaction with the text as crucial in making meaning of a text.

(2) This approach focuses on interaction with the larger text of the gospel and on its final form. The concern is not so much with how a text got to be as it is as with what an audience makes of it. Audience-oriented criticism attends to what happens to the audience as it encounters the finished text in the reading process. Interpreters have sought to describe the education of readers through the sequence of the gospel. Rather than view the text as an object they emphasize the event of interacting with it.

(3) This approach concentrates on the world of the text and the world and roles which the authorial audience engages in encountering the text. It also recognizes the importance of gender, social class, ethnicity, age, etc. which an actual audience brings to the text as it interacts with the roles of the authorial audience.

(4) This approach understands the gospel as a story which draws the audience into its world. The story challenges or confirms or disinterests the audience's understandings and values through the process of reading. The act of reading is active and dynamic.

(5) This approach recognizes that texts can have multiple meanings. Audiences choose roles in reading a text. Reading as the authorial audience is one strategy. Audiences in different situations find various meanings through their interaction with a text. A recognition of multiple meanings is not, though, the same as saying a text can mean anything. The author shapes the text to limit the range of available meanings without restricting them to only one.[7]

(6) Audience-oriented approaches examine various aspects of the audience's interaction with the text. Part Two contains the four most commonly discussed areas: (i) how the audience makes sense of the points of view it encounters; (ii) how it connects and orders the various actions of the gospel into a plot; (iii) how it interprets the significance of the various settings employed through the gospel; and (iv) how it understands the motivations, actions, and conflicts of the characters.

WHO IS THE AUDIENCE?

In audience-oriented/reader-response work one of the most confusing aspects concerns "the reader" or "the audience."[8] Scholars use these terms in a variety of ways.

For instance, some scholars talk about the reading experience of a "first-time" or "virginal" reader. Others have discussed the "ideal" or "model" reader, the reader as a member of "interpretive communities," or scholar-readers. Most common is the term "implied reader." There are four ways of thinking about the reader of Matthew's gospel.

(1) *The original readers for whom the text was written.* This approach attempts to enter into the readers' experience and circumstances and hear the text for the first time as they did. It recognizes that these readers shared the world, ideas, values, and experiences of the author. The strength of this approach is its realization that texts are affected by their circumstances of origin. Its limitation is that any such attempt at reconstruction always bears the marks of the circumstances of the reconstructers. Further, it is most unlikely that Matthew's readers are hearing the stories about Jesus for the first time.

(2) *The reader of today.* This approach recognizes that Matthew has something important to say today. The experiences, values, and questions of the contemporary reader, whether those of a middle class, suburban, professional, educated congregation, or of a poor, uneducated, oppressed, grass roots, base community struggling to gain some measure of human rights are uppermost in the interpretive process. This approach often pays little attention to the circumstances of the text's origin.

(3) *The implied reader.* This term assumes a model of communication which distinguishes the following entities in the communication process:[9]

real author — implied author—text—implied reader — real reader

Real Author: the historical person who created the gospel

Implied Author: a literary version of the real author. In reading the gospel readers gain a sense of an author who shaped the content and point of view of the text.

Implied Reader: this is an imaginary person. It is a reader created by the text, the reader who responds "to the text at every point with whatever emotion, understanding, or knowledge the text ideally calls for . . . the imaginary person in whom the intention of the text is to be thought of as always reaching its fulfillment." In Matthew this person exists between the resurrection and the return of Jesus (24:15; 27:8; 28:15) and is a disciple.[10]

Real Reader: any "flesh-and-bones" reader.

In this approach scholars try to identify and describe this fulfillment of the text in the implied reader.

There are, though, some unsatisfactory features in this third approach. It posits something that is essentially unrealistic. It is impossible for any reader to "grasp all the complex interrelationships that may occur within a text."[11] Moreover, it assumes a largely passive role for the reader in that the text determines the reader's response without recognizing what the reader brings to the text (gender, ethnicity, socio-economic circumstances, etc.) or the reader's active role in determining the text's meaning. That is, it leaves no room for the experiences or engagement of the reader to affect the understanding of the text. The lack of theoretical recognition that readers contribute to the meaning of texts is betrayed by any attempt to describe the implied reader's interaction with the text. Those descriptions are always going to be marked by the circumstances and concerns of the one offering them.

(4) *The authorial audience.* As explained in chapter 1, the authorial audience is the audience which the author has in mind, when he or she writes.[12] This audience is the author's construct. It is assumed by the text rather than present in it, though the text provides evidence for its contours. In the case of Matthew's gospel, it bears some correspondence to Matthew's community or communities in so far as it is the author's impression of that community. The author assumes certain things of this contextualized implied audience. He decides what it knows and what needs to be explained if it is to understand the gospel. He shapes the gospel accordingly.

In reading as the authorial audience, we, an actual audience, try to understand as much of the experience and knowledge assumed of the authorial audience as possible before and during reading. We make explicit much of the knowledge (cultural values, religious and social experiences, traditions, narrative conventions, etc.) assumed of the authorial audience. We consent to take on this role, at least to the extent we can reconstruct it.

Two things are important about this approach: (1) It recognizes that in joining and reading as the authorial audience, the actual audience actively participates in interpreting the text. Understanding the roles and knowledge required of the authorial audience is not a passive task. It remains our work, our construction, our selections. Of course, these roles and knowledge are shaped to a significant degree by the text as we have seen, but an actual audience is actively engaged in identifying and reconstructing them.

(2) Reading as the authorial audience provides a basis for the actual audience's reflection on the text. Adopting the role of the authorial audience is not necessarily a privileged or definitive reading. Rather, it provides the basis for the actual audience to agree or disagree strongly or partially. The view of the author as expressed in the text and that of the actual audience come together in their interaction with the text. In that process we formulate meaning.

For example, if because of our religious commitments we view this text as especially authoritative, we will want to identify and agree with the roles of the authorial audience, perhaps subordinating our own perspectives to the text's or having our already-formulated perspectives, identity, and lifestyle confirmed. If we view the gospel as only somewhat authoritative we might have aspects of our own ways of understanding and living confirmed, newly articulated, or challenged. We might find something life-giving or we might find little to interest us. If we do not regard the gospel as authoritative in any way or find its viewpoint at odds with our own, we may be persuaded in part by the text or we may dismiss or resist it completely. Reading as the authorial audience provides a foundation for the actual audience's diverse interaction with the text.

NOTES

1. For an evaluation from a redaction critic, see Stanton, *Gospel for a New People*, 36–53; also Petersen, *Literary Criticism*, 9–23, esp. 17–20.

2. See the description of how redaction critics approach a pericope or section by Gail Paterson Corrington, "Redaction Criticism," in *To Each Its Own Meaning: An Introduction to Biblical Criticisms and Their Application* (ed. S. McKenzie and S. Haynes; Louisville: Westminster/John Knox, 1993) 87–99, esp. 91.

3. Stanton, *Gospel for a New People,* 47–49; J. E. Davison, "Anomia and the Question of an Antinomian Polemic in Matthew," *JBL* 105 (1985) 617–35; J. Barclay, "Mirror Reading a Polemical Letter: Galatians as a Test Case," *JSNT* 31 (1987) 73–93.

4. For discussion, J. Resseguie, "Reader-Response and the Synoptic Gospels," *JAAR* 52 (1982) 411–34; Eagleton, *Literary Theory,* 54–90; T. J. Keegan, *Interpreting the Bible: A Popular Introduction to Biblical Hermeneutics* (New York: Paulist, 1985) 73–130; R. Detweiler, ed., *Semeia 31: Reader Response Approaches to Biblical and Secular Texts* (Decatur: Scholars, 1985); E. McKnight, *The Bible and the Reader: An Introduction to Literary Criticism* (Philadelphia: Fortress, 1985); E. McKnight, *Post-Modern Use of the Bible: The Emergence of Reader-Oriented Criticism* (Nashville: Abingdon, 1988); Moore, *Literary Criticism and the Gospels;* Powell, *What Is Narrative Criticism?* M. A. Powell, "Toward a Narrative-Critical Understanding of Matthew," *Int* 46 (1992) 341–46; D. M. Gunn, "Narrative Criticism," and E. McKnight, "Reader-Response Criticism," in *To Each Its Own Meaning* (ed. McKenzie and Haynes) 171–219.

5. Powell, *What Is Narrative Criticism?* 6–18; idem, "Toward a Narrative-Critical Understanding of Matthew," 341–46.

6. It is important to realize that there is much continuing debate about all these emphases.

7. In addition to Rabinowitz's approach used in this book, see the essays on Textual Determinacy in *Semeia* 62 (1993).

8. R. Fowler, "Who is 'The Reader' in Reader Response Criticism?" *Semeia* 31 (1985) 5–23.

9. I am following Kingsbury, *Matthew as Story,* 31–32, 37–40. See also Powell, *What Is Narrative Criticism?* 19–21. J. D. Kingsbury, "Reflections on 'The Reader' of Matthew's Gospel," *NTS* 34 (1988) 442–60.

10. Kingsbury, *Matthew as Story,* 38–39.

11. Powell, *What Is Narrative Criticism?* 20.

12. P. J. Rabinowitz, "Truth in Fiction: A Reexamination of Audiences," *Critical Inquiry* 4 (1977) 121–41; idem, "Whirl Without End: Audience-Oriented Criticism," in *Contemporary Literary Theory* (ed. G. D. Atkins and L. Morrow; Amherst: University of Massachusetts, 1989) 81–100; idem, *Before Reading.*

Bibliography

Albright, W. F. and C. S. Mann. *Matthew*. AB. Garden City: Doubleday, 1971.

Allen, W. *The Gospel According to S. Matthew*. Edinburgh: T. & T. Clark, 1907.

Allison, D. "Review of D. Harrington, *The Gospel of Matthew*." *Biblica* 75 (1994) 115–18.

_____. *The New Moses: A Matthean Typology*. Minneapolis: Fortress, 1993.

_____. "Jesus and Moses (Mt 5:1–2)." *ExpT* 98 (1987) 203–5.

Anderson, J. C. *Matthew's Narrative Web: Over, and Over, and Over Again*. JSNTSup 91. Sheffield: JSOT, 1994.

Aristotle. *The Poetics*. Loeb Classical Library. Cambridge: Harvard University, 1939.

Aune, D. *The New Testament in Its Literary Environment*. Philadelphia: Westminster, 1987.

_____. "Greco-Roman Biography." In *Greco-Roman Literature and the New Testament: Selected Forms and Genres*. SBLSBS 21. Edited by D. Aune. Pages 107–26. Atlanta: Scholars, 1988.

Bacon, B. W. *Studies in Matthew*. London: Constable, 1930.

Bailey J. L. and L. D. Vander Broek. *Literary Forms in the New Testament*. Louisville: Westminster/John Knox, 1992.

Baird, W. *History of New Testament Research: From Deism to Tübingen*. Volume 1. Minneapolis: Fortress, 1992.

Balch, D., ed. *Social History of the Matthean Community: Cross-Disciplinary Approaches.* Minneapolis: Fortress, 1991.

Barclay, J. "Mirror Reading a Polemical Letter: Galatians as a Test Case." *JSNT* 31 (1987) 73–93.

Barton, S. C. *Discipleship and Family Ties in Mark and Matthew.* SNTSMS 80; Cambridge: Cambridge University, 1994.

Bauer, W., W. F. Arndt, F. W. Gingrich, and F. W. Danker. *A Greek-English Lexicon of the New Testament and Other Early Christian Literature.* 2d ed. Chicago: University of Chicago, 1979.

Beker, J. C. "The Challenge of Paul's Apocalyptic Gospel for the Church Today." *Journal of Religious Thought* 40 (1983) 9–15.

Bellinzoni, A. J., ed. *The Two Source Hypothesis.* Macon: Mercer University, 1985.

Boring, M. E. "The Historical-Critical Method's 'Criteria of Authenticity': The Beatitudes in Q and Thomas as a Test Case." *Semeia* 44 (1988) 9–44.

Bornkamm, G. *Jesus of Nazareth.* London/New York: Hodder & Stoughton, 1960.

Bornkamm, G., G. Barth, and H. J. Held. *Tradition and Interpretation in Matthew.* Philadelphia: Westminster, 1963.

Brandon, S. G. F. *The Fall of Jerusalem and the Christian Church.* London: SPCK, 1957.

Brooks, S. H. *Matthew's Community: The Evidence of His Special Sayings Source.* JSNTSup 16. Sheffield: JSOT, 1987.

Brown, R. E. *The Death of the Messiah.* 2 vols. New York: Doubleday, 1994.

_____. *The Birth of the Messiah.* New York: Doubleday, 1977, 1993.

Brown, R. E. and J. P. Meier. *Antioch and Rome.* New York: Paulist, 1983.

Bultmann, R. "The Primitive Christian Kerygma and the Historical Jesus." In *The Historical Jesus and the Kerygmatic Christ.* Edited by C. Braaten and R. Harrisville. Pages 15–42. New York: Abingdon, 1964.

_____. *The History of the Synoptic Tradition.* Revised edition. Reprint 1963. Peabody, Mass.: Hendrickson, 1994.

_____. *Theology of the New Testament.* London: SCM, 1952.

_____. *Jesus and the Word.* New York: Charles Scribner's Sons, 1934.

Burnett, F. W. "Characterization and Reader Construction of Characters in the Gospels." *Semeia* 63 (1993) 3–28.

_____. "Exposing the Anti-Jewish Ideology of Matthew's Implied Author: The Characterization of God as Father." *Semeia* 59 (1992) 155–91.

Burridge, R. A. *What Are the Gospels? A Comparison with Graeco-Roman Biography.* SNTSMS 70. Cambridge: Cambridge University, 1992.

Butler, B. C. *The Originality of St Matthew.* Cambridge: Cambridge University, 1951.

Cahill, L. "The Ethical Implications of the Sermon on the Mount." *Int* 41 (1987) 144–56.

Carter, W. "Matthew 4:18–22 and Matthean Discipleship: An Audience-Oriented Perspective." *CBQ* forthcoming.

_____. "To See the Tomb": A Note on Matthew's Women At the Tomb (28:1)." *ExpT* (1996) forthcoming.

_____. "Recalling the Lord's Prayer: The Authorial Audience and Matthew's Prayer as Familiar Liturgical Experience." *CBQ* 57 (1995) 514–30.

_____. "Challenging by Confirming, Renewing by Repeating: The Authorial Audience's Interaction with the Parables of "the Reign of the Heavens" in Matthew 13 as Embedded Narratives." In *SBLSP*. Edited by E. Lovering. Pages 399–424. Atlanta: Scholars, 1995.

_____. *Households and Discipleship. A Study of Matthew 19–20.* JSNTSup 103. Sheffield: JSOT, 1994.

_____. *What Are They Saying About Matthew's Sermon on the Mount?*. Mahwah: Paulist, 1994.

_____. "The Crowds in Matthew's Gospel." *CBQ* 55 (1993) 54–67.

_____. "Kernels and Narrative Blocks: The Structure of Matthew's Gospel." *CBQ* 54 (1992) 463–81.

_____. "The Prologue and John's Gospel: Function, Symbol and the Definitive Word." *JSNT* 39 (1990) 35–58.

_____. "Rome (and Jerusalem): The Contingency of Romans 3:21–26." *Irish Biblical Studies* 11 (1989) 54–68.

Carter, W. and J. P. Heil, *Reading Matthew's Parables,* forthcoming.

Charlesworth, J., ed. *The Messiah: Developments in Earliest Judaism and Christianity.* Minneapolis: Fortress, 1992.

Chatman, S. *Story and Discourse*. Ithaca: Cornell University, 1978.

Clark, K. W. *The Gentile Bias and Other Essays*. Leiden: E. J. Brill, 1980.

Cohen, S. *From the Maccabees to the Mishnah*. Philadelphia: Westminster, 1987.

Cook, M. J. "Interpreting 'Pro-Jewish' Passages in Matthew." *HUCA* 53 (1984) 135–46.

Corrington, G. P. "Redaction Criticism." In *To Each Its Own Meaning: An Introduction to Biblical Criticisms and Their Application*. Edited by S. McKenzie and S. Haynes. Pages 87–99. Louisville: Westminster/John Knox, 1993.

Cox, P. *Biography in Late Antiquity: A Quest for the Holy Man*. Berkeley: University of California, 1983.

Crosby, M. *House of Disciples: Church, Economics, Justice*. Maryknoll: Orbis, 1988.

Cullmann, O. *The Christology of the New Testament*. Philadelphia: Westminster, 1963.

Culpepper, A. *Anatomy of the Fourth Gospel: A Study in Literary Design*. Philadelphia: Fortress, 1983.

Dahl, N. "The Passion Narrative in Matthew." In *The Interpretation of Matthew*. Edited by G. Stanton. Pages 42–55. Philadelphia and London: Fortress and SPCK, 1983.

Darr, J. "Narrator as Character: Mapping a Reader-Oriented Approach to Narration in Luke–Acts." *Semeia* 63 (1993) 43–60.

Davies, W. D. *The Setting of the Sermon on the Mount*. Cambridge: Cambridge University, 1966.

Davies, W. and D. Allison, *The Gospel According to Saint Matthew*. 2 vols. Edinburgh: T. & T. Clark, 1988, 1991.

Davison, J. E. "Anomia and the Question of an Antinomian Polemic in Matthew." *JBL* 105 (1985) 617–35.

de Jonge, M. "Christ." *Anchor Bible Dictionary*. 1.914–18.

———. "Messiah." *Anchor Bible Dictionary*. 4.777–88.

Detweiler, R., ed. *Semeia 31; Reader Response Approaches to Biblical and Secular Texts*. Decatur: Scholars, 1985.

Deutsch, C. *Hidden Wisdom and the Easy Yoke: Wisdom, Torah and Discipleship in Matthew 11.25–30*. JSNTSup 18; Sheffield: JSOT, 1987.

Dibelius, M. *Die Formgeschichte des Evangeliums*. Tübingen: J. C. B. Mohr, 1919. English translation: *From Tradition to Gospel*. London: Ivor Nicholson and Watson, 1934.

Donahue, J. "Recent Studies on the Origin of "Son of Man" in the Gospels." *CBQ* 48 (1986) 484–98.

Donaldson, T. *Jesus on the Mountain: A Study in Matthean Theology.* JSNTSup 8; Sheffield: JSOT, 1985.

Donfried, K., ed. *The Romans Debate.* Revised and expanded edition. Peabody, Mass.: Hendrickson, 1991.

Downey, E. *A History of Antioch in Syria.* Princeton: Princeton University, 1961.

Duling, D. "Matthew and Marginality." In *SBLSP.* Edited by E. H. Lovering. Pages 642–71. Atlanta: Scholars, 1993.

―――. "Matthew." *Anchor Bible Dictionary.* 4.618–22.

―――. "The Therapeutic Son of David: An Element in Matthew's Christological Apologetic." *NTS* 24 (1977–78) 392–410.

―――. "Solomon, Exorcism, and the Son of David." *HTR* 68 (1975) 235–52.

Dunn, J. D. G. *Romans 1–8.* WBC 38A. Dallas: Word, 1988.

―――. *The Evidence for Jesus.* Philadelphia: Westminster, 1985.

―――. *Christology in the Making.* Philadelphia: Westminster, 1980.

Eagleton, T. *Literary Theory: An Introduction.* Minneapolis: University of Minnesota, 1983.

Eco, U. *The Role of the Reader.* Bloomington: University of Indiana, 1979.

Edwards, J. R. "The Use of προσέρχεσθαι in the Gospel of Matthew." *JBL* 106 (1987) 65–74.

Edwards, R. A. "Narrative Implications of *Gar* in Matthew." *CBQ* 52 (1990) 636–55.

―――. "Uncertain Faith: Matthew's Portrait of the Disciples." In *Discipleship in the New Testament.* Edited by F. Segovia. Pages 47–61. Philadelphia: Fortress, 1985.

Egan, K. "What Is a Plot?" *New Literary History* 9 (1978) 455–73.

Farmer, R. "The Kingdom of God in the Gospel of Matthew." In *The Kingdom of God in 20th-Century Interpretation.* Edited by W. Willis. Pages 119–30. Peabody, Mass: Hendrickson, 1987.

Farmer, W. *The Synoptic Problem: A Critical Analysis.* New York: Macmillan, 1964.

Fenton, J. C. *Saint Matthew.* Philadelphia: Westminster, 1963, 1977.

Fetterley, J. *The Resisting Reader: A Feminist Approach to American Fiction.* Bloomington: Indiana University, 1978.

Fitzmyer, J. "The Priority of Mark and the 'Q' Source in Luke." In *Jesus and Man's Hope* vol. 1. Edited by D. Miller. Pages 131–70. Pittsburgh: Perspective, 1970.

Fossum, J. "Son of God." *Anchor Bible Dictionary.* 6.128–37.

Fowler, R. "Who is 'The Reader' in Reader Response Criticism?" *Semeia* 31 (1985) 5–23.

France, R. T. *Matthew: Evangelist and Teacher.* Grand Rapids: Zondervan, 1989.

Frankemölle, H. *Jahwebund und Kirche Christi.* NTA 10. Münster: Aschendorf, 1974.

Freed, E. D. "The Women in Matthew's Genealogy." *JSNT* 29 (1987) 3–19.

Freedman, D. N., ed. *Anchor Bible Dictionary.* 6 vols. New York: Doubleday, 1992.

Fuller, R. "Classics and the Gospels: The Seminar." In *The Relationships Among the Gospels: An Interdisciplinary Approach.* Edited by W. Walker. Pages 173–92. San Antonio: Trinity University, 1978.

_____. *The Foundations of New Testament Christology.* New York: Charles Scribner's Sons, 1965.

Funk, R. and R. Hoover. *The Five Gospels.* New York: Macmillan, 1993.

Gaechter, P. *Das Matthäus-Evangelium: Ein Kommentar.* Innsbruck: Tyrolia, 1963.

Garland, D. *Reading Matthew: A Literary and Theological Commentary on the First Gospel.* New York: Crossroad, 1993.

_____. *The Intention of Matthew 23.* NovTSup 52. Leiden: E. J. Brill, 1979.

_____. "Review of J. D. Kingsbury, *Matthew.* Proclamation: Philadelphia: Fortress, 1975." *RevExp* 74 (1977) 567–78.

Genette, G. *Narrative Discourse: An Essay in Method.* Ithaca: Cornell University, 1980.

_____. "Time and Narrative in *A la recherche du temps perdu.*" In *Aspects of Narrative.* Edited by J. H. Miller. Pages 93–118. New York: Columbia University, 1971.

Gerhardsson, B. *The Mighty Acts of Jesus According to Matthew.* Lund: C. W. K. Gleerup, 1979.

Gerhart, M. "Generic Studies: Their Renewed Importance in Religious and Literary Interpretation." *JAAR* 45 (1977) 309–22.

Gill, C. "Character-Development in Plutarch and Tacitus." *Classical Quarterly* 33 (1983) 469–87.

González, J. *The Story of Christianity*. 2 vols. San Francisco: Harper & Row, 1985.

Goodspeed, E. J. *Matthew, Apostle and Evangelist*. Philadelphia: John C. Winston, 1959.

Goulder, M. *Midrash and Lection In Matthew*. London: SPCK, 1974.

Grant, F. C. *The Gospels: Their Origin and Their Growth*. London: Faber & Faber, 1957.

Grundmann W. and G. Stählin. "ἁμαρτάνω, ἁμάρτημα, ἁμαρτία." *TDNT*. 1.267–316.

Guelich, R. *The Sermon on the Mount*. Dallas: Word, 1982.

_____. "The Matthean Beatitudes: 'Entrance-Requirements' or Eschatological Blessings?" *JBL* 95 (1976) 415–34.

Gundry, R. "A Responsive Evaluation of the Social History of the Matthean Community in Roman Syria." In *Social History of the Matthean Community: Cross-Disciplinary Approaches*. Edited by D. Balch. Pages 62–67. Minneapolis: Fortress, 1991.

_____. *Matthew: A Commentary on His Literary and Theological Art*. Grand Rapids: Eerdmans, 1982.

Gunn, D. M. "Narrative Criticism." In *To Each Its Own Meaning: An Introduction to Biblical Criticisms and Their Application*. Edited by S. McKenzie and S. Haynes. Pages 171–95. Louisville: Westminster/John Knox, 1993.

Gustafson, J. M. "The Place of Scripture in Christian Ethics: A Methodological Study." *Int* 24 (1970) 430–55.

Guthrie, D. *New Testament Introduction: The Gospel and Acts*. Chicago: Inter-Varsity, 1965.

Hagner, D. *Matthew 1–13*. WBC 33A. Dallas: Word, 1993.

Hahn, F. *The Titles of Jesus in Christology*. New York: World, 1969.

Hare, D. R. A. *Matthew*. Interpretation. Louisville: Westminster/John Knox, 1993.

_____. *The Theme of Jewish Persecution of Christians in the Gospel according to St Matthew*. SNTSMS 6. Cambridge: Cambridge University, 1967.

Hare, D. and D. Harrington. " 'Make Disciples of All the Gentiles' (Mt 28:19)." *CBQ* 37 (1975) 359–69.

Harrington, D. J. *The Gospel of Matthew*. Sacra Pagina 1. Collegeville: Liturgical, 1991.

_____. "The Jewishness of Jesus: Facing Some Problems." *CBQ* 49 (1987) 1–13.

Harris, B. F. "The Idea of Mercy and its Graeco-Roman Context." In *God Who Is Rich In Mercy: Essays Presented to D. B. Knox*. Edited by P. T. O'Brien and D. G. Peterson. Pages 89–105. Sydney: Macquarie University, 1986.

Hawkins, J. *Horae Synopticae: Contributions to the Study of the Synoptic Problem*. 2d ed. Grand Rapids: Baker, 1968.

Heichelheim, F. M. "Roman Syria." In *An Economic Survey of Ancient Rome*. Edited by T. Frank. Pages 121–257. Baltimore: Johns Hopkins, 1938.

Heil, J. P. *The Death and Resurrection of Jesus: A Narrative-Critical Reading of Matthew 26–28*. Minneapolis: Fortress, 1991.

_____. *Jesus Walking on the Sea: Meaning and Gospel Functions of Matt 16:22–33, Mark 6:45–52 and John 6:15b–21*. AB 87. Rome: Biblical Institute, 1981.

_____. "Significant Aspects of the Healing Miracles in Matthew." *CBQ* 41 (1979) 276–87.

Hendrickx, H. *The Passion Narratives of the Synoptic Tradition*. London: Geoffrey Chapman, 1984.

Hengel, M. *Studies in the Gospel of Mark*. Philadelphia: Fortress, 1985.

_____. *The Atonement*. Philadelphia: Fortress, 1981.

_____. *The Son of God*. Philadelphia: Fortress, 1976.

_____. *Judaism and Hellenism*. Philadelphia: Fortress, 1974, 1981.

Hill, D. "The Figure of Jesus in Matthew's Story: A Response to Professor Kingsbury's Literary-Critical Probe." *JSNT* 21 (1984) 37–52.

_____. "Son and Servant: An Essay on Matthean Christology." *JSNT* 6 (1980) 2–16.

_____. *The Gospel of Matthew*. NCB. Grand Rapids: Eerdmans, 1972.

Iser, W. "Interaction between Text and Reader." In *The Reader in the Text: Essays on Audience and Interpretation*. Edited by S. Suleiman and I. Crosman. Pages 106–119. Princeton: Princeton University, 1980.

_____. *The Act of Reading: A Theory of Aesthetic Response*. Baltimore: Johns Hopkins, 1978.

Jacobson, A. "The Literary Unity of Q." *JBL* 101 (1982) 365–89.

Johnson, L. T. "The New Testament's Anti-Jewish Slander and the Conventions of Ancient Rhetoric." *JBL* 108 (1989) 419–41.

————. *The Writings of the New Testament.* Philadelphia: Fortress, 1986.

Johnson, M. D. "Reflections on a Wisdom Approach to Matthew's Christology." *CBQ* 36 (1974) 44–64.

————. *The Purpose of Biblical Genealogies.* SNTSMS 8. Cambridge: Cambridge University, 1969.

Judge, E. A. "The Quest for Mercy in Late Antiquity." In *God Who Is Rich In Mercy: Essays Presented to D. B. Knox.* Edited by P. T. O'Brien and D. G. Peterson. Pages 107–121. Sydney: Macquarie University, 1986.

Kähler, M. *The So-Called Historical Jesus and the Historic Biblical Christ.* Translated by C. Braaten. Philadelphia: Fortress, 1964.

Käsemann, E. *New Testament Questions of Today.* Philadelphia: Fortress, 1969.

————. *Essays on New Testament Themes.* Philadelphia: Fortress, 1964, 1982.

Katz, S. "Issues in the Separation of Judaism and Christianity after 70 C. E.; A Reconsideration." *JBL* 103 (1984) 43–76.

Keck, L. E. "Toward the Renewal of New Testament Christology." *NTS* 32 (1986) 362–77.

————. "Ethics in the Gospel According to Matthew." *Iliff Review* 40 (1984) 39–56.

Keegan, T. J. *Interpreting the Bible: A Popular Introduction to Biblical Hermeneutics.* New York: Paulist, 1985.

Kennedy, G. "Classical and Christian Source Criticism." In *The Relationships Among the Gospels: An Interdisciplinary Approach.* Edited by W. Walker. Pages 125–155. San Antonio: Trinity University, 1978.

Kiley, M. "Why 'Matthew' in Matt 9, 9–13?" *Biblica* 65 (1984) 347–51.

Kilpatrick, G. D. *The Origins of the Gospel According to St. Matthew.* Oxford: Clarendon, 1946.

Kimelman, R. "*Birkat Ha-Minim* and the Lack of Evidence for an Anti-Christian Jewish Prayer in Late Antiquity." In *Jewish and Christian Self-Definition.* Volume 2. Edited by E. P. Sanders, A. Baumgarten, A. Mendelson. Pages 226–44. Philadelphia: Fortress, 1981.

Kingsbury, J. D. "The Plot of Matthew's Story." *Int* 46 (1992) 347–56.

———. "Conclusion: Analysis of a Conversation." In *Social History of the Matthean Community*. Edited by D. Balch. Pages 259–69. Minneapolis: Augsburg Fortress, 1991.

———. *Matthew as Story*. 2d ed., revised and expanded. Philadelphia: Fortress, 1988.

———. "Reflections on 'The Reader' of Matthew's Gospel." *NTS* 34 (1988) 442–60.

———. "The Developing Conflict between Jesus and the Jewish Leaders in Matthew's Gospel: A Literary-Critical Study." *CBQ* 49 (1987) 57–73.

———. "The Place, Structure, and Meaning of the Sermon on the Mount within Matthew." *Int* 41 (1987) 131–43.

———. "The Parable of the Wicked Husbandmen and the Secret of Jesus' Divine Sonship in Matthew: Some Literary-Critical Observations." *JBL* 105 (1986) 643–55.

———. *Matthew*. Proclamation Commentaries. Philadelphia: Fortress, 1986.

———. "The Figure of Jesus in Matthew's Story: A Literary-Critical Probe." *JSNT* 21 (1984) 3–36.

———. "The Figure of Peter in Matthew's Gospel as a Theological Problem." *JBL* 98 (1979) 67–83.

———. "Observations on the 'Miracle Chapters' of Matthew 8–9." *CBQ* 40 (1978) 559–73.

———. "The Verb ἀκολουθεῖν ("To Follow") as an Index of Matthew's View of the Old Testament." *JBL* 97 (1978) 56–73.

———. "The Title 'Son of David' in Matthew's Gospel." *JBL* 95 (1976) 591–602.

———. *Matthew: Structure, Christology, Kingdom*. Philadelphia: Fortress, 1975.

———. *The Parables of Jesus in Matthew 13*. Richmond: John Knox, 1969.

Kittel, G. and G. Friedrich, eds. *Theological Dictionary of the New Testament*. 10 vols. Translated by G. Bromiley. Grand Rapids: Eerdmans, 1964–76.

Knox, B. "Silent Reading in Antiquity." *GRBS* 9 (1968) 421–35.

Kraeling, C. "The Jewish Community at Antioch." *JBL* 51 (1932) 130–60.

Kümmel, W. *Introduction to the New Testament*. London: SCM, 1975.

_____. *The New Testament: The History of the Investigation of its Problems*. Nashville: Abingdon, 1972.

Kürzinger, J. "Das Papiaszeugnis und die Erstgestalt des Matthäusevangeliums." *BZ* 4 (1960) 19–38.

_____. "Irenäus und sein Zeugnis zur Sprache des Matthäusevangeliums." *NTS* 10 (1963–64) 108–115.

Ladd, G. E. *Theology of the New Testament*. Guildford and London: Lutterworth, 1974.

Lischer, R. "The Sermon on the Mount as Radical Pastoral Care." *Int* 41 (1987) 157–69.

Loader, W. "Son of David, Blindness, Possession, and Duality in Matthew." *CBQ* 44 (1982) 570–85.

Lohr, C. "Oral Techniques in the Gospel of Matthew." *CBQ* 23 (1961) 403–35.

Lotman, J. M. "Point of View in a Text." *New Literary History* 6 (1975) 339–52.

Louw, J. P. and E. Nida. *Greek-English Lexicon of the New Testament*. 2 vols. New York: United Bible Societies, 1988.

Luz, U. "The Son of Man in Matthew: Heavenly Judge or Human Christ." *JSNT* 48 (1992) 3–21.

_____. *Matthew 1–7*. Minneapolis: Fortress, 1989.

_____. "The Disciples in the Gospel According to Matthew." In *The Interpretation of Matthew*. Edited by G. Stanton. Pages 98–128. Philadelphia: Fortress, 1983.

MacMullen, R. *Roman Social Relations*. New Haven: Yale University, 1974.

Manson, T. W. *The Sayings of Jesus*. London: SCM, 1949.

Marxsen, W. *Introduction to the New Testament*. Philadelphia: Fortress, 1968.

Massaux E. *The Influence of the Gospel According to Saint Matthew on Christian Literature before Saint Irenaeus*. 3 vols. Macon: Mercer University, 1990–93.

Matera, F. "The Plot of Matthew's Gospel." *CBQ* 49 (1987) 233–53.

_____. *Passion Narratives and Gospel Theologies*. New York: Paulist, 1986.

McArthur, H. "The Origin of the 'Q' Symbol." *ExpT* 88 (1977) 119–20.

McKnight, E. "Reader-Response Criticism." In *To Each Its Own Meaning: An Introduction to Biblical Criticisms and Their Application.* Edited by S. McKenzie and S. Haynes. Pages 197–219. Louisville: Westminster/John Knox, 1993.

_____. *Post-Modern Use of the Bible: The Emergence of Reader-Oriented Criticism.* Nashville: Abingdon, 1988.

_____. *The Bible and the Reader: An Introduction to Literary Criticism.* Philadelphia: Fortress, 1985.

_____. *What Is Form Criticism?.* Philadelphia: Fortress, 1969.

Meeks, W. "Hypomnēmata from an Untamed Sceptic: A Response to George Kennedy." In *The Relationships Among the Gospels: An Interdisciplinary Approach.* Edited by W. Walker. Pages 157–72. San Antonio: Trinity University, 1978.

Meeks W. and R. L. Wilken. *Jews and Christians in Antioch.* Missoula: Scholars, 1978.

Meier, J. P. "Matthew and Ignatius: A Response to William R. Schoedel." In *Social History of the Matthean Community: Cross-Disciplinary Approaches.* Edited by D. Balch. Pages 178–86. Minneapolis: Fortress, 1991.

_____. *The Vision of Matthew.* New York: Crossroad, 1979, 1991.

_____. "Nations or Gentiles in Matthew 28:19?" *CBQ* 39 (1977) 94–102.

_____. *Law and History in Matthew's Gospel.* AnBib 71. Rome: Biblical Institute, 1976.

_____. "Salvation-History in Matthew: In Search of a Starting Point." *CBQ* 37 (1975) 203–15.

Menzies, A., ed. *Ante-Nicene Fathers.* Volume 9. Reprint 1896. Peabody, Mass.: Hendrickson, 1995.

Meyer, P. D. "The Gentile Mission in Q." *JBL* 89 (1970) 405–17.

Momigliano, A. *The Development of Greek Biography.* Cambridge: Harvard University, 1971.

Moo, D. *The Old Testament in the Gospel Passion Narratives.* Sheffield: Almond, 1983.

Moore, S. *Literary Criticism and the Gospels: The Theoretical Challenge.* New Haven: Yale University, 1989.

Moule, C. F. D. *The Birth of the New Testament.* London: A. & C. Black, 1981.

Murphy-O'Connor, J. *St. Paul's Corinth.* Good News Studies 6. Wilmington: Michael Glazier, 1983.

Neill, S. and N. T. Wright. *The Interpretation of the New Testament.* 2d ed. Oxford: Oxford University, 1988.

Neirynck, F. "The Symbol Q (=Quelle)." *ETL* 54 (1978) 119–25.

Nepper-Christensen, P. *Das Matthäusevangelium: Ein judenchristliches Evangelium?.* ATD 1. Aarhus: Universitetsforlaget, 1954.

Neusner, J. *From Politics to Piety: The Emergence of Pharisaic Judaism.* Englewood Cliffs: Prentice-Hall, 1973.

Neusner, J., W. Green, E. Frerichs., eds. *Judaisms and Their Messiahs at the Turn of the Christian Era.* Cambridge: Cambridge University, 1987.

Neyrey, J. "The Thematic Use of Isa 42,1–4 in Matthew 12." *Biblica* 63 (1982) 457–73.

Nickelsburg, G. W. E. "Resurrection: Early Judaism and Christianity." *Anchor Bible Dictionary.* 5.684–91.

———. "Son of Man." *Anchor Bible Dictionary.* 6.137–50.

———. *Resurrection, Immortality and Eternal Life in Intertestamental Judaism.* Cambridge: Harvard University, 1972.

Nickelsburg, G. W. E. and M. E. Stone. *Faith and Piety in Early Judaism: Texts and Documents.* Philadelphia: Fortress, 1983.

Nickle, K. F. *The Synoptic Gospels.* Atlanta: John Knox, 1980.

Norris, F. W. "Artifacts from Antioch." In *Social History of the Matthean Community: Cross-Disciplinary Approaches.* Edited by D. Balch. Pages 248–58. Minneapolis: Fortress, 1991.

Oakman, D. E. "The Countryside in Luke–Acts." In *The Social World of Luke–Acts: Models for Interpretation.* Edited by J. Neyrey. Pages 151–79. Peabody, Mass.: Hendrickson, 1991.

Overman, J. *Matthew's Gospel and Formative Judaism: A Study of the Social World of the Matthean Community.* Minneapolis: Fortress, 1990.

Pelling, C., ed. *Characterization and Individuality in Greek Literature.* Oxford: Clarendon, 1990.

Perkins, P. *Resurrection: New Testament Witness and Contemporary Reflection.* Garden City: Doubleday, 1984.

Perrin, N. *Jesus and the Language of the Kingdom.* Philadelphia: Fortress, 1976.

———. *What Is Redaction Criticism?* Philadelphia: Fortress, 1969.

Perry, M. "Literary Dynamics: How the Order of a Text Creates its Meaning." *Poetics Today* 1 (1979–1980) 35–64, 311–64.

Petersen, N. *Literary Criticism for New Testament Critics*. Guides to Biblical Scholarship. Philadelphia: Fortress, 1978.

_____. " 'Point of View' in Mark's Narrative." *Semeia* 12 (1978) 97–121.

Petrie, C. S. "The Authorship of 'The Gospel According to Matthew': a Reconsideration of the External Evidence." *NTS* 14 (1967–68) 15–33.

Plummer, A. *An Exegetical Commentary on the Gospel According to St. Matthew*. London: E. Stock, 1909.

Polman, G. H. "Chronological Biography and *AKMĒ* in Plutarch." *Classical Philology* 69 (1974) 169–77.

Powell, M. A. "Expected and Unexpected Readings in Matthew: What the Reader Knows." *The Asbury Theological Journal* 48 (1993) 31–52.

_____. *God With Us: A Pastoral Theology of Matthew's Gospel*. Minneapolis: Fortress, 1995.

_____. "The Plot and Subplots of Matthew's Gospel." *NTS* 38 (1992) 187–204.

_____. "Toward a Narrative-Critical Understanding of Matthew." *Int* 46 (1992) 341–46.

_____. *What Is Narrative Criticism?*. Guides to Biblical Scholarship. Minneapolis: Fortress, 1990.

Przybylski, B. *Righteousness in Matthew and His World of Thought*. SNTSMS 41. Cambridge: Cambridge University, 1980.

Rabinowitz, P. J. "Whirl Without End: Audience-Oriented Criticism." In *Contemporary Literary Theory*. Edited by G. D. Atkins and L. Morrow. Pages 81–100. Amherst: University of Massachusetts, 1989.

_____. *Before Reading: Narrative Conventions and the Politics of Interpretation*. Ithaca: Cornell University, 1987.

_____. "Truth in Fiction: A Reexamination of Audiences." *Critical Inquiry* 4 (1977) 121–41.

Rajak, T. *Josephus: The Historian and His Society*. Philadelphia: Fortress, 1984.

Rengstorf, K. "Die Stadt der Mörder (Mt 22:7)." In *Judentum, Urchristentum, Kirche: Festschrift für Joachim Jeremias*. BZNW 26. Edited by W. Eltester. Pages 106–29. Berlin: Töpelmann, 1960.

Resseguie, J. "Reader-Response and the Synoptic Gospels." *JAAR* 52 (1982) 411–34.

Richardson, C. C., trans. and ed. *Early Christian Fathers*. Philadelphia: Westminster, 1953.

Roberts, A. and J. Donaldson. *The Ante-Nicene Fathers*. Reprint, 1885. Peabody, Mass.: Hendrickson, 1995.

Roetzel, C. *The World That Shaped the New Testament*. Atlanta: John Knox, 1985.

Rohde, J. *Rediscovering the Teaching of the Evangelists*. London: SCM, 1968.

Rohrbaugh, R. "The Pre-Industrial City in Luke–Acts." In *The Social World of Luke–Acts: Models for Interpretation*. Edited by J. Neyrey. Pages 125–49. Peabody, Mass: Hendrickson, 1991.

Saldarini, A. J. *Matthew's Christian-Jewish Community*. Chicago: University of Chicago, 1994.

Sanders, E. P. *Jesus and Judaism*. Philadelphia: Fortress, 1985.

_____. *Paul and Palestinian Judaism*. London: SCM, 1977.

Saunders, S. *"No One Dared Ask Him Anything More:" Contextual Readings of the Controversy Stories in Matthew*. Ph.D. diss., Princeton Theological Seminary, 1990.

Schaff, P. *Nicene and Post-Nicene Fathers*. First and Second Series. Reprint, 1899. Peabody, Mass.: Hendrickson, 1995.

Schmidt, K. *Der Rahmen der Geschichte Jesu*. Berlin: Trowitzsch, 1919.

Schmitt, J. "In Search of the Origin of the Siglum Q." *JBL* 100 (1981) 609–611.

Schoedel, W. "Ignatius and the Reception of the Gospel of Matthew in Antioch." In *Social History of the Matthean Community: Cross-Disciplinary Approaches*. Edited by D. Balch. Pages 129–77. Minneapolis: Fortress, 1991.

Schweitzer, A. *The Quest of the Historical Jesus*. 3d ed. London: A. & C. Black, 1906, 1954.

Schweizer, E. *Jesus*. London: SCM, 1971.

_____. "Matthew's Church." In *The Interpretation of Matthew*. Edited by G. Stanton. Pages 129–55. Philadelphia and London: Fortress and SPCK, 1983.

_____. "The 'Matthean' Church." *NTS* 20 (1974) 216.

Segal, A. "Matthew's Jewish Voice." In *Social History of the Matthean Community: Cross-Disciplinary Approaches*. Edited by D. Balch. Pages 3–37. Minneapolis: Fortress, 1991.

Sellew, P. "Eusebius and the Gospels." In *Eusebius, Christianity, and Judaism*. Edited by H. Attridge and G. Hata. Pages 110–38. Detroit: Wayne State University, 1992.

Senior, D. *The Passion of Jesus in the Gospel of Matthew*. Wilmington: Michael Glazier, 1985.

_____. *What Are They Saying About Matthew?*. New York/Ramsey: Paulist, 1983.

_____. "The Death of Jesus and the Resurrection of the Holy Ones." *CBQ* 38 (1976) 312–29.

Slingerland, H. D. "The Transjordanian Origin of St. Matthew's Gospel." *JSNT* 3 (1979) 18–28.

Stanton, G. *A Gospel for a New People: Studies in Matthew*. Edinburgh: T. & T. Clark, 1992.

_____. "The Communities of Matthew." *Int* 46 (1992) 379–91.

_____. *The Gospels and Jesus*. Oxford, Oxford University, 1989.

_____. "The Origin and Purpose of Matthew's Gospel: Matthean Scholarship from 1945 to 1980." In *ANRW* II.25.3. Edited by W. Haase. Pages 1889–95. Berlin and New York: Walter de Gruyter, 1985.

_____., ed. *The Interpretation of Matthew*. Philadelphia and London: Fortress and SPCK, 1983.

Stark, R. "Antioch as the Social Situation for Matthew's Gospel." In *Social History of the Matthean Community: Cross-Disciplinary Approaches*. Edited by D. Balch. Pages 189–210. Minneapolis: Fortress, 1991.

Stein, R. "The 'Criteria' for Authenticity." In *Gospel Perspectives*. Edited by R. T. France and D. Wenham. Pages 225–63. Sheffield: JSOT, 1980.

Stendahl, K. *The School of St. Matthew*. Philadelphia: Fortress, 1954, 1968.

Stillwell, R. "Houses of Antioch." *Dumbarton Oaks Papers* 15 (1961) 47–57.

Stonehouse, N. *Origins of the Synoptic Gospels: Some Basic Questions*. Grand Rapids: Eerdmans, 1963.

Strauss, D. F. *The Life of Jesus Critically Examined*. Edited by P. Hodgson. Philadelphia: Fortress, 1973.

Strecker, G. *Der Weg der Gerechtigkeit*. FRLANT 82. Göttingen: Vandenhoeck & Ruprecht, 1962.

Streeter, B. H. *The Four Gospels: A Study of Origins*. New York: Macmillan, 1925.

Styler, G. M. "The Priority of Mark." In C. F. D. Moule, *The Birth of the New Testament*. Pages 285–316. London: A. & C. Black, 1981.

Suggs, M. J. *Wisdom, Christology and Law in Matthew's Gospel*. Cambridge: Harvard University, 1970.

Suleiman, S. "Redundancy and the 'Readable' Text." *Poetics Today* 1 (1980) 119–42.

Suleiman, S and I. Crosman, eds., *The Reader in the Text: Essays on Audience and Interpretation*. Princeton: Princeton University, 1980.

Syreeni, K. "Between Heaven and Earth: On the Structure of Matthew's Symbolic Universe." *JSNT* 40 (1990) 3–13.

Talbert, C. *What Is a Gospel? The Genre of the Canonical Gospels*. Philadelphia: Fortress, 1977.

Talbert, C., ed. *Reimarus: Fragments*. Philadelphia: Fortress, 1970.

Tatum, W. B. *In Quest of Jesus*. Atlanta: John Knox, 1982.

Thompson, W. G. "Reflections on the Composition of Matt 8:1–9:34." *CBQ* 33 (1971) 365–88.

_____. *Matthew's Advice to a Divided Community*. AnBib 44. Rome: Biblical Institute, 1970.

Torrey, C. C. *Our Translated Gospels*. New York and London: Harper & Brothers, 1936.

Travis, S. "Form Criticism." In *New Testament Interpretation*. Edited by I. H. Marshall. Pages 153–64. Exeter: Paternoster, 1979.

_____. *The Revival of the Griesbach Hypothesis*. Cambridge: Cambridge University, 1983.

Tuckett, C., ed. *The Messianic Secret*. Issues in Religion and Theology 1. Philadelphia: Fortress, 1983.

_____. *Reading the New Testament: Methods of Interpretation*. Philadelphia: Fortress, 1987.

Uspensky, B. *A Poetics of Composition*. Berkeley: University of California, 1973.

van Tilborg, S. *The Jewish Leaders in Matthew*. Leiden: E. J. Brill, 1972.

Via, D. O. *Self-Deception and Wholeness in Paul and Matthew*. Minneapolis: Fortress, 1990.

Viviano, B. "Where was the Gospel According to St. Matthew Written?" *CBQ* 41 (1979) 533–46.

Wainwright, E. M. *Towards a Feminist Critical Reading of the Gospel According to Matthew.* BZNW 60. Berlin, New York: Walter de Gruyter, 1991.

Walker, R. *Die Heilsgeschichte im ersten Evangelium.* FRLANT 91. Göttingen: Vandenhoeck & Ruprecht, 1967.

Walker W. and R. Norris, D. Lotz, R. Handy. *A History of the Christian Church.* 4th ed. New York: Charles Scribner's Sons, 1985.

Weiss, J. *Jesus' Proclamation of the Kingdom of God.* Reprint, 1892. Philadelphia: Fortress, 1971.

White, L. "Grid and Group in Matthew's Community: The Righteousness/Honor Code in the Sermon on the Mount." *Semeia* 35 (1986) 61–90.

White, L. M. "Crisis Management and Boundary Maintenance: The Social Location of the Matthean Community." In *Social History of the Matthean Community: Cross-Disciplinary Approaches.* Edited by D. Balch. Pages 211–47. Minneapolis: Fortress, 1991.

Wilkins, M. J. *The Concept of Discipleship in Matthew's Gospel as Reflected in the Use of the Term Mathētēs.* Leiden: E. J. Brill, 1988.

Williams, S. *Jesus' Death as Saving Event: The Background and Origin of a Concept.* HDR 2. Missoula: Scholars, 1975.

Wink, W. "Beyond Just War and Pacifism: Jesus' Nonviolent Way." *RevExp* 68 (1992) 197–214.

Wittig, S. "Formulaic Style and the Problem of Redundancy." *Centrum* 1 (1973) 123–36.

Wrede, W. *The Messianic Secret.* Reprint, 1901. Greenwood: Attic, 1971.

Zumstein, J. *La condition du croyant dans l'évangile selon Matthieu.* OBO 16. Göttingen: Vandenhoeck & Ruprecht, 1977.

Index of Modern Authors

Index of Scripture References